3rd Edition

Elementary

MARKET LEADER

Business English Teacher's Resource Book

Irene Barrall

Pearson Education Limited
Edinburgh Gate
Harlow
Essex CM20 2JE
England
and Associated Companies throughout the world.

www.pearsonlongman.com
www.market-leader.net

First published 2004

Third edition 2012

ISBN: 978-1-408-21973-7

Set in MetaPlus 9.5/12pt

Printed and bound by Neografia in Slovakia

Acknowledgements
*We are grateful to the following for permission to reproduce
copyright material:*

Text
Extract 3 from 'Dear Lucy: should I go back to my old job?', The
Financial Times, 17/08/2011 (Lucy Kellaway), © The Financial
Times Limited. All Rights Reserved; Extract 10 adapted from
'Email after hours? That's overtime', The Financial Times,
18/01/2012 (Joe Leahy), © The Financial Times Limited. All Rights
Reserved.

In some instances we have been unable to trace the owners of
copyright material, and we would appreciate any information that
would enable us to do so.

Project managed by Chris Hartley

Introduction

Market Leader is an extensive business English course designed to bring the real world of international business into the language-teaching classroom. It has been developed in association with the *Financial Times*, one of the world's leading sources of professional information, to ensure the maximum range and authenticity of international business content.

1 Course aims

In addition to new authentic reading texts and listening material, the Third Edition features a number of exciting new resources:

- specially filmed interviews with business practitioners for each unit
- *Skills* video dialogues on the DVD-ROM for every unit
- *Working across cultures* – regular input and tasks to develop students' intercultural awareness and skills
- four *Revision* units, one after every three main units
- an interactive *i-Glossary* on DVD-ROM
- additional photocopiable tasks in this Teacher's Resource Book
- *Active Teach* software to deliver the course digitally, through an interactive whiteboard or computer.

This course is intended for use either by students preparing for a career in business or by those already working who want to improve their English communication skills. *Market Leader* combines some of the most stimulating recent ideas from the world of business with a strongly task-based approach. Role plays and case studies are regular features of each unit. Throughout the course, students are encouraged to use their own experience and opinions in order to maximise involvement and learning.

2 The main course components

Course Book

This provides the main part of the teaching material, divided into 12 topic-based units. The topics have been chosen following research among teachers to establish which are the areas of widest possible interest to the majority of their students. The Course Book provides input in reading, speaking and listening, with guidance for writing tasks too. Every unit contains vocabulary development activities and a rapid review of essential grammar. There is a regular focus on key business functions, and each unit ends with a motivating case study to allow students to practise language they have worked on during the unit. For more details on the Course Book units, see *Overview of a Course Book unit*.

After every three units is a spread called *Working across cultures*. Here, students are introduced to key intercultural concepts, developing their awareness and skills in order to function effectively in international business situations. There are also four *Revision* units in the Course Book that revise and consolidate the work done in the main units and culture spreads.

Audio and DVD-ROM materials

All the listening material from the Course Book is available on the audio CDs. A number of these tracks provide students with exposure to non-native English accents which they may find challenging to understand, but which will help them build confidence in their own speaking. All of the audio files are also provided in fully downloadable MP3 format on the DVD-ROM, allowing transfer to personal computers and portable audio players.

The DVD-ROM is an integral part of the course. All 12 interviews from the Course Book can be viewed on the DVD-ROM with the option of subtitles, depending on the user's preference. The interviews (which form the main listening focus of each unit) provide an opportunity for students to get expert perspectives on the latest business practice through English. None of the interviews is scripted and, as such, they expose students to authentic examples of natural speech.

The DVD-ROM also provides video of the *Skills* dialogues from each unit. Students can use these to develop their own communication skills in typical business situations. In addition, the DVD-ROM provides students with interactive, self-study practice activities. These allow them to revisit problem areas and reinforce work done in class in their own time. The activities provide further listening practice, opportunities for task repetition and instant, personalised feedback. The DVD-ROM also includes the *i-Glossary*, an interactive mini-dictionary which provides definitions and pronunciation of all the key vocabulary listed at the back of the Course Book and which encourages further self-study.

Vocabulary Trainer

This is an online, self-study tool that lets students take control of their own learning. Once students have created a personal account, the Vocabulary Trainer tests them on the meaning, spelling, collocation and use of vocabulary learned in class. Their development is automatically recorded so they can chart their own progress outside the classroom.

Practice File

This gives extra practice in the areas of grammar and vocabulary, together with a complete syllabus in business writing. In each unit, students work with text models and useful language, then do a writing task to consolidate the learning. Additionally, the Practice File provides regular self-study pronunciation work (with an audio CD and exercises) and a valuable survival language section for students when travelling.

Teacher's Resource Book

This book provides teachers with an overview of the whole course, together with detailed teaching notes, background briefings on business content, the *Text bank* and the *Resource bank*.

The *Text bank* provides an extra *FT* reading text per unit, followed up with comprehension and vocabulary exercises. The *Resource bank* provides photocopiable worksheet-based communication activities linked to particular sections of the Course Book units:

- *Listening bank*: extra activities based on each Course Book *Listening* interview
- *Speaking bank*: extra activities based on each *Skills* section
- *Writing bank*: a model answer to the case-study *Writing* task, together with an additional writing exercise

Test File

Six photocopiable tests are available to teachers and course planners to monitor students' progress during the course. There is an *Entry test*, four *Progress tests*, which test both skills and language knowledge, and an *Exit test*, which reviews the work done throughout the course.

Test Master CD-ROM

Included in the Teacher's Resource Book, the Test Master CD-ROM is a useful assessment resource to accompany the course. It includes digital, editable versions of the Test File tests, enabling valid, tailored assessment. It also contains the accompanying audio files and a further 12 unit tests. These tests assess students' progress in terms of the *Vocabulary, Language focus* and *Skills* sections of their corresponding units. Full keys and audio scripts are also provided to make marking the tests as straightforward as possible.

Active Teach

The *Active Teach* software provides digital access to a range of course components via an interactive whiteboard or computer. Components include the Course Book, video and audio with printable scripts, the i-Glossary interactive activities based on the Course Book content, editable tests, the Teacher's Resource Book and the phonetic chart. It also includes the *Writing file*, which provides good models for writing work, and *Help* videos to make using the software as easy as possible.

Using *Active Teach* facilitates student engagement and enables the clear giving of instructions and valuable feedback. It is ideal for use on a laptop in one-to-one classes.

3 Overview of a Course Book unit

A typical unit consists of the following sections:

Starting up

Students have the opportunity to think about the unit topic and to exchange ideas and opinions with each other and with the teacher. There is a variety of stimulating activities such as answering quiz questions, reflecting on difficult decisions, prioritising options and completing charts. Throughout, students are encouraged to draw upon their life and business experience as appropriate.

Vocabulary

Essential business vocabulary is presented and practised through a wide variety of creative and engaging exercises. Students learn new words, phrases and collocations and are given tasks which help to activate the vocabulary they already know or have just learned. There is further vocabulary practice in the Practice File.

Reading

Students read interesting and relevant authentic texts from the *Financial Times* and other business sources. They develop their reading skills and acquire essential business vocabulary. The texts provide a context for language work and discussion later in the unit.

Listening

The authentic listening texts are based on interviews with businesspeople and experts in their field. Students develop listening skills such as prediction, listening for specific information and note-taking. They can, if they prefer, watch the interviews on the DVD-ROM.

Language focus

These sections develop students' awareness of the common problem areas at pre-intermediate level. They focus on accuracy and knowledge of key areas of grammar. If students already know the grammar point, this section serves as a quick check for them and the teacher. If they need more explanation, they are referred to the *Grammar reference* at the back of the Course Book. There is further grammar practice in the Practice File and in the *Essential Business Grammar and Usage* book (see *Extending the course*).

Skills

This section helps learners to develop their communication skills in the key business areas of presentations, meetings, negotiations, telephoning and social English. Each section contains a *Useful language* box which provides students with the phrases they need to carry out the business tasks in the regular role-play activities. Each of the *Skills* dialogues is available in video on the DVD-ROM, as well as in audio form.

Case studies

Each unit ends with a case study linked to the unit's business topic. The case studies are based on realistic business problems or situations and are designed to motivate and actively engage students. Students use the language and communication skills which they have acquired while working through the unit. Typically, students will be involved in discussing business problems and recommending solutions through active group work.

Each case study ends with a realistic writing task. These tasks reflect the real world of business correspondence and will also help those students preparing for business English exams. Models of writing text types are given in the *Writing file* at the end of the Course Book.

4 Using the course

Accessibility for teachers

Less-experienced teachers can sometimes find teaching business English a daunting experience. *Market Leader* sets out to provide the maximum support for teachers.

The *Business brief* section at the beginning of each unit in the Teacher's Resource Book gives an overview of the business topic, covering key terms (given in bold, and which can be checked in the *Longman Dictionary of Business English*) and suggesting a list of titles for further reading and information.

Authenticity of content

One of the principles of the course is that students should deal with as much authentic content as their language level allows. Authentic reading and listening texts are motivating for students and bring the real world of business into the classroom, increasing students' knowledge of business practice and concepts. Due to its international coverage, the *Financial Times* has been a rich source of text, video and business information for the course.

The case studies present realistic business situations and problems and the communication activities based on them – group discussions, simulations and role plays – serve to enhance the authenticity of the course.

Flexibility of use

An essential requirement of business English materials is that they cater for the wide range of needs which students have, including different areas of interest and specialisation, different skills needs and varying amounts of time available to study. *Market Leader* offers teachers and course planners a unique range of flexible materials to help meet these needs. There are suggestions in this book on how to use the unit material extensively or intensively, with fast-track routes through the units focusing mainly on speaking and listening skills. The lesson notes include suggestions on extending the classwork through the DVD-ROM and photocopiable materials in the *Text bank* and *Resource bank* sections of this book. In addition, this book gives suggestions on how to extend the course using components including the Practice File, the *Essential Business Grammar and Usage* book, and the *Market Leader* specialist series, which develops vocabulary and reading skills (see *Extending the course*).

5 Case studies that work

The following teaching tips will help when using case studies:

1 Draw on the students' knowledge of business and the world.

2 Ensure that all students have understood the case and the key vocabulary.

3 Encourage students to use the language and communication skills they have acquired in the rest of the unit. A short review of the key language will help.

4 Focus on communication and fluency during the case-study activities. Language errors can be dealt with at the end. Make a record of important errors and give students feedback in a sympathetic and constructive way.

5 Allow students to reach their own conclusions. Many students expect there to be a correct answer. The teacher can give their own opinion but should stress that there usually is no single 'right' answer.

6 Encourage creative and imaginative solutions to the problems.

7 Encourage students to use people-management skills such as working in teams, leading teams, delegating and interacting effectively with each other.

8 Students should identify the key issues of the case and discuss all the options before reaching a decision.

6 Extending the course

Some students will require more input or practice in certain areas, either in terms of subject matter or skills, than is provided in the Course Book. In order to meet their needs, *Market Leader* provides a wide range of optional extra materials and components to choose from.

Essential Business Grammar and Usage

For students needing more work on their grammar, this book provides reference and practice in all the most important areas of business English usage. It is organised into structural and functional sections. The book complements the *Language focus* sections of the Course Book.

Market Leader specialist titles

Many students will need to learn the language of more specialised areas of business English. To provide them with authentic and engaging material, *Market Leader* includes a range of special-subject books which focus on reading skills and vocabulary development. Each book includes two tests and a glossary of specialised language.

Longman Dictionary of Business English New Edition

This is the most up-to-date source of reference in business English today. Compiled from a wide range of text sources, it allows students and teachers rapid access to clear, straightforward definitions of the latest international business terminology. The fully updated New Edition includes an interactive CD-ROM with 35,000 key words pronounced in both British and American English, together with practice material for both the Business Vantage and BULATS exams, and is now available as an iPhone or iPod touch app to download from the Pearson website.

Market Leader website: www.market-leader.net

The *Market Leader* companion website provides up-to-date information about the Course Books and specialist titles and offers a wide range of materials teachers can use to supplement and enrich their lessons. In addition to tests for each level and supplementary *Text bank* pages, the website provides links to websites relevant to units and topics in the Course Book and also downloadable glossaries of business terms.

The *Premier Lessons* subscription area of the website has a bank of ready-made lessons with authentic texts from the *Financial Times* that have student worksheets and answers. These lessons are regularly updated and can be searched in order to find relevant texts for the unit, topic and level that students are studying. *Premier Lessons* can be used in the classroom or for self-study.

Contents

CONTENTS

Resource bank

UNIT 1 Introductions

AT A GLANCE

	Classwork – Course Book	Further work
Lesson 1 *Each lesson (excluding case studies) is about 45 to 60 minutes. This does not include administration and time spent going through homework.*	**Starting up** Students listen to four businesspeople and match the speakers to their business cards. **Vocabulary: Nationalities** Students match countries and nationalities. **Listening: Meeting business contacts** A consultant introduces himself and then talks about meeting new business contacts.	**Practice File** Vocabulary (page 4) **i-Glossary** (DVD-ROM) **Course Book Listening** (DVD-ROM) **Resource bank: Listening** (page 175)
Lesson 2	**Reading: Angela Ahrendts** Students read an article about the American CEO of Burberry and complete comprehension questions. Students then use the information to ask and answer questions. **Language focus 1: *to be*** Students are introduced to positive and negative forms of the verb *to be*.	**Text bank** (pages 132–133) **Practice File** Language review (page 5)
Lesson 3	**Language focus 2: *a/an* with jobs; *wh-* questions** Students look at the use of *a/an* before vowels and consonants and are introduced to question words *what*, *who* and *where*. **Skills: Introducing yourself and others** Students listen to three conversations where people introduce themselves and others. They then practise introductions.	**Course Book Skills Dialogues** (DVD-ROM) **Resource bank: Speaking** (page 163)
Lesson 4 *Each case study is about 30 minutes to 1 hour.*	**Case study: A job fair in Singapore** Students find out information about people at a job fair. **Writing** Students write an e-mail about a person from the conference.	**Resource bank: Writing** (page 189) **Practice File** Writing (page 7)

For a fast route through the unit focusing mainly on speaking skills, just use the underlined sections.

For one-to-one situations, most parts of the unit lend themselves, with minimal adaptation, to use with individual students. Where this is not the case, alternative procedures are given.

BUSINESS BRIEF

The tone of a business relationship can be set by an initial introduction. It is important to make a good impression right from the first handshake.

When meeting businesspeople for the first time, is it better to be formal or informal? If in doubt, advise students to adopt a more formal approach. Here are some points to remember when making business introductions in English-speaking Western countries:

- Introduce businesspeople in order of professional rank – the person of highest authority is introduced to others in the group in descending order, depending on their professional position. Gender does not affect the order of introductions.

- When possible, stand up when introductions are being made.

- If clients are present, they should be introduced first.

- The name and title of the person being introduced is followed by the name and title of the other person. It is also helpful to include a small piece of information about each person to start the conversation.

- If you are being introduced to someone, shake hands and say *Hello* (informal) or *Pleased to meet you* / *How do you do* (formal), followed by the person's name.

- Treat business cards with respect. Take a moment to read them and carefully put them somewhere safe.

- Address people by their first names only if they indicate that they want you to.

Of course, in practice we often break these rules – but knowing they exist provides a starting point.

It is also worth remembering that many aspects of etiquette are not universal – **cultural norms** vary from country to country. What passes for good manners in one country may be frowned on in another. A firm handshake may be appreciated in the USA, the UK and Australia, but a French businessperson is more likely to offer a single, light handshake. In Japan, it is more usual to bow. Preparation is important in order to avoid **culture clash**. Doing some background research to get acquainted with local **business etiquette** and **social customs** can spare the blushes of both visitor and host and avoid causing offence.

Elementary students may find introducing themselves and others intimidating. Help students to navigate these situations by highlighting key phrases such as those in the Useful language box (see Course Book page 12). Drill pronunciation and intonation, and give students plenty of opportunity to use the language with short role plays. A few well-practised phrases may help to give students enough confidence to make that first impression count.

Read on

Jeanette S. Martin and Lillian H. Chaney: *Global Business Etiquette: A Guide to International Communication and Customs*, Greenwood Press, second edition 2012

Roy. A. Cook and Gwen. O. Cook: *Guide to Business Etiquette*, Prentice Hall, second edition 2010

http://www.kwintessential.co.uk/cultural-services/articles

Articles which look at various aspects of general global etiquette

http://www.modern-manners-and-etiquette.com

Etiquette tips covering a variety of business and social contexts

LESSON NOTES

Warmer

- This activity will build students' confidence by reminding them of international English and basic English words that they already know.

- Divide the class into two teams. Name one team 'noughts' (O) and the other 'crosses' (X).

- Draw a noughts-and-crosses grid on the board.

- Demonstrate that teams need to get three noughts or crosses in a row (horizontally, vertically or diagonally).

- To place a nought or a cross on the grid, teams have to say the English word for a picture that you draw.

- Demonstrate by drawing a television and asking the 'crosses' team to call out what the object is. If they say the correct word, write *television* on the board (say the word as you write it to model pronunciation) and ask one of the team to come to the board and place a cross on the grid.

- Continue until one team wins. Possible words to include are: *pen*, *book*, *pizza*, *football*, *camera*, *hamburger*, *car*. Include other English words that your class knows.

- If teams reach a stalemate, then draw a picture on the board and the first team to say the word wins.

Overview

- Introduce students to the Overview section on page 6. Point to each heading and elicit or explain a little about each. Point to the sections you will be covering in this lesson, using the table on page 8 of this book as a guide.

Quotation

- Point to the picture and ask what the people are doing (shaking hands).

- Write the quotation on the board.

- Ask the class to say it.

- Check that students know who James Bond is.

- See if students can name any other actors who played James Bond (*Roger Moore, George Lazenby, Timothy Dalton, Pierce Brosnan and Daniel Craig*).

Starting up

Students listen to four businesspeople and match the speakers to their business cards, then practise the alphabet and spelling names.

- If this is your first lesson with the group and they have not done a listening exercise before, take time over Exercises B and C. Reassure the class that they will hear the listening more than once.

- If you have a business card, show it to the class and try to elicit what it is. If not, draw a large business card on the board. Ask students what information is normally on a business card (*name, position, company, contact details*). Complete the card with details about yourself. Encourage students to show their own business cards to the class if they have them.

A

- This is a warmer exercise designed to remind students of the language they are likely to hear in introductions. The sentences come from the listening in Exercise B, so will 'sensitise' students to what they will hear and familiarise them with the names.

- Allow students to work in pairs to complete the four sentences. Make sure that students are aware that there are two words in the box (*you* and *she*) that they will not need.

- You can either check students' answers now, or let them check themselves when they listen in Exercise B.

> **1** I'm   **2** My   **3** name's   **4** from

- Draw students' attention to *Good morning* and *How do you do*. Ask students if they say this when they first meet someone or when they say goodbye (*when they first meet someone*). Can students think of other phrases that have a similar meaning to *Good morning*? (*Hi, Hello, Good afternoon, Good evening.*) See if they know any phrases that are similar to *How do you do?* (*Pleased to meet you.*)

- Ask what the opposite of *hello* is (*goodbye, bye*).

- See if students can say two ways to introduce themselves (*Hello, I'm … /My name's …*).

- Model how to say the sentences and ask students to repeat.

B 🔊 CD1.1–1.4

- Play the recording from beginning to end and ask students how many speakers they can hear (*four*).

- Play the first part of the listening (recording 1.1) and elicit which business card matches the speaker. (*Speaker 1 is Emma Schneider, card B.*)

- Ask students to complete the exercise in pairs. Play the recording at least twice and ask them if they need to hear it again.

- Play the recording again. Pause after each speaker and elicit the answers.

> **1** B   **2** D   **3** A   **4** C

C 🔊 CD1.1–1.4

- Briefly check students know each of the places a–d.

LESSON NOTES

- Do this as a quick-fire whole-class exercise.

> **1** d **2** a **3** c **4** b

- Ask questions to find out what words or phrases helped students to decide on each location and write these on the board.

- See if students can add one or two more words/phrases connected to each location.

D

- On the board write:
  Hello, my name's ..., I'm from ...

- Introduce yourself to the class using the prompts.

- Divide the class into pairs. Tell students to take turns to tell their partner about themselves. Circulate, monitor and encourage.

- Depending on your class, you could ask students to change partners two or three times to continue practising the language. This is also useful to help the class get to know each other.

> **One-to-one**
>
> If this is your first lesson with your student, use the exercises as an opportunity to get to know each other better. This would also be a good time to check or supplement the information in the needs analysis, if there is one.

E ◀)) CD1.5

- Write the alphabet on the board and ask students if they can say it in English. You can either do this in chorus, or by going round the class asking each student to say a letter. Pay particular attention to letters that are likely to cause students problems.

- Once you are happy that students are reasonably confident with the English alphabet, ask them to look at the way the letters are grouped in this exercise and see if students can explain why they are grouped like that. (*Each group contains the same vowel sound.*) If necessary, encourage students to read each group aloud.

- Play the recording, then ask students to repeat the letter groups.

F ◀)) CD1.6

- Write your name on the board and ask students to spell it.

- In pairs, ask students to spell their own name or company name for their partner.

- Point to Shi Jiabao's business card and ask students to say the e-mail address.

- Explain to students that they are going to hear four people speaking. Each of them is going to say a sentence that includes a name that they spell out. (Two of the names have already appeared in Exercises A and B, but you may prefer not to tell students this.) Tell students that they will also hear an e-mail address.

- Play the recording and ask students to write just the four names and the e-mail address that are spelled out.

- Play the recording again if necessary and check answers.

> **1** Emma **2** Payton **3** Anyukov
> **4** Davieson; sosa@rtas.com.ar

G

- Students work in pairs to spell out three names and e-mail addresses each.

- Have one or two pairs come to the front to model; one student speaks, while the other writes the name on the board.

- For extra practice, ask pairs to continue with names of friends or colleagues. Student A says and spells the name, and Student B writes the name down. Alternatively, this could be done as a class activity, with a student coming to the board to write down names spelled by other students.

Vocabulary: Nationalities

Students complete a chart of countries and nationalities and ask and answer questions about companies.

A

- Look at the chart together. Highlight the endings in each section: *-an*, *-ese*, *-i* and *-ish*.

- Point to the first example. Say: 'The country is Brazil, the nationality is Brazilian.'

- Point to the second example. Say: 'The nationality is German, the country is ...?' (*Germany*).

- Point to the next entry in the chart (India). Ask students to find the nationality from the box (*Indian*).

- Divide the class into groups of three or four.

- Get students to complete the chart using countries and nationalities from the box.

- Check the answers together.

LESSON NOTES

Country	Nationality
	-an
Brazil	Brazilian
Germany	German
India	Indian
Mexico	Mexican
Italy	Italian
Russia	Russian
Korea	Korean
	-ese
Japan	Japanese
China	Chinese
	-i
Kuwait	Kuwaiti
Oman	Omani
	-ish
Poland	Polish
Spain	Spanish
Sweden	Swedish
Turkey	Turkish
	others
France	French
Greece	Greek
the UK	British
the USA	American

- Ask students if they know any other countries and nationalities and write them on the board.

B 🔊 CD1.7

- Play the recording for students to check their answers. Ask students what they notice about the stress patterns of each ending (with *-(i)an*, *-i* and *-ish* endings, the stress falls on the syllable before the ending; with *-ese* endings, the stress is on the ending).

- Spend some time comparing the word stress for countries and nationalities.

- For extra practice, ask students to 'test' each other in pairs, taking it in turns to prompt one another:

  A: She's Brazilian.   *B: Yes, and he's from Brazil, too.*

  A: He's from Germany.   *B: Yes, and she's German, too.*

C

- Ask students to say the names of the companies in the box with you.

- Highlight the example, particularly the short answers *Yes, it is* and *No, it isn't.*

- Get two students to read the example to the class.

- Write *Ikea* on the board. Ask students to suggest a question and answer about the company similar to the example.

- Divide the class into pairs. Tell Student A to turn to page 132 and Student B to turn to page 138. Explain to students that they should take turns to ask a question about a company.

- They should use the information in the Activity file to answer their partner's questions.

- Circulate and monitor, helping if necessary.

- Have a brief feedback session with the class. Ask students to expand on their answers and say what else they know about each company.

Sony – Japanese
Chanel – French
Ikea – Swedish
Zara – Spanish
Prada – Italian
Gazprom – Russian
Michelin – French
Mercedes – German
McDonald's – American
Samsung – Korean
Petrobras – Brazilian
Tesco – British
Tata Group – Indian
Telcel – Mexican

D

- Ask students to call out ideas for famous companies. Write suggestions on the board.

- In pairs or small groups, get students to discuss which companies they think are most famous and which country they are from. If students have suggested a lot of companies, you could ask students to discuss which are the top three most famous.

- Have a quick feedback session and help with pronunciation where needed.

 i-Glossary

LESSON NOTES

Listening: Meeting business contacts

The listening is in two parts. In the first part, the speaker, consultant Jeremy Keeley, introduces himself. In the second part, he talks about meeting new business contacts and exchanging business cards.

In the first part, students listen for general understanding, and in the second part, they complete an extract by listening for specific information.

A 🔊 CD1.8

- Set the context of the recording by focusing on the photograph of Jeremy Keeley. Ask students to read the instructions carefully and then point to the photograph and ask: *What's his name? What's his job?*

- Tell students that they will hear the listening more than once.

- Check students understand the meaning of *true* and *false*.

- Play the recording as many times as necessary (twice is optimum). After the initial listening, it is useful to pause regularly to elicit whether the statements are true or false.

- Choose students around the class to correct the false statements.

> 1   F (He lives in St Albans.)
>
> 2   F (He has three teenagers.)
>
> 3   T
>
> 4   F (It works for organisations across the UK and Europe.)
>
> 5   T
>
> 6   T

B 🔊 CD1.9

- Before playing the second part of the listening, you could ask students to look at the exercise and see if they can predict any of the missing words.

- Play the recording all the way through and give students time to complete the extract.

- Play it again, pausing after the missing words to allow students to check their answers.

- Ask individual students to read out parts of the extract and check answers around the class.

> 1 how   2 Where   3 What   4 what   5 why
> 6 wait   7 offers   8 exchange

C

- Check that students understand the words. Demonstrate with actions where necessary.

- Divide students into pairs and ask them to discuss the question. Have a brief feedback session with the whole class.

- ◎ Students can watch the interview with Jeremy Keeley on the DVD-ROM.

- ➡ Resource bank: Listening (page 175)

Reading: Angela Ahrendts

This article is about the CEO of Burberry, Angela Ahrendts. After completing a chart with information from the article, students do a true/false comprehension exercise and use the text to ask and answer questions.

In a work environment, students need to be able to read a variety of documents in different ways. The reading sections in the Course Book give students an opportunity to develop their reading skills. Some activities get students to read for general gist, others to scan for specific information or answer comprehension questions that require a more detailed understanding of the text.

It may be useful to treat each paragraph differently. For example, you could read one paragraph with the whole class and get students to read the other parts individually or in pairs.

Depending on time, you could also exploit the articles further by focusing on useful language or by asking students to respond to ideas in the text.

A

- Write *Burberry* on the board. Ask students if they know the company. Write down any ideas on the board.

- Reassure students that they do not need to understand every word. The aim is to get a general sense of the article and complete the exercises.

- However, you may wish to pre-teach some terms (*leader, luxury brand, married, son, daughter, quiet time, back-to-back meetings, takeaway*). Alternatively, use this as an opportunity to introduce the class to dictionary work.

- Point to the article. Ask students: *What's the title?* (From small town to global leader) and *How many paragraphs are there in the article?* (five).

- Focus on the top photograph and ask: *What's her name?* (Angela Ahrendts).

- Read the first paragraph with the class. Ask students: *Is Angela Ahrendts German?* (No, she's American.)

- Ask the class to read the rest of the article to themselves.

LESSON NOTES

- Ask students to complete the chart. Highlight the example. They can do this individually, then compare answers in pairs. Check the answers around the class.

Angela Ahrendts	
Age	50
Job	CEO of Burberry
Nationality	American
Family	Married to Greg. They have three children: one son, Jennings (15), and two daughters (14 and 11).
Interests outside work	Her family – likes having takeaway pizza with her children, playing basketball with them, visiting her family in Indiana.

B

- Read the sentences with the class and check understanding. Clarify meaning where necessary (*global*, *teenagers*, *away on business*).

- Ask students to read the article again and decide whether the sentences are true or false.

- Tell students to correct the sentences that are false.

- Ask students to work in pairs and compare their answers.

- Go through the answers with the class.

> 1 F (It's a British company, with its headquarters in London.)
>
> 2 T
>
> 3 F (One of her daughters is just 11.)
>
> 4 F (They go to an American international school in London.)
>
> 5 T
>
> 6 F (She is away on business for about one week every month.)
>
> 7 F (She is so busy that she only has time for work and her family.)
>
> 8 T

- This may also be a good point to check what other vocabulary for the family students know (*mother, father, husband, wife, sister, brother,* etc.).

C

- Ask individual students to read out the example questions and ask them to find the answers in the text (*Yes, she is*; *Indiana in the USA*).

- On the board write:
  Angela Ahrendts is a CEO.
  Is Angela Ahrendts a CEO?

- Ask students to read out one or two more sentences from the article that use *to be*. Write the sentences on the board and elicit how to say them as questions. Ask the questions and elicit short answers.

- On the board write:
  Burberry's headquarters are in London

- Ask: *What question do you need to ask to get this as an answer?* (Where are Burberry's headquarters?). Students will do more work on question words on page 11, but this may be a good opportunity to find out what question words they know.

- Ask students to work in pairs. Give them a few moments to look at the article and prepare five questions. Make sure that students know that they should both write the questions on separate pieces of paper, as they will need them in the next exercise. Circulate and help.

D

- Divide the class into new pairs and get students to ask and answer questions about Angela Ahrendts and her life.

- Circulate, paying attention to word order, question formation and short answers.

- Books closed. Ask pairs what they remember about Angela Ahrendts. Have a feedback session and encourage students to use sentences (*She is a CEO, She is American,* etc.).

➡ Text bank (pages 132–133)

Language focus 1: *to be*

Students look at the present simple positive and negative forms. To practise, they complete sentences about a woman called Maristella and listen to the answers before completing a chart about themselves and writing a paragraph about their partner. They also look at question forms.

- Give students a few moments to read the Language focus box.

- Emphasise that *to be* is usually used to describe people and things. You could give the examples *Burberry is a global company* (describes a company), *I'm a teacher* (describes a person), *We're in the classroom* (describes the class), etc.

- Focus on the form of the present simple. Highlight the contracted forms of *to be*.

LESSON NOTES

A

- Look at the example together. Invite students to call out suggestions for item 2 (*I'm*). Make sure students understand that they should use the short forms.

> 1 name's 2 I'm 3 I'm 4 I'm 5 I'm
> 6 They're 7 husband's 8 he's 9 sister's
> 10 She's 11 We're 12 son's

B 🔊 CD1.10

- Play the recording twice for students to check their answers.
- Elicit the long form of each of the answers.

C

- Tell the class some things about yourself, using the chart as a guide.
- Write the categories on the board. Clarify any unfamiliar vocabulary. Indicate that you want students to call out information about you. Add the information to the board. Demonstrate introducing yourself to a student, using the information (*Hello, I'm ...*).
- Ask students to complete the chart about themselves.
- Divide the class into pairs. Get students to use the information in the chart to tell their partner about themselves. They should make notes on what their partner says.
- Circulate and monitor. Note any problem areas to clarify with the class.

D

- Ask students to write a paragraph about their partner, using the notes they made in Exercise C.
- Tell students to use the first paragraph of the text from Exercise A as a model, but remind them that they are now using the third person form; write the sentence *He's/She's interested in ...* on the board to enable them to include information about their partner's interests and favourite sports.
- Ask students if they know any other ways of talking about likes and dislikes (e.g. *I like ...* , *I enjoy ...*).

E

- Point out that this exercise is concerned with negative forms of *to be*.
- Refer students back to the Language focus box.
- Go through the example with the class. Then tell students to complete the rest individually before comparing their answers with a partner.

- Elicit answers from the pairs.

> 1 she isn't 4 I'm not
> 2 they aren't 5 it isn't
> 3 he isn't 6 she isn't

F

- Briskly match the questions and answers around the class.

> 1 c 2 a 3 e 4 d 5 b

G

- Draw students' attention to the example.
- Refer students back to the information about Maristella in Exercise A. Ask students to suggest another question and write it on the board. Elicit the answer. If students respond with a short form, indicate that you want more information.
- Give students a few moments to prepare questions individually. More confident classes can ask the questions without preparation.
- Divide the class into pairs and tell students to take turns to ask and answer questions.
- Circulate and monitor.

Language focus 2: *a/an* with jobs, *wh-* questions

Students look at the use of *a* before a consonant and *an* before a vowel in the context of jobs. They also look at the key question words (*what, who, where*) and their use with *to be*.

- Read the information in the Language focus box with the class.
- When presenting *a/an*, model the /ə/ sound of *a*. Write two or three jobs, such as *designer* and *engineer*, on the board and elicit whether they take *a* or *an*.
- Ask students to translate *what*, *who* and *where* into L1.
- Check whether students know any other *wh-* question words (*why, when, how* are usually included here, too).
- Model the intonation of the example questions.
- Ask students: *Is the verb before or after the question word?* (after)
- Highlight the contracted forms and elicit the long forms (e.g. *What's = What is*).

LESSON NOTES

A

- Encourage the class to check any unfamiliar jobs in a dictionary and model pronunciation for them.
- Tell students to decide whether each job is preceded by *a* or *an*.
- Check the answers around the class.

a	an
cashier	accountant
consultant	architect
director	artist
doctor	engineer
journalist	executive
lawyer	office worker
manager	optician
personal assistant (PA)	
pilot	
receptionist	
research analyst	
sales assistant	
technician	
telephone operator	
trainee	

B

- Quickly teach or revise vocabulary for the family (*mother, father, brother, sister, son, daughter, husband, wife*).
- Ask a student to read out the example.
- Tell the class about your job and the jobs of your family and friends.
- Divide the class into pairs. Tell students to take turns to talk about their job and the jobs of their family and friends.
- Get one or two pairs to tell you about the jobs of people they know.
- If appropriate, ask students to work in groups and list the jobs of everyone in the class. Nominate individuals to tell you the job of someone in the class.

C 🔊 CD1.11–1.13

- Go through the questions in the chart and check understanding.

- Tell students that they are going to hear three people talk about their jobs.
- Students listen and complete the table.
- Play the recording again to give students the opportunity to check their answers.
- Check answers around the class.

Pierre	Gustavo	Silvia
an engineer	a lawyer	an architect
Switzerland	Argentina	Sicily
Singapore	New York	Rome
an IT consultant	a journalist	a househusband

D

- Ask: *What is Pierre's job?* Elicit the answer (*an engineer*).
- Divide the class into pairs and get students to ask and answer questions about Pierre, Gustavo and Silvia.
- Circulate and help. Note any areas where students need more practice.
- You could nominate two or three pairs to ask and answer questions.

Skills: Introducing yourself and others

In this section, the class listens to three conversations. Students listen first for general information and say whether statements are true or false. They then listen for specific information and complete three extracts from the conversations. Finally, students use the language to practise similar conversations.

A 🔊 CD1.14–1.16

- Point out that the focus of this section is on people introducing themselves and other people in a natural way.
- Elicit any phrases students already have for introducing themselves and other people.
- Play Conversation 1 (recording 1.14). Pause to elicit how many people are speaking (*three*).
- Ask for a volunteer to read the two statements about Conversation 1. Ask students whether the statements are true or false. Encourage students to correct the statements using complete sentences (*Jim Davis works in sales; Paula will be an intern (in the company) for three months*).
- Play the other two conversations, pausing after each to elicit whether the statements are true or false and get students to correct false statements.

LESSON NOTES

Conversation 1

1   F (Jim Davis works in sales.)

2   F (Paula will be an intern for three months.)

Conversation 2

3

4   F (Jonathan Ross is an assistant to Lucy Collins.)

Conversation 3

5   F (They work for the same company.)

6   T

B 🔊 CD1.14–1.16

- Focus on the Useful language box. Read the phrases together and clarify any unfamiliar vocabulary.

- Play the three conversations again and pause after each while students fill in the gaps.

- Ask students to compare their answers with a partner.

- Play the recording a final time for students to check.

> 1 This   2 Nice   3 name's   4 director   5 do
> 6 introduce   7 colleague   8 Pleased   9 in
> 10 work   11 going   12 colleagues

C

- Look at the audio scripts on pages 158–159. Ask students to read through the three conversations. Ask students: *Which conversation is most informal (friendly and relaxed)? Which is most formal (serious and official)?* Encourage students to give reasons for their answers.

> – Most informal conversation: Conversation 3
>   Reason. The language is informal. For example, they greet each other with the words *Hi*, which is an informal greeting.
>
> – Most formal conversation: Conversation 2
>   Reason: The use of formal language. For example *introduce* and *colleague*. Formal language is used to make the introduction. Also Lucy introduces herself formally, giving her position in the company.

- Ask students to choose one of the conversations to read in pairs. Encourage them to copy the intonation from the recording.

- Ask students to practise the conversations again. This time, encourage them to include other phrases from the Useful language box.

- Choose one or two pairs to read out their conversations.

D

- Divide the class into pairs. Once again, focus students on the Useful language box.

- Give students time to read the information on pages 134 and 140 and to prepare their conversations.

- Encourage students to try to improvise. Allow less-confident students to write the dialogue together before reading it, but then encourage them to try again without referring to their notes.

- Choose one or two pairs to read out their conversations. Praise phrases that students use.

◎ Students can watch the conversations on the DVD-ROM.

➡ Resource bank: Speaking (page 163)

CASE STUDY

A job fair in Singapore

Students role-play being at a job fair in Singapore. They talk about three young people who are looking for a job in sales. They then choose one of the candidates to talk to and give reasons for their choice. Finally, they role-play a conversation between a director of a company and the job seeker.

Background

- Read the background information together with the class. Clarify where necessary.

- Ask questions to check that students understand (*What sort of company is Treadlight? Where is the job fair? Why are you there? What job do the three young people want?* etc.).

- Point to the information about Jenny Wong. Ask check questions such as *What is her name? Where is she from? Is she an accountant?*

Task

- Ask students to work in pairs. Highlight the examples in the first section and ask individual students to read them out.

- Get students to talk about the three people.

- Circulate and help if necessary.

- In their pairs, students use the prompts in the second section to decide which candidate they want to meet.

- Give students a few minutes to make their decision. Encourage them to think of a reason why they chose their candidate.

- Get students to discuss their choice with their partner. Check that they understand that they can disagree with their partner's choice.

- Write the Student A question prompts from the third section on the board. Ask students to suggest ideas for the first question (*Where do you come from?*).

- Divide the class into two groups. Tell Group A that they are employees of Treadlight Film Company and ask them to use the prompts to make questions. More confident classes may wish to add an extra question. Tell Group B that they are job seekers. Ask them to look at the question prompts and think of answers to the questions. They can base their answers on the people in the profiles or use their own ideas.

- Ask students to work in A/B pairs and role-play the conversation. Remind the student playing the Treadlight Film Company employee to introduce himself/herself at the start of the conversation.

- Circulate and help where needed. Have a brief feedback session to ask pairs what went well with the conversation and what they would change.

- If you have time, you could ask students to change roles and role-play the conversation again.

Writing

- Ask students for ideas about how to begin and end an e-mail. Write suggestions on the board. If students suggest the formal phrases often used in a letter (*Dear, Yours sincerely, Yours faithfully,* etc.), contrast these with the more informal phrases typically used in an e-mail (*Hello, Hi, Regards, Best wishes,* etc.).

- Read the instructions and the example together. Refer students to the Writing file. Spend some time looking at the model together. Focus on how to begin and end the e-mail and compare with the phrases suggested by the class.

- Tell students to write an e-mail about one of the candidates to their boss.

- Circulate, helping and encouraging.

- In pairs, ask students to compare their e-mails.

- Ask one or two students to read out their e-mail.

- If practical, collect in the written e-mails and check for any areas where students may need extra work.

➡ Writing file (Course Book page 126)

➡ Resource bank: Writing (page 189)

Work and leisure

AT A GLANCE

	Classwork – Course Book	Further work
Lesson 1 *Each lesson (excluding case studies) is about 45–60 minutes. This does not include administration and time spent going through homework.*	<u>**Starting up**</u> Students make word partnerships and listen to four people talking about what they want from work. **Vocabulary 1: Days, months, dates** Students practise days, months and dates and use the prepositions *in*, *at* and *on* with time phrases. **Reading: Describing your routine** Students read an article about Eugene Kaspersky, President and CEO of Kaspersky Lab, a Russian security software company.	**Practice File** Vocabulary (page 8) **i-Glossary** (DVD-ROM) **Text bank** (pages 134–135)
Lesson 2	**Language focus 1: Present simple** Students look at the present simple to talk about habits and work routines. **Vocabulary 2: Leisure activities** Students use leisure activities, verbs and time phrases to talk about leisure time. **Listening: Working and relaxing** Students listen to an interview with Ros Pomeroy, where she describes what she likes about her job and what she likes to do to relax.	**Practice File** Language review (page 9) **i-Glossary** (DVD-ROM) **Resource bank: Listening** (page 176) **Course Book Listening** (DVD-ROM)
Lesson 3	**Language focus 2: Adverbs and expressions of frequency** Students complete exercises using adverbs and expressions of frequency and listen to three people talking about their typical day. <u>**Skills: Talking about work and leisure**</u> Students match questions and answers about work and leisure, then listen to a conversation about what Tim does at the weekend. Afterwards, they talk about their own work and leisure activities.	**Practice File** Language review (page 9) **Resource bank: Speaking** (page 164) **Course Book Skills Dialogues** (DVD-ROM)
Lesson 4 *Each case study is about 30 minutes to 1 hour.*	<u>**Case study: Hudson Design Inc.**</u> Students role-play an interview between a member of the Human Resources department and unhappy employees of a website design company. **Writing** Students use the information from the case study to write an e-mail to the Human Resources team.	**Resource bank: Writing** (page 190) **Practice File** Writing (page 10)

For a fast route through the unit focusing mainly on speaking skills, just use the underlined sections.

For one-to-one situations, most parts of the unit lend themselves, with minimal adaptation, to use with individual students. Where this is not the case, alternative procedures are given.

BUSINESS BRIEF

It has never been easy to balance work and leisure. During the late 20th century, the concept of a **job for life** was largely replaced by **short-term** or **fixed-term contracts**. Recent economic upheavals have made many workers feel that their **job security** is less secure. Some find themselves with too much free time on their hands when company **restructures** lead to **redundancies**.

Despite these challenges, **workforce** values in the 21st century do seem to be shifting. Employees are less willing to trade all other aspects of life for purely professional or financial gains. **Work–life balance** has become a new goal for many. The average length of the European working week is decreasing, from 40.5 hours in 1991 to 37.5 hours in 2010. **Self-employed** workers in Europe can expect to work longer hours, with 42 per cent working more than 48 hours a week. Similarly, longer hours are more usual in **manufacturing** (with 20 per cent of the workforce working more than 48 hours a week) than in **service industries** (where 15 per cent work more than 48 hours a week).*

New technologies have proved a double-edged sword. E-mail, laptops and smartphones have intensified the pace of work and allow people to be contacted anywhere at any time. However, they have also allowed employers and employees to explore different ways of working. **Teleworking** seems like a natural application of modern technology. It can help to balance employment with **domestic** commitments and allow greater time for leisure activities by cutting down on the time spent **commuting**. Some **flexible working practices**, such as **flexitime** or **part-time** work, have also become well established. Some people choose to **downshift** by moving to a less demanding job or decreasing hours and pay, in order to enjoy a less pressurised **lifestyle** and to improve their **quality of life**.

Work remains an integral and, for most of us, essential part of our everyday life. We are arguably armed with more tools and opportunities than ever before to share the time we give to work and the time we give to ourselves and family. Yet getting that balance right remains a difficult task.

Read on

*http://www.eurofound.europa.eu/pubdocs/2010/74/en/3/EF1074EN.pdf

A report on European working conditions carried out by the European Foundation for the Improvement of Living and Working Conditions.

http://www.ons.gov.uk/ons/dcp171766_258996.pdf

Details of a survey from the Office of National Statistics about the balance between work and leisure

http://www.businesslink.gov.uk/bdotg/action/layer?topicId=1074409708

Meet the need for work–life balance, a series of documents exploring issues connected to work–life balance from the perspective of employers and employees

Ian Sanders: *Juggle, Rethink work, Reclaim your life,* Capstone, 2009

LESSON NOTES

Warmer

- It is useful to recycle vocabulary or grammar from previous lessons to help students consolidate language.

- Books closed. Divide the class into groups.

- Ask groups to write as many jobs as they can in two minutes. Get them to include *a/an*.

- Groups take turns to call out countries and nationalities. Write ideas on the board. Check pronunciation. Revise spelling by occasionally asking: *How do you spell that*?

- Depending on your class, you can make the activity competitive by awarding groups a point for correctly using *a/an* and another point for thinking of a job that the other groups do not have on their lists.

Overview

- Tell students that they will be studying language for work and leisure today.

- Ask students to look at the Overview section on page 14. Point to each heading and elicit or explain a little about each. Point to the sections you will be covering in this lesson, using the table on page 19 of this book as a guide.

Quotation

- Write the quotation on the board and read it with the whole class.

- Divide the class into pairs. Ask students to discuss whether they agree or not. Keep this brief.

- Ask students as a class if they agree or disagree with the quotation. Encourage students to give reasons where possible.

Starting up

This section looks at what people want from work. Students make word partnerships and use the language to talk about the most important things about work for themselves.

A

- Books closed. Divide the class into pairs. Write the examples on the board and elicit one or two further ideas and add these to the list.

- Give students five minutes to list things that they think are important in a job (such as salary or holiday). Encourage them to use dictionaries. Have a brief feedback session.

- Students might not be able to contribute much language at this stage; if so, allow them to look at the boxes in Exercise B for ideas. However, it is useful to ask students to attempt this exercise 'blind' at first to ascertain their level of vocabulary in this area.

B ◀)) CD1.17–1.20

- Books open. Explain to students that certain words often go together to form common expressions.

- Point to section 1 and explain that *high salary* is a word partnership. Ask students what words they think make other word partnerships in that section.

- Do the same with the other three sections.

---

1 high salary, long holidays, helpful colleagues

2 company car, mobile phone, parking facilities

3 friendly boss, travel opportunities, job security

4 fast promotion, flexible hours, sports facilities

- Play the recording for students to check.

- If necessary, pause the recording after each of the speakers and elicit the word partnerships.

C

- Focus on the example. Do item 2 with the class to demonstrate.

- Ask students to complete the exercise individually.

- If students find this difficult, point out that sentences 1–3 are from section 1, sentence 4 is from section 2 and sentences 5 and 6 are from section 4.

- Check the answers around the class.

---

2 long holidays   3 helpful colleagues
4 travel opportunities   5 fast promotion
6 flexible hours

- Check students' understanding of the remaining word partnerships.

D

- Tell students about some of the things that you want from work. Write the list on the board.

- Get students to work individually and use the word partnerships from Exercise B to make their own list of things that they want from work.

- After a few minutes, divide the class into pairs.

- Ask students to compare their lists with a partner and to choose the five most important things from the combined lists.

- Elicit ideas around the class. Compare and contrast opinions.

LESSON NOTES

Vocabulary 1: Days, months, dates

Students look at vocabulary for days and months, prepositions of time and time phrases.

A

- Do this briskly with the whole class.

- Books closed. Model and drill pronunciation by asking students to take turns saying the days of the week with a partner.

- Ask students to name the days that are the weekend.

- This may be a good opportunity to point out that days and months are written with a capital letter.

> Friday 5, Monday 1, Saturday 6, Tuesday 2, Sunday 7, Thursday 4, Wednesday 3
>
> The weekend is Saturday and Sunday.

- You may wish to tell your class that in Muslim societies, the weekend is Friday and the week starts on Saturday. In Jewish society, the weekend is Saturday and the week starts on Sunday.

B

- Go through the months checking that students know the correct order and pronunciation. Do the same for the seasons.

- Ask students to complete the exercise with a partner.

- The answer key describes northern hemisphere seasons. If appropriate, allow for different answers for the southern hemisphere.

- Encourage students to dictate the months that go with each season as you write them on the board. Answers will depend on the hemisphere that you live in.

- Books closed. Ask students questions such as: *Is April in winter?*

- Ask students what their favourite season or month is.

Spring	Summer	Autumn	Winter
March, April, May	June, July, August	September, October, November	December, January, February

C

- Look at the example, then do the next two items with the whole class to demonstrate how to do the exercise.

- Ask students to complete the exercise individually. Circulate and monitor, helping where necessary.

> **2** in **3** on **4** on **5** in **6** on **7** in
> **8** at (BrE) / on (AmE) **9** at (BrE) / on (AmE)

D 🔊 CD1.21

- Play the recording for students to check their answers.

- Write on the board *15th February* and elicit how to say the date (*the 15th of February*). Point out that we say *in February* but *on (the) 15th (of) February*.

- Highlight the differences between the use of *at* and *on* in British and American English.

- Also highlight that we say *in the morning/afternoon/ evening* but *on Monday morning*.

- Books closed. Say some time phrases (*night*, *the afternoon*, *Friday evening*, etc.). Ask students to call out the preposition that goes with the phrase. Write some other dates on the board and get students to say them.

E

- Draw attention to the example. Ask students to use the prepositions to complete the sentences. Get students to compare the remaining answers.

- Check the answers around the class.

- Ask students to say the dates of special holidays in their country.

> **2** at (BrE) / on (AmE) **3** on **4** in **5** on

F

- Read the instructions together. Check students understand *busy* and *quiet*.

- Ask two students to read the example questions and responses to the class.

- Indicate that you want students to ask you the question. Respond and ask students to suggest other possible questions and responses (*When are you busy/ quiet at the weekend /in January /during the week?* etc.).

- Divide the class into pairs. Students take turns to ask and respond to questions about when they are busy and quiet.

- Circulate and monitor. Note any areas where students may need more practice.

G

- Write the three bullet points on the board and explain to students that they are going to write a short paragraph answering the questions.

- The first two should be fairly straightforward, as students have just discussed this in Exercise F.

- The third question may need more thought. Ensure that students understand it and perhaps elicit some examples (e.g. *when I wake up on the first morning of a holiday, when the first snow falls*). You may also need to help them with language to express why

LESSON NOTES

they enjoy these moments (e.g. *because it makes me feel …*).

- You could model this by talking about your day.

- When students have finished writing their paragraphs, ask them to compare with a partner. Encourage them to point out any errors they spot (you may need to monitor this).

◉ i-Glossary

Reading: Describing your routine

Students read about the CEO of Kaspersky Lab, a Russian security software company.

This could be a good opportunity to compare Eugene Kaspersky's routine with students' own.

A

- Students will have come across the term *CEO* in Unit 1. To recycle, write the letters *CEO* on the board and ask students what they stand for (*Chief Executive Officer*). If necessary, explain that this is the person in charge of running a company.

- Ask students to imagine what the life of a CEO of a big company might be like. Encourage them to brainstorm the sort of daily routine he or she might have and write a schedule on the board.

- Check that students understand the meaning of the next two questions. Get students to work in small groups and discuss. Keep this brisk and have a brief feedback session.

- Ask students to look at the title of the article and the photo. Have any of them heard of Eugene Kaspersky? Who do they think he is?

- Read the first paragraph together. Point to the photograph and ask: *What's his name? What's his job? Where is the company based? How many countries does the company have offices in? Does the company have a competitor?*

B

- Ask students to read the rest of the article. Give them five minutes for this. Then ask students what Eugene does in a typical day at work (*He travels*, *he attends meetings*, *he goes to trade shows*, *he sometimes gives presentations*, *he spends time talking to colleagues*.). Look at the schedule they wrote in Exercise A and ask students if any of Eugene's activities appear there.

- Ask how much time he spends travelling (*50%*). See if students know any other ways to say this (*He spends half his time travelling*.). Ask where he is based when he isn't travelling (*Moscow*).

- Get students to say how Eugene relaxes when he's in Moscow (*He goes to the gym*.). Ask whether holidays

are important to Eugene (*yes*). Encourage students to say where he goes on holiday in winter and summer (*In winter he goes skiing and in summer he goes to the mountain*.).

- You could ask individual students around the class questions such as: *Do you attend meetings / give presentations / go to the gym / go skiing?* Students answer yes or no.

C

- Have students read the questions and check that they understand *formal* and *informal* and *24/7*.

- Ask students to read the article again to find the answer to the first question. Get them to compare their ideas with a partner. Encourage them to say what information in the text makes them think this (*Many people in the office are friends, some go on holiday together, people dress informally, Kaspersky normally wears shirts and jeans*.). Ask: *What clothes do people usually wear to the office? What do they wear at the weekend?*

- As a class, discuss questions 2 and 3. Again ask students to say what information in the text helped them to answer the question.

- If you have time, you could discuss whether students think it is a good idea to take a holiday where they can't use the Internet or mobile phones.

---

1 Informal – the article tells us that *The Moscow office is like a big family* and that Kaspersky spends time in the office talking informally to people at their desks or in the company restaurant. Kaspersky also dresses informally at work.

2 In other countries – the article says *Most of the company's sales are outside Russia*.

3 No – he works hard, but he also thinks it's important to relax. He tries to take two days off a month and has holidays in the winter and summer. He doesn't get up early and goes to the gym at the end of the office day to relax.

D

- Read the statements with the whole class.

- Highlight the example.

- Ask students to complete the exercise individually.

- Stop and give students the opportunity to compare answers together. Then check the answers around the class.

- Ask students to identify where in the article they found the answers.

LESSON NOTES

2　F (He normally wears shirts and jeans. He only wears a suit for very important meetings.)

3　F (The article says that he doesn't get up early, especially after a business trip.)

4　T (When he's in Moscow, he goes to the gym with his personal trainer at the end of the office day.)

5　T (He travels a lot and doesn't get much sleep on business trips, so he needs to relax when he is in Moscow.)

6　F (He also goes skiing in the winter.)

E

● Ask students to complete the exercise and read through the article again to check.

● Check the answers together.

1 b　2 a　3 d　4 c　5 g　6 e　7 h　8 f

● Invite students to add more examples of nouns to go with the verbs *attend*, *give*, *spend* and *go*.

F

● Tell students about your typical day and holiday.

● Divide the class into pairs.

● Ask students to use the prompts to tell their partner about their day and holiday. If they don't want to use real information they can use their imagination.

● Ask two or three stronger students to tell the class about their partner using *he* or *she*.

➡ Text bank (pages 134–135)

Language focus 1: Present simple

Students are introduced to the present simple.

A

● Emphasise the use of the present simple for habits and routines – things that happen on a regular basis. To demonstrate, tell the class again about your typical day.

● Ask students to repeat back the parts that they remember and write the sentences on the board. Elicit and underline the verbs.

● Use the Language focus box as a guide and elicit or present all the forms of *travel*, *attend* and *work*.

● Look at the example together.

● Ask students to complete the article about Darren Throop's working day.

● Get students to compare their answers with a partner.

● Ask the class to dictate the completed article to you. Write it on the board.

2 does　3 makes　4 checks　5 drives　6 has
7 spends　8 finishes　9 travels　10 likes

● Ask the class one or two questions about Darren Throop (*Does he go to the gym? Does he get up at 8.30?* etc.). Elicit short answers (*Yes, he does. / No, he doesn't.*).

● If time allows, divide students into pairs. Ask them to take turns to ask and answer questions about Darren Throop's day.

B

● This exercise gives students practice in all forms of the present simple positive.

● Tell students that it is important to read the information carefully to find the correct form of the verbs in brackets to use.

● Highlight the example and elicit the answer to item 2 (*works*). Then have students complete the exercise individually.

● Check the answers around the class.

2 works　3 work　4 live　5 travel　6 drives
7 like　8 play　9 go

C

● Use Exercise B as a model to write a paragraph about yourself on the board. Pause occasionally to invite the class to guess or provide information about you.

● Tell students to write a paragraph about themselves. You may wish to get students to do this for homework. Collect in the written work to check any areas that need more work.

Vocabulary 2: Leisure activities

This section introduces vocabulary for leisure activities, as well as the verbs *going to*, *playing*, *watching* and *listening to*. Students talk about the activities using *love*, *like*, *quite like* and *don't like*.

A

● Books closed. Ask students what leisure activities (things to do when they are not studying or working) they can think of. They can use dictionaries to help. Write suggestions on the board.

● Books open. Get students to look at Exercise A. Quickly run through any activities which were not on the list to check understanding.

LESSON NOTES

- Highlight the example and do the next two together (*watching*; *going to*). Ask students to work with a partner and complete the exercise.

- Check the answers around the class.

> **2** watching **3** going to **4** listening to
> **5** playing **6** going to **7** playing/watching
> **8** going to **9** going to / listening to
> **10** playing **11** watching **12** playing

- Can the class add any other activities to the verbs (e.g. *going to the theatre, playing squash, listening to the radio*)?

B

- Highlight the *-ing* ending of the verb following *love* and *like*. At this stage, it is not necessary to go into *like/love + to +* infinitive (e.g. *I like to run at the weekend*).

- Talk about the activities that you love, like, quite like and don't like using time phrases.

- In pairs, get students to talk about leisure activities using the verbs in box 1 and the time phrases in box 2. Circulate and encourage.

- Spend some time comparing ideas around the class. Use this as an opportunity to practise the third person form (*Tariq doesn't like playing golf at the weekend, Lena loves going to restaurants in the evening*, etc.).

 i-Glossary

Listening: Working and relaxing

Students listen to an interview in three parts. The listening recycles vocabulary and verbs for leisure activities. Students practise different skills with each part of the listening. In the first, they take notes; in the second, they listen for specific information; the third part is used in a prediction exercise.

A ◀)) CD1.22

- Point to the picture of Ros Pomeroy. Tell students that they are going to hear an interview with her in three parts. Ask students to suggest ideas about what she likes in her job.

- Play the first part of the recording and elicit the answer around the class.

> There is no such thing as a typical day.

- Ask students if they think it is a good or bad thing not to have a typical day.

B ◀)) CD1.22

- Do the first one together to demonstrate the activity.

- Play the recording again while students complete the notes.

- Ask the class to dictate the notes while you write the information on the board.

> **1** meetings **2** running **3** discussion **4** office
> **5** computer **6** phone

- If you have time, confident classes could use the information to work in pairs and make true and false statements about Ros (e.g. *She doesn't have meetings; False, she does have meetings.*).

C ◀)) CD1.23

- Look at the questions together and check understanding (in particular, *enough* and *overall*).

- Tell students they are going to hear the second part of the interview.

- Play it twice and give students the opportunity to compare answers with a partner before checking with the whole class.

> **1** Ros works very long hours; she has teenage children.
>
> **2** Yes, she does.

D

- Ask students to work in pairs and say what they think Ros likes doing to relax.

- Give students two or three minutes to think of ideas and have a feedback session. Encourage students to express their ideas in sentences (*I think she likes playing golf,* etc.).

E ◀)) CD1.24

- Play the final part of the interview and elicit answers.

> She likes reading the newspaper and going running.

- Get the class to recap things that they know about Ros from the three parts of the listening. They can do this in writing, as a whole-class activity dictating information as you write it on the board, or as a speaking activity with a partner. Students could then check their information by referring to the audio script on page 159.

F

- Ask students to suggest more activities to relax and write them on the board. Ask them to guess which ones you do to relax.

- Say what you like to do to relax using whole sentences.

- Divide the class into pairs and ask students to tell their partner what they like to do to relax.

LESSON NOTES

- Get two or three confident students to share information about their partner.

- ◉ Students can watch the interview with Ros Pomeroy on the DVD-ROM.

- ➜ Resource bank: Listening (page 176)

Language focus 2: Adverbs and expressions of frequency

Students are shown the use and form of the adverbs *always*, *usually*, *often*, *sometimes* and *never*. Expressions of frequency are introduced. The class listens to three speakers talking about a typical day.

- Refer students to the Language focus box. Give them a few moments to read through it.

- Read the information about adverbs and expressions of frequency together.

A

- Books closed. Write the first sentence on the board and ask a student to insert *usually* in the correct place.

- Remind students that the adverb usually goes before the main verb. When *to be* is used, the adverb goes after the verb.

- Tell students to complete the exercise individually.

- Check the answers around the class. Spend time clarifying and going over the explanations where necessary.

> **2** They **always** start their first meeting at nine o'clock.
>
> **3** We are **never** late for meetings.
>
> **4** I am **often** busy in the afternoon.
>
> **5** The office **sometimes** closes at 3 p.m.

B

- Look at the example together. Explain that students need to choose the adverb that gives sentence b) the same meaning as sentence a).

- Ask students to cross out the incorrect word in each sentence b). Get students to compare answers in pairs, then check the answers around the class.

- Read the correct sentences together.

> **2** usually   **3** sometimes   **4** never   **5** often

- Draw attention to the position of the adverbs and expressions of frequency in each sentence.

C 🔊 CD1.25–1.27

- Look at the questions together. Check students' understanding.

- Pre-teach any vocabulary you think your class may have problems with (e.g. *diary, desk*).

- Tell students that they will hear three people talking about a typical day. Point out that the speakers are from different countries.

- Play Mark's interview (recording 1.25). Pause after his response to each question, eliciting the answers.

- Play Isabelle's and Dan's interviews and ask students to complete the chart.

- Play the recordings again for students to check. Then elicit the answers around the class.

	Mark	Isabelle	Dan
1	Say hello to colleagues Check e-mail	Check e-mail and diary Have coffee with colleagues	Have a meeting with team Check BlackBerry Reply to e-mails
2	Some days go home for lunch Other days have lunch with colleagues in restaurant	Have sandwich at desk	Company restaurant Go out for lunch with visitors twice a week
3	Go to fashion shows in Paris and New York	Never travel	Visit sales office in South Africa three times a year Go to Europe once a month, for a week
4	Meet friends for a meal Go clubbing	Spend time with children Invite friends round for dinner Go to cinema	Read a lot Listen to music Play golf on Sunday mornings

D

- Nominate a student to ask you the four questions in Exercise C. Answer in the same manner as in the recording.

- Divide the class into pairs.

- Get students to ask and answer the questions.

- Circulate and encourage.

E

- Go through the list of prompts and check that students understand the questions.

- Ask one or two students the first two questions.

LESSON NOTES

- Encourage students to suggest other possible questions.

- Divide the class into pairs.

- Ask students to take it in turns to ask and answer the questions with their partner.

- Ask two or three students to talk about their partner using *he* or *she*.

- For more practice, you could ask students to move around the class asking and answering the questions.

Skills: Talking about work and leisure

Students are introduced to and listen to additional useful phrases to talk about how they spend their time and their preference for activities. They then ask and answer questions about work and leisure.

A

- Read the questions and answers with the class. Explain any words your class may have problems with (such as *best*, *free time*, *flexible*, *between*).

- Ask students to match the questions and answers individually. Check the answers around the class.

> 1 b   2 e   3 f   4 a   5 c   6 d

B

- Encourage the class to ask you the questions in Exercise A. Answer about yourself.

- Get students to look at the questions and make a note of their own answers.

- Divide the class into pairs.

- Ask students to take turns to ask and answer the questions. Circulate and help if necessary.

C ◀)) CD1.28

- Play the recording. Pause and ask how many speakers there are (*two*).

- Play it all the way through and get students to tick the questions and answers from Exercise A that they hear in the listening.

- Briskly check answers around the class.

> Questions: 1, 2, 3, 5, 6
>
> Answers: b, c, e, f

D ◀)) CD1.28

- Go over the words in the box and check understanding (e.g. *interested (in)*, *into*).

- Before playing the recording again, ask students to look at the exercise and suggest the words from the box to go into the gaps.

- Play the recording twice for students to check.

> 2 really   3 love   4 interested   5 enjoy
> 6 into   7 watching   8 playing

E

- Read through the Useful language box together.

- Nominate students to read the examples and check understanding.

- Divide the class into pairs.

- Tell students to use phrases from the Useful language box to talk about their work or studies. Circulate and monitor.

- Write on the board:
  I really enjoy …
  I like …
  I don't enjoy …
  I don't like …

- In pairs or small groups, ask students to finish the sentences with ideas about their English lessons.

F

- Get students to ask you questions about what you do in your free time. Use phrases from the Useful language box to answer.

- Ask questions around the class such as: *What do you do in the evening? How often do you go to the cinema? Do you like tennis?*

- Give students about five minutes to prepare questions individually.

- Divide the class into pairs and get students to ask and answer the questions.

G

- Students change partners and tell their new partner about the first person's likes and dislikes. They can change partners again and tell their new partner about their first partner.

- If time allows, students could write short sentences about their partners. Tell students to use *he* or *she* instead of their partner's name.

- Get students to take turns reading out their sentences. Ask the class to guess who the student is describing.

- To make identification more challenging, collect in the descriptions and distribute them at random around the class. Then continue as above.

◎ Students can watch the conversation on the DVD-ROM.

➡ Resource bank: Speaking (page 164)

CASE STUDY

Hudson Design Inc.

A team from Human Resources is interviewing employees at a website design company to find out what problems people have with working conditions in the company.

Background

- Check students understand what type of company Hudson Design is.

- Ask students if they think it would be an interesting place to work. Can they think of any disadvantages of working for a website design company?

- Pre-teach any vocabulary you think your class may need.

- Read the background information with the whole class.

- Clarify where necessary.

- Ask a few check questions such as: *Are the employees happy? Why not? Why is the company worried? What department is interviewing people? What departments are they interviewing?*

🔊 CD1.29

- Play the interview between a member of the Human Resources team and a company employee.

- Get students to work in pairs or small groups and discuss the questions.

Likes: A lot of variety in his job; meets interesting people; his colleagues are his friends

Dislikes: Long hours without a break; doesn't spend enough time with his daughter; doesn't have enough time for leisure and his family

What can he do to solve his problem?

Suggested answers

Talk to his boss and negotiate a better work schedule.

Try to work from home more often.

Task

- Read the first two task instructions together.

- Give students five or 10 minutes to read their role cards and prepare for the interview. Go round the class helping where necessary.

- Depending on your class, you could ask students to prepare in same-role groups.

- When students are ready, ask them to role-play the interview. Circulate and encourage.

- After the interviews, divide the class into two groups (interviewers and employees). Ask each group to make a list of problems and decide which ones are important. Give a time limit of 10 minutes, but if groups are getting involved in the discussion, let it go on a little longer.

- Ask each group to briefly present their ideas. Note ideas on the board and ask the whole class to choose the three working conditions they want to change.

One-to-one

Do the interview as above, taking one of the roles yourself. For Task 3, role-play as a meeting and encourage your student to do most of the talking. Finally, ask your student to identify the three working conditions that he/she would change.

Writing

- Ask students who were interviewers in the Task to choose one of the role cards from page 135. Give them a minute to familiarise themselves with their job.

- Using the information in their role cards, ask students to list their likes and dislikes about their job. They will already have thought about the latter when discussing the problems, so if time is short, ask them to focus on the positive points.

- Then ask them to think about how they would like things to change. They can either stick with the three working conditions they chose at the end of the Task, or choose ones more specific to their job.

- Students then use this information to write the e-mail. The main body of the e-mail should have three paragraphs, corresponding to the three bullet points. However, ensure that students also use appropriate introductory and closing phrases for an internal e-mail.

- You may wish to get students to do this for homework. Collect in the e-mails to check any areas that need more work.

➡ Writing file (Course Book page 126)

➡ Resource bank: Writing (page 190)

Problems

AT A GLANCE

	Classwork – Course Book	Further work
Lesson 1 *Each lesson (excluding case studies) is about 45–60 minutes. This does not include administration and time spent going through homework.*	**Starting up** Students match jobs and problems and listen to four people speaking about problems they have at work. **Vocabulary: Adjectives; *too/enough*** Students look at adjectives and their opposites and use *too* and *enough*. **Listening: Typical work problems** An interview with Jeremy Keeley, a specialist in change leadership. He talks about problems he has at work and problems in companies.	**Practice File** Vocabulary (page 12) **i-Glossary** (DVD-ROM) **Course Book Listening** (DVD-ROM) **Resource bank: Listening** (page 177)
Lesson 2	**Reading: Workplace problems** Three call-centre workers answer the question: 'What are the biggest problems for you at work?' **Language focus 1: Present simple: negatives and questions** Students match questions and answers, make negative sentences and practise the question forms in a role play.	**Text bank** (pages 136–137) **Practice File** Language review (page 13)
Lesson 3	**Language focus 2: *have; some* and *any*** Students look at the use of *have* with *some* and *any* and also *have* to talk about possession. **Skills: Telephoning: solving problems** Students listen to a telephone call where the caller asks to be put through at reception and requests information. They then listen to four phone calls and match them to problems before role-playing a phone conversation talking about problems with an order.	**Practice File** Language review (page 13) **Course Book Skills Telephoning** (DVD-ROM) **Resource bank: Speaking** (page 165)
Lesson 4 *Each case study is about 30 minutes to 1 hour.*	**Case study: High-Style Business Rentals** Students listen to guests commenting on their stay with a company that rents apartments to businesspeople. They compare the experiences with the promises in the company's online advertisement. Then they role-play a telephone conversation between a guest and the manager of the company. **Writing** Students write an internal e-mail to the High-Style Business Rentals head office. They explain the problems and say they want a meeting to discuss future advertising policy.	**Resource bank: Writing** (page 191) **Practice File** Writing (page 14)

For a fast route through the unit focusing mainly on speaking skills, just use the underlined sections.

For one-to-one situations, most parts of the unit lend themselves, with minimal adaptation, to use with individual students. Where this is not the case, alternative procedures are given.

BUSINESS BRIEF

BUSINESS BRIEF

Problems are a fact of life. So **problem-solving** is an essential life skill, both at home and in the office. Many pressurised managers in the modern business world may benefit from training in **conflict resolution** to resolve disagreements.

It is wise to deal with sensitive matters face to face. E-mails and memos may contain sentiments we would modify if speaking to the person directly or may convey an unintended negative tone. Social psychologist Albert Merabian says that words account for seven per cent of communication, tone 38 per cent and body language 55 per cent.* These elements are particularly useful in understanding and resolving potential conflict situations, but can be lost in **online communication**.

In a cross-cultural business context, problems can occur due to cultural misconceptions. Trying to enforce one culture's way of doing things can cause bad feelings. It is always a good idea to research possible cultural differences. For example, short, direct meetings are acceptable in Germany, Switzerland and the USA. However, other cultures, such as those in the Middle East and Latin America, are **relationship-orientated**. Meetings tend to be longer here, as **social interaction** is a vital part of the business process, and a deal may take more than one meeting to **finalise**.

Many problems can be traced back to misunderstandings and loss of perspective. If a **communication breakdown** does occur, it can be helped by:

active listening	Consult people and really listen to what they have to say.
reformulation	Repeat back key points to make sure that no misinterpretation has occurred.
focus	Concentrate on the problem, not on personalities – separate personal differences from the situation in hand.

Sometimes it is useful to employ basic skills that reflect how we would like other people to treat us; be polite, don't shout and respect other people. Problems will still occur, but a peaceful resolution may be easier to find.

Read on

*from 'E-mail can worsen problems' by Yvonne Fontyn, *Business Day* (South Africa) August 20, 2002

Rob Van Haastrecht and Martin Scheepbouer: *Thinking Backwards: The Art of Problem-Solving in Business*, Marshall Cavendish International, 2011

Joan Van Aken, Hans Berends, Hans Van Der Bij: *Problem-Solving in Organizations: A Methodical Handbook for Business and Management Students*, Cambridge University Press, second edition 2012

John Adair: *Decision-Making and Problem-Solving Strategies*, Kogan Page, revised edition 2010

Ken Watanabe: *Problem-solving 101: A Simple Guide for Smart People*, Vermillion, 2009

James M. Higgins: *101 Problem-solving Techniques: The Handbook of New Ideas for Business*, New Management Pub Co, 2005

LESSON NOTES

Warmer

- On the board, write some jobs (e.g. *police officer*, *firefighter*, *nurse*, *teacher*, etc.). Get students to call out more suggestions and write these on the board (maximum 10). Ask students to number the jobs in order from most to least difficult (1 = most difficult). Then get students to work in pairs or small groups and compare their ideas. Where possible, encourage students to give reasons for their choices. Finally, ask pairs/groups to choose the top three jobs that they think are difficult. Ask students to brainstorm what they think is difficult about each job.

Overview

- Tell students that they will be studying language for talking about problems today.

- Ask students to look at the Overview section on page 22. Point to each heading and elicit or explain a little about each. Point to the sections you will be covering in this lesson, using the table on page 29 of this book as a guide.

- Check any unfamiliar vocabulary (such as *adjectives*). Ask whether anybody knows what it means.

Quotation

- Read the quotation and ask students to repeat it.

- Books closed. Get students to dictate the quotation while you write it on the board.

- Ask students if they have heard of Duke Ellington (*an American musician and composer 1899–1974*) and what type of music he played (*jazz*).

Starting up

This section introduces the concept of everyday problems.

Students listen to four people talk about problems that they have at work.

A

- Books closed. Write the jobs (a–d) on the board. Ask students to work in pairs and suggest problems people who do these jobs might have at work. Write ideas on the board.

- Books open. Read through the problems in the box (1–8) and check students understand. Ask them to see if any of their ideas are mentioned.

- With the whole class, match the first two problems in the box to one of the jobs.

- Get students to complete the exercise individually and check ideas with a partner.

- There are a number of possible answers. Have a feedback session with the whole class to compare ideas.

Suggested answers

a) 1, 3, 4, 5, 6

b) 3, 7, 8

c) 1, 2, 7

d) 2, 4, 5

B 🔊 CD1.30–1.33

- Play the four recordings all the way through. Ask students how many different voices they can hear (*four*).

- Pre-teach any vocabulary your class may have problems with (e.g. *stock*, *production*).

- Play the first speaker again (recording 1.30) and point to the example. Elicit which other problem the speaker mentions (*2 difficult customers*).

- Play the second speaker (recording 1.31) and pause to ask what job the speaker has (*office worker*) and what problems are mentioned (*4 computer crashes* and *6 missing documents*).

- Continue with the recordings, pausing after each speaker to give students time to complete the information.

- Ask students to compare their answers with a partner.

- Play the recordings again to check. Elicit the answers around the class.

1 Person c, problems 7 and 2

2 Person a, problems 4 and 6

3 Person d, problems 1 and 5

4 Person b, problems 8 and 3

C

- Make a list on the board of all the problems in Exercise A. Ask students to add other problems that can occur at work or when studying.

- Get students to work in pairs and say what problems they have at work or in their studies.

- If the question is not appropriate for your class (for example, because they work for the same company), you may wish to focus on problems that they had when studying.

Vocabulary: Adjectives; *too*/*enough*

Students match adjectives and their opposites and make sentences using *too* and *enough*.

A

- Check students understand the six adjectives in the box.

- Highlight the example and do sentence 2 with the class to demonstrate.

- Get students to do the exercise in pairs. Then check the answers around the class.

> **2** fast   **3** clean   **4** broken   **5** confusing   **6** noisy

B

- Write on the board: *We are a big/small class*. Elicit which adjective is true. Underline it and point out that *big* and *small* are adjectives because they describe the noun (*class*).

- Ask students: *What is the opposite of big?* (small). Write the phrase on the board.

- Ask students to work in pairs, taking it in turns to ask and answer about the opposites.

- Point to various objects around the class and ask students to call out adjectives to describe them.

- In pairs, ask students to take it in turns to name an object; their partner thinks of as many adjectives as they can to describe it (e.g. car: *fast*, *big*, *safe*, etc.).

- Books closed. Say an adjective and ask students to say the opposite adjective.

C

- Look at the sentences and the example. Then draw a house on the board. Say: *It's too small*. Elicit another way to say this (*It isn't big enough*).

- Highlight the words in brackets at the end of each sentence. Make sure that students are aware that although some of the answers can be expressed in two possible ways, they only need to write one.

- Ask students to complete the sentences in pairs.

- Check the answers with the whole class. If more than one answer is possible, elicit both versions.

> **2** They're too heavy.
>
> **3** It's too early.
>
> **4** It's too slow. / It isn't fast enough.
>
> **5** It's too dangerous./ It isn't safe enough.
>
> **6** It's too big./ It isn't small enough.
>
> **7** It's too expensive./ It isn't cheap enough.
>
> **8** It's too noisy./ It isn't quiet enough.

D

- Refer students back to the list of problems they made in Starting up, Exercise C. Ask them to list those that they have experienced themselves. Allow them to add to the list if they can think of any others.

- Encourage them to talk about the problems in pairs, using *too* and *enough*.

- Circulate to monitor and assist as necessary.

- ◉ i-Glossary

Listening: Typical work problems

Students listen to a specialist in change leadership talk about the problems he has at work.

A CD1.34

- Point to the picture of Jeremy Keeley and ask: *What's his job?* (He's a specialist in change leadership.) Check students understand what he does (*He helps companies deal with change.*).

- Tell students that they are going to hear Jeremy talk about his job and that the listening will be in three parts. Reassure students that they don't need to understand every word. However, you may wish to pre-teach key words that you think your class may have problems with (e.g. *complicated*, *resolve*, *urgent*).

- Books closed. Write on the board: *He is an employee and he runs his boss's business.*

- Play the first part of the interview (recording 1.34) and ask students to say whether the sentence is true or false (*false*). Ask students to correct the sentence (*He is a consultant and he runs his own business.*).

- Books open. Get students to read through the statements. Clarify where necessary.

- Play the recording again and get students to say which statements are true (*2, 3 and 4*). Ask them to correct the first statement while you write it on the board (*Jeremy often works on his own.*).

- Ask students to suggest some adjectives to describe Jeremy's job (e.g. *interesting*, *busy*, *difficult*, etc.).

> **1** F (He is often on his own.)   **2** T   **3** T   **4** T

B ◀)) CD1.35

- Books closed. Dictate these adjectives to the class: *boring, complicated, fast, slow, easy, difficult, efficient*.

- Play the recording and ask students to tick the adjectives they hear (*complicated, fast, difficult, efficient*).

LESSON NOTES

- Books open. Give students time to look at the notes. See if they can fill any of the gaps. Play the recording again and ask students to complete the notes.

- Check answers around the class. You could ask one or two students to read the completed notes.

---

1 change **2** equipment **3** property **4** prices
5 costs

C 🔊 CD1.36

- Read through the questions with the class.

- Play the third part of the interview and pause to elicit answers.

---

1 Complicated problems where lots of people need to be involved

2 A computer system had to be introduced that affected millions of customers and their bills, and at the last moment a problem arose that affected the whole system.

3 Technical team, project team, business team and suppliers

◉ Students can watch the interview with Jeremy Keeley on the DVD-ROM.

➡ Resource bank: Listening (page 177)

Reading: Workplace problems

Students read three people's responses to the question 'What are the biggest problems for you at work?'.

A

- Write on the board: *call centre* and ask students to think about some of the things that people do in this job (e.g. answer phones, talk to customers, take orders, deal with complaints, etc.).

- Run through the words in the box and check students understand. Encourage the class to call out the words that they think describe work in a call centre. Write these on the board.

- If time allows, you could ask students to think of more words to add to the list.

Suggested answers
badly paid, boring, noisy, stressful

B – C

- Books closed. Write the question on the board (*What are the biggest problems for you at work?*). Ask students to work in pairs and suggest problems that a person working in a call centre might have (e.g. rude/angry customers, long hours, etc.) and write these on the board.

- If necessary, pre-teach *call-centre agent*, *workstation*, *headphones*, *screen*. The photo in the Course Book can be used for some of these.

- Books open. Get students to quickly read the three texts to see if they mention their ideas.

- Reassure students that they don't need to understand every word in the three texts.

- Ask students to read the texts again and complete the chart. Point out that not all the problems are mentioned in the texts. Get them to compare their questions with a partner. Check answers around the class.

Problems	Name	Problems	Name
long working day	✓ V	angry customers	✓ V
breaks too short		low pay	
long hours at workstation	✓ B	no time between calls	✓ K
boring work	✓ K	high staff turnover	✓ K
no promotion	✓ K	a lot of noise	✓ B

D

- Get two or three students to read Reply 1 to the class.

- Ask students to say the physical problems that Birgit mentions.

- Get students to mime the part of the body connected to the problem.

---

hearing problems, backache, headaches

E

- Ask students to underline the adjectives in the three replies in Exercise A.

- Get students to compare their answers with a partner.

- Have a feedback session with the whole class.

---

noisy, well paid, boring, stressful

F

- Give students time to think about problems in their workplace or place of study.

- Focus on the example. Ask students to suggest other ways to ask the question (*What problems do you have at work/college? Do you have any problems at work/college?*).

- Get students to work in pairs and take turn to ask and answer the questions. This could be a good opportunity to teach appropriate responses (e.g. *Oh really*, *I see*, *OK*, etc.).

- If you think your class will be uncomfortable talking about their own job or college, they could brainstorm other jobs to discuss.

➡ Text bank (pages 136–137)

Language focus 1: Present simple: negatives and questions

Students focus on the form and use of present simple negatives and questions. Word order can be a problem, in particular, omission of the auxiliary *do*.

- Read through the Language focus box with the whole class and clarify where necessary.

- Point out that *do* changes form in questions and negatives but the main verb does not change form, e.g. *Does he go?* not *Does he goes?* and *She doesn't have* not *She doesn't has*.

- Write the following examples from the reading on page 24:
  It's not easy to talk to customers.
  You don't get time to think.

- Elicit the difference between the two sentences. Point out that the auxiliary *do* is not used with *to be*.

- Highlight the use of *don't/doesn't* in negatives. Write these sentences on the board:
  You have an office.
  She lives in Milan.
  They work for Microsoft.

- Put students in pairs and ask them to make the sentences negative (*You don't have an office. She doesn't live in Milan. They don't work for Microsoft.*).

- Make the first sentence into a question (*Do you have an office?*). Encourage students to say the question forms for the next two sentences (*Does she live in Milan?, Do they work for Microsoft?*). Highlight the use of *do* with questions. Point out or elicit that the answer to a question starting with the verb *do* is usually *yes* or *no*.

- Explain that when questions begin with a question word (such as *where*), they usually need a longer, more detailed answer.

- Point out that a conversation often starts with one or two closed questions and then uses open questions to continue. For example:
  A: Do you like sport?
  B: Yes.
  A: What sports do you play?
  B: Tennis and football.

A

- Books closed. Ask the class to call out any question words they know and write them on the board.

- Divide the class into pairs.

- Books open. Look at the example together.

- Ask students to work in pairs to match the questions and answers.

- Check the answers around the class.

> 2 f   3 e   4 b   5 a   6 c

- Ask students to take turns reading out the questions and answers with a partner.

B

- This exercise focuses on word order.

- Look at the example together.

- Do item 2 with the whole class, on the board.

- Students may find this type of exercise difficult. Circulate and help where necessary.

- Ask students to compare their questions with a partner. Check the answers around the class.

> 2   Does Pierre work in sales?
>
> 3   How often do you travel abroad?
>
> 4   How do you spell *business*?
>
> 5   When does the meeting finish?

C

- Some students may prefer to write the questions first.

- Encourage students to ask you the questions. Check the word order and the form of *do*.

> 2   When do you finish work?
>
> 3   Where do you work?
>
> 4   Who do you report to?
>
> 5   How often do you work at the weekend?

- Divide the class into pairs. Give students time to read their role cards.

- Demonstrate the activity with a confident student.

- Get students to take turns to ask and answer the questions.

- Circulate and help where needed.

- If everyone in the class works, you could get them to ask and answer the questions again with information about themselves.

LESSON NOTES

D

● Highlight the example. Point out that in items 4 and 5, students should not repeat the name or noun phrase in the sentences. Instead, replace *Susan* with *she* and *Our management team* with *it* or *they*.

● Tell students to complete the exercise individually. Then check the answers around the class.

> 2 We waste a lot of paper, but we don't waste (a lot of) electricity.
>
> 3 They agree about most things, but they don't agree about money.
>
> 4 Susan sends a lot of e-mails, but she doesn't send (a lot of / any) faxes.
>
> 5 Our management team discusses business strategy, but they don't / it doesn't discuss employee problems.

E

● Ask five students to each read a sentence aloud. Ensure students understand the sentences and clarify any difficult vocabulary (e.g. *work in teams*).

● Students work individually to tick the sentences that are true for themselves and to change the ones that are false. If students are not in work, ask them to transform all the sentences to the opposite (negative to positive, and positive to negative) for practice.

● Circulate and monitor, making sure that students are forming negatives correctly.

> 1 I don't agree with my manager about everything.
>
> 2 I often work in teams.
>
> 3 I don't always come to work/college on time.
>
> 4 I like giving presentations.
>
> 5 I take work home in the evening or at the weekend.

● Students work in pairs to compare their answers and discuss where there are differences. If none of your students is in work, you can either ask them to imagine a work situation or omit this stage.

Language focus 2: *have; some* and *any*

Students look at the form and use of *have* and *some/any*.

● Give students time to read through the Language focus box.

● List one or two things that you have in the classroom. Encourage students to call out suggestions.

● Ask students: *Do we have a photocopier in the classroom?* Elicit *No* and say: *We don't have a photocopier.*

● Ask students to list some other things that the classroom has and doesn't have.

● If students ask about *Have you got ...? /We haven't got ...*, tell them that this form is common in British English and is also correct.

A

● Get students to make sentences about Marco, using *has / doesn't have*.

● Read the example together and ensure that students understand how to interpret the ticks and crosses.

● Check the answers together.

> 2 Marco doesn't have an iPhone. He has an iPad.
>
> 3 Marco has an interesting job. He doesn't have a high salary.
>
> 4 Marco doesn't have a nice boss. He has some great colleagues.
>
> 5 Marco doesn't have a desktop computer at work. He has a laptop.

● If you feel students can cope with it, ask them to join the pairs of sentences using the conjunctions *and* and *but*. Remind them that a positive sentence with a negative sentence needs *but*, whereas two positive or two negative sentences need *and*.

● You could choose one or two sentences and ask/ elicit questions and responses (*Does Marco have a company car? Yes he does; Does he have an iPhone? No, he doesn't*).

B

● Look at the example together and complete the second question with the class.

● Get students to complete the questions.

● Circulate and help where needed.

● Check answers with the class.

LESSON NOTES

2   What kind of car does she have?

3   Does the company have a restaurant?

4   Do all the rooms have air conditioning?

5   Do I have time to finish this?

C

● Quickly check the vocabulary in Exercise A.

● Divide the class into pairs.

● Get the students to talk about the items in their pairs.

● Circulate and help where needed.

D

● Look at the example together and ask students to suggest another question (e.g. *Do you have a sat-nav?*).

● Divide the class into pairs. Ask students to prepare five questions.

● Pairs circulate and ask three people the survey questions.

● Have a feedback session where students report their results to the class.

Skills: Telephoning: solving problems

Students listen to a call where a person gets through on the phone and asks for information. They then listen to four short phone calls. The Useful language box includes phrases for getting through, giving details of a problem and finding solutions.

A 🔊 CD1.37

● Play the recording all the way through and ask students how many speakers they hear (*three: the receptionist, Marcia and Harry*).

● Play it again and get the whole class to answer the questions. Write the name on the board.

1   She needs the name of the new marketing assistant.

2   J-E-F-F H-A-Y-D-O-N

B 🔊 CD1.37

● Before listening again, see if students can remember the phrases that Marcia uses. Write suggestions on the board.

● Play the recording again and get students to check the phrases on the board.

● Ask students to look at the audio script on page 160 to check.

1   My name's Marcia Jones, Hove Stores.

2   Could you spell his name for me, please?

3   Sorry, could you repeat that, please?

4   I'll speak to you soon, Harry. Bye.

● You could ask students to work in groups of three and read the audio script, then change roles and read again.

C 🔊 CD1.38–1.41

● Play the recordings all the way through and ask students how many phone calls they hear (*four*).

● Play the calls again, pausing after each call for students to complete the exercise.

● Ask students to compare their answers with a partner.

● Check the answers with the whole class.

a) 4   b) 1   c) 2   d) 3

D 🔊 CD1.38–1.41

● Play the recordings again; pause at the end of Call 1 (recording 1.38) and ask students to suggest the missing word in the sentence.

● Play the rest of the calls and have students complete the exercise individually.

● Play the recordings again, pausing after each of the sentences in the exercise to check the answers.

1 boss   2 arrange   3 delivery   4 deal
5 instructions   6 catch; repeat   7 figures
8 look into; invoice

E 🔊 CD1.38–1.41

● Focus on the Useful language box.

● Point out that some of the expressions in the recording may not use exactly the same words as those in the Useful language box.

● Play the recordings and tell students to tick the expressions they hear.

● Ask students to compare their answers with a partner and play the recordings once more to check.

● Look at the audio script with the whole class and check the phrases.

LESSON NOTES

Call 1

Can I speak to ..., please?

I've got a problem.

Call 2

This is ...

Sorry about that.

Thanks for your help. Bye.

Call 3

Good morning, ... speaking.

Sorry to hear that.

Which model is it?

Call 4

Can I speak to ..., please?

Sorry about that.

- Less-confident students may prefer to prepare this exercise in writing first. If so, encourage students to write short notes and use these to have the conversation. As students become more confident, ask them to try the conversation again without using their notes.

- Circulate and encourage. Note any areas that may need revision.

- ◎ Students can watch the phone calls on the DVD-ROM

- ⇥ Resource bank: Speaking (page 165)

- As a follow-up exercise, you could ask students what problems they have making telephone calls in English (people speak too fast, vocabulary problems, etc.). On the board, write:
Speak slowly, please.
Do you speak [students' language]?
Sorry?

- Ask students to decide which phrase they can use if:
  a) they want the person to repeat.
  b) they don't understand anything the person says.
  c) the person speaks too fast.

- This would be a good point to tell students how important it is to prepare before making telephone calls in English. You could compile a list of useful telephone vocabulary with the class which students can keep at work, either on their desk or in a drawer for easy access.

F

On the board, write the headings *Sales Representative* and *Customer*.

- Tell students that there is a problem with an order. The customer telephones the sales representative to explain the problem. Ask the class to suggest what the problem could be.

- Refer students to the Useful language box. Elicit some phrases that the sales representative and the customer could use.

- Divide the class into pairs.

CASE STUDY

High-Style Business Rentals

Students describe problems with apartments that are rented to businesspeople working abroad.

Background

- Books closed. Ask students what sort of accommodation they stay in when on they travel abroad for work or on holiday (*hotel*, *villa*, etc.).

- On the board, write *rental apartments*. Ask students what facilities they expect to have in an apartment. Write the list on the board. In pairs, ask students to decide which things are good to have and which things are very important to have.

- Tell students to open their books at page 28. Point to the picture of the apartment and ask students to suggest adjectives to describe it.

- Read through the information about the apartments with the whole class.

- Check any unfamiliar vocabulary (e.g. *spacious, ceilings, decorations, terrace, sauna, reservation*). Ask students to suggest what each word or phrase means from the context.

- Get students to identify the adjectives in the brochure.

- Ask students if they like the apartments. Would they like to stay there?

🔊 CD1.42–1.45

- Now ask students to listen to the comments made by High-Style guests and make notes.

Task

- Read the instructions for part 1 together.

- Divide the class into pairs.

- Get students to compare the brochure with the notes and say what is different.

- Circulate and help where needed.

- Elicit ideas and write them on the board.

- Ask the pairs to decide which of the problems are most important.

- Give students a few minutes to read their role cards and write notes to help them with the telephone call.

- Write on the board the headings *Manager at High-Style Business Rentals* and *Guest*. Ask students to suggest phrases that the guest could say and phrases that the manager could say to start the telephone call.

- If possible, position students so that they are back to back to role-play the telephone call.

- Circulate and monitor.

Writing

- Ask students to make a list of the problems encountered by High-Style guests (they should find this very straightforward after doing part 1 of the Task).

- Students write the e-mail from Diana Nolan to Jason Parker. Remind them that this is an internal e-mail, so does not have to be formal.

- Refer students to the Writing file as necessary.

- Ensure students include the three points mentioned.

- Collect students' e-mails and check for areas that need more work.

⮕ Writing file (Course Book page 126)

⮕ Resource bank: Writing (page 191)

WORKING ACROSS CULTURES 1

Eating out

Introduction

As this is probably the first *Working across cultures* unit that you have done with students, explain that it is to help them consider different attitudes or ways of behaving that other cultures may have. This is important when travelling or doing business with people from different countries.

This cultural-awareness unit focuses on the language of different cultural attitudes to eating out. It provides a useful introduction to allow students to think about different ways that different cultures approach common experiences.

A

- Nominate students to ask you the three questions and respond.
- Get students to work in groups and discuss the questions.
- You could ask a member of the group to tell the class a little about one of the other members (e.g. *Tariq's favourite dish is ...*) or to talk about similarities and differences in their group.

B

- Go through the questions and clarify where needed.
- You may wish to give students time to read through the quiz and decide their own answers first.
- Get students to work in pairs and take it in turns to ask and answer the questions in the quiz.
- Ask students if they were surprised at any of the answers.
- You could write some of the issues from the quiz on the board (e.g. *dinner time*, *leave food on plate*, *chewing gum*, *paying for a meal*, *interrupting*). If students are from different nationalities, they could work in pairs with someone from a different country and compare ideas about the topics on the board.

> 1 c 2 a 3 d 4 b 5 c 6 b 7 d 8 b 9 d

C – D 🔊 CD1.46

- Ask students to suggest some topics that the speaker might talk about. Write ideas on the board. Play the recording and ask students to listen to see if their ideas are mentioned.
- Play the recording again and get students to complete the topics in the chart.
- Circulate and help where needed.
- Highlight the examples in the second column.

- Play the first part of the recording again and complete the first item in the example column together.
- Play the rest of the recording and ask students to complete the examples individually.
- Circulate and help where needed.
- Ask students to compare their answers with a partner, then check answers with the class.

	Topics	Examples
1	Arrival	Denmark: not good to arrive late
		Italy: OK to arrive for dinner up to 30 minutes late
2	Seating	Germany: wait until you are shown where to sit
3	How much to eat	Norway, Malaysia, Singapore: rude to leave food on your plate
		Egypt, China: leave a little food to show you are full
4	What you use to eat	Arab cultures: don't eat with your left hand
5	Drinking	Korea, Japan, Russia: it's rude to pour your own drink
6	Body language	Germany: bad to rest your elbows on table
7	Leaving	China: common to leave soon after your meal
		Colombia: polite to stay for a while

Task

- Go through the task with the whole class and make sure that they understand.
- Nominate students to read the notes for guests when being entertained by someone from China. If anyone in your class is from China, ask if they agree with the notes. Can they add any other advice?
- Give students time to prepare their talk. They can use the notes or make their own notes, using the topics from Exercise C.
- Circulate and help where necessary.
- Ask students to suggest ways to introduce the talk (e.g. *I'm here to talk about entertaining in (country)*).
- Students take turns to give their talk to their partner. You could ask the students listening to think of a question to ask at the end of the talk.

UNIT A Revision

1 Introductions

Vocabulary

1 France   2 Turkish   3 Japanese   4 Kuwait
5 Oman   6 an American   7 British   8 China
9 Greece   10 Swedish

to be

1 are   2 'm   3 'm not   4 Are   5 is   6 aren't
7 isn't

Wh- questions

1 Where   2 What   3 What   4 Who   5 Where
6 Who

2 Work and leisure

Vocabulary

1 on   2 at   3 on   4 in   5 on   6 at*   7 in
8 in   9 at*

* *on* is used in US English

Adverbs and expressions of frequency

1 e   2 a   3 d   4 c   5 b

Skills

1   What do you do in your free time?

2   When do you finish work?

3   What do you like best about your job?

4   What do you do in your job?

5   Do you meet your colleagues after work?

6   How many hours a week do you work?

Writing

Suggested answer

Hi, I'm [name]. I work in the sales and marketing
division. I'm [nationality]. I live in [area] and I
come to work by [transport]. I'm married with two
children. They go to the international school. I like
playing sports. At the weekend, I play golf or go
swimming. I don't enjoy watching sports, though.
Let's go for a drink after work sometime.

3 Problems

Vocabulary

2   His hotel room isn't big enough.

3   The office is too noisy.

4   The report is too confusing.

5   Her laptop isn't fast enough.

6   We were too late to get seats on the train.

7   The spaces in the car park aren't wide enough.

8   The electrical cable is too short.

Present simple: negatives and questions

1 Do   2 doesn't   3 does   4 don't   5 Do
6 does   7 Does   8 doesn't

Have; *some* and *any*

1 don't have   2 any   3 doesn't have   4 has
5 doesn't   6 Do   7 have   8 some

Skills

1 c   2 a   3 d   4 b   5 h   6 e   7 g   8 f

Writing

Suggested answer

My office has six desks, a table and 10 chairs. It
doesn't have any plants. It has some bookshelves
with lots of books. It has six computers. It has a
meeting room next door. It has two doors and five
windows. It has a notice board on the wall.

Cultures 1: Eating out

A   1 d   2 h   3 g   4 a   5 f   6 c   7 e   8 b

B   1 e   2 d   3 c   4 f   5 a   6 e   7 b   8 a
    9 f   10 b   11 c   12 d

AT A GLANCE

	Classwork – Course Book	Further work
Lesson 1 *Each lesson (excluding case studies) is about 45–60 minutes. This does not include administration and time spent going through homework.*	<u>**Starting up**</u> Students talk about things they like and don't like when travelling on business. **Vocabulary: Travel details** Students practise saying flight details and match verbs and travel phrases. Students listen and answer questions about travel information.	**Practice File** Vocabulary (page 16) **i-Glossary** (DVD-ROM)
Lesson 2	**Listening: A business traveller** Students listen and complete information about Liz Credé's business travels. **Language focus 1: *can/can't*** Students put a dialogue into the correct order, then listen to check. Then they role-play a conversation using *can/can't*. **Reading: Business hotels** Students read about facilities in the Hilton Tokyo.	**Course Book Listening** (DVD-ROM) **Resource bank: Listening** (page 178) **Practice File** Language review (page 17) **Text bank** (pages 138–139)
Lesson 3	**Language focus 2: *there is / there are*** Students complete sentences using *there is / there are* and carry out a role play about a new job abroad. <u>**Skills: Making bookings and checking arrangements**</u> Students listen and answer questions about booking a hotel room before role-playing a similar situation.	**Practice File** Language review (page 17) **Course Book Skills Dialogues** (DVD-ROM) **Resource bank: Speaking** (page 166)
Lesson 4 *Each case study is about 30 minutes to 1 hour.*	<u>**Case study: The Gustav Conference Centre**</u> A Manager and Assistant Manager allocate conference rooms to three companies. **Writing** Students write an e-mail to one of the guests confirming arrangements.	**Resource bank: Writing** (page 192) **Practice File** Writing (page 18)

For a fast route through the unit focusing mainly on speaking skills, just use the underlined sections.

For one-to-one situations, most parts of the unit lend themselves, with minimal adaptation, to use with individual students. Where this is not the case, alternative procedures are given.

BUSINESS BRIEF

Around 3,500 years ago, Polynesians paddled across the open ocean in canoes, searching for new **trading partners,** and the age of business travel began. The modern businessperson is more likely to choose flying as the quickest way of getting from A to B. Although safer than a canoe, this can still pose hazards. **Frequent fliers** are likely to encounter a number of hurdles that can lead to increased stress levels. First, you have to actually get on the plane. Most airlines overbook to minimise seat wastage and **no-shows**. This means that if all the passengers who actually booked seats turn up, there could be a shortage of places. If there are not enough volunteers to give up their seats, then you may find yourself **bumped** – denied boarding and put on a later flight.

Once in the air, travelling conditions and health become the main issues. The cabin environment can be cramped and low in both pressure and oxygen. **Jetlag** was once considered the most unpleasant effect of **long-haul** travel. Now travellers also have to contend with worries about DVT (deep vein thrombosis), which has been linked to prolonged immobility in planes, cars or trains. On the plus side, some airlines appear to be acknowledging that extra leg room is important to customers and are willing to take out seats to increase passenger comfort and safety.

In recent years, there has also been a lot of media coverage regarding the **carbon footprint** of travellers. As people become more aware of the natural resources consumed in air travel and the pollution it creates, there is pressure for travellers to limit their journeys and to travel in the most environmentally friendly way possible.

Many countries are experiencing a slump in **corporate travel**, causing repercussions in the **airline sector**. Some companies are cutting costs by restricting travel or purchasing **lower fares**. **Web-conferencing** and **teleconference** technology are beginning to be used more widely by companies. In the future, this may reduce the frequency of travelling to face-to-face meetings. Some airlines are countering by investing in new technology that allows business travellers to work online while **in transit,** making optimum use of the time spent in the air.

In 1928, the first commercial airline had luxury upholstered seats and elegant reading lamps. But the flight from San Francisco to Chicago took 23 hours. So, despite any disadvantages, modern air travel remains the quickest option available.

Read on

The National Business Travel Association aviation committee white paper on *The critical condition of the airline industry*, 17th October 2002

Michelle G. Martin*: Travel Tips for the Busy Business Traveler*, CreateSpace, 2011

Rob Davidson and Beulah Cope: *Business Travel*, Financial Times/Prentice Hall, 2002

LESSON NOTES

Warmer

- Elicit some countries or places that students have travelled to on business or on holiday.
- Ask how they travelled (e.g. *by plane, by car,* etc.).
- Draw a suitcase on the board. Divide the class into pairs or small groups. Ask students to discuss what objects they always take with them when they travel.

Overview

- Tell students that they are going to study the language of travel today.
- Ask students to look at the Overview section on page 36. Give them a few moments to read the list of points. Point to the areas that you are covering in this lesson, using the table on page 41 of this book as a guide.

Quotation

- Write the quotation on the board and ask students what they think it means (*You see a lot of things living every day, but if you travel, you see more, because you see how people live in different places.*).
- Ask students what they think *much* means (*a lot*).
- Divide the class into pairs. Ask students if they agree or disagree with the quotation.

Starting up

This section introduces the theme of the unit. Students use key vocabulary in listening and speaking practice.

A

- Nominate students to ask you the three questions and respond.
- Give students time to prepare their answers to the questions individually.
- Then divide the class into pairs and tell students to take turns asking and answering the questions.
- Circulate and monitor.

B

- Go through the bullet points and clarify any activities students are unfamiliar with.
- Look at the examples together. Draw attention to *don't mind* (= don't dislike), which may be new to students.
- Give them time to write 10 short sentences.
- Divide the class into pairs. Students take turns asking questions (e.g. *Do you like checking in?*) and responding (*I love /like /don't mind /don't like /hate checking in*).
- Books closed. See what students can remember about their partner's likes and dislikes.

C ◀)) CD1.47–1.54

- Write the places (a–e) on the board. Tell students to work in small groups and ask them to think of phrases they might hear at these places.
- Play the recordings all the way through and ask students to listen for any of the phrases they noted.
- Read the instructions together. Point out that students will hear some of the places more than once.
- Play the recordings. Pause after recording 1.47 to highlight the example.
- Ask students to complete the activity individually.
- Play the recordings again. Pause after each one and check the answer around the class.

> 2 e   3 b   4 a   5 c   6 e   7 c   8 d

Vocabulary: Travel details
Students practise saying flight details.

A ◀)) CD1.55–1.58

- You may wish to quickly revise the alphabet and numbers in English before doing this exercise.
- Ask students to brainstorm vocabulary connected to train journeys and flights, in particular things connected to stations and airports (e.g. *platform, terminal, arrivals, departures, check in*). Write ideas on the board.
- Play the recordings from beginning to end and ask students to listen to see if any of the words on the board are used.
- Read the questions with the class. Clarify where necessary.
- Play the recordings again. Pause after each one to check the answers with the whole class.

> 1 14:40   2 JA327   3 14:16   4 platform 5
> 5 9.30 a.m.   6 11.45 a.m.   7 BA341   8 Terminal 5

- Books closed. Ask the questions again. How many times and numbers can the class remember? Open books again and check.

B

- Books closed. Ask students to call out some things that they can do at an airport.
- Write the verbs (1–10) on the board. Don't write phrases (a–j). Say the verbs with the whole class and check students' understanding. See if they can think of any travel words to go with the verbs.

LESSON NOTES

- Books open. Read the verbs and phrases with the class and check students' understanding.

- Focus on the example. Do item 2 together (*confirm their flight*).

- Divide the class into pairs.

- Ask students to match verbs 1–5 with the phrases a–e in the second column.

- Circulate and help where needed.

- Then ask students to match verbs 6–10 with phrases f–j in the fourth column.

- Check the answers together.

> 2 d 3 e 4 a 5 c 6 i 7 j 8 f 9 g 10 h

C

- Look at the actions in Exercise B. Draw students' attention to the example.

- Then ask students which action they think comes next (*confirm their flight*).

- Divide the class into pairs and ask students to put the actions 1–10 into the order that they usually happen.

- Check the answers around the class and write the order on the board.

> 3 confirm their flight
>
> 4 queue at the check-in
>
> 5 go through security
>
> 6 do some shopping
>
> 7 watch an in-flight movie
>
> 8 collect their luggage
>
> 9 take a bus or taxi
>
> 10 check in at the hotel

D

- Go through the nouns from the box and check students' understanding.

- Highlight the example and do item 2 with the whole class to demonstrate (*flight*). Then ask students to do the exercise individually.

- Check the answers together. See if students know any other phrases that could be used in these situations.

- Model how to say the phrases and get students to repeat.

> 2 flight   3 luggage   4 seat   5 passport
> 6 centre   7 receipt   8 reservation   9 call
> 10 bill   11 password

E

- You could divide the class into two groups, A and B, to look at the information cards and prepare questions together. If your class is confident, students can prepare individually.

- Divide the class into A/B pairs and get students to do the role play.

- Ask one or two pairs to do the role play for the class.

- ◉ i-Glossary

Listening: A business traveller

Students listen to an interview with a business traveller and answer questions.

A 🔊 CD1.59

- Tell students that they are going to hear an interview with Liz Credé, an organisation development consultant. The interview is in two parts.

- Ask students to say what country Amsterdam and Chicago are in (*the Netherlands and the USA*).

- Read the questions with the class. Clarify where necessary.

- Play the first part of the interview. Pause to check the answers with the whole class.

> 1 a) to work with clients   b) to visit colleagues
>
> 2 a) every month   b) twice a year
>
> 3 The Singapore office, because it's based in the old town and not the business district, and it has a lot of character

B

- On the board write: *flying business class* and *staying in the same hotel*.

- Ask students to say why they think Liz likes doing these things. Write suggestions on the board.

C 🔊 CD1.60

- Students listen to the second part of the interview and answer the questions from Exercise B.

LESSON NOTES

> She likes flying business class because she can go to a business lounge and have a meal, and on the plane, she can have a seat that turns into a bed so she can sleep.
>
> She likes going to the same hotel because it's great to be recognised, where they know her name and know what she likes to do.

- If time allows, you may wish to get students to read the audio script with a partner.

D

- Ask students to suggest some attractive locations and write them on the board.
- Choose one location and ask students to say what they like/don't like about it.
- Ask students to work in pairs and say where they would most like to go for a business conference. Encourage them to say what they like about their location.
- ◎ Students can watch the interview with Liz Credé on the DVD-ROM.
- ➡ Resource bank: Listening (page 178)

Language focus 1: *can/can't*

Students learn about *can* and *can't* for ability, permission and possibility.

- Give students a few moments to read through the Language focus box.
- Books closed. On the board, write: *He can speak English*. Elicit the negative (*He can't speak English*.) and the question form (*Can he speak English?*).
- Focus on *Can he speak English?* and *He can speak English*. Model the pronunciation of *can* at the beginning and middle of a sentence /kən/. Contrast with *Yes, he can* /kæn/.

A

- Ask the class to call out the names of languages and write them on the board.
- Highlight the example. Encourage students to ask you similar questions.
- Tell students to move around the class asking about different languages (*Can you speak ...?*). If space is a problem, divide the class into A/B pairs. After a few minutes, ask all Student As to move and sit next to a new partner. Repeat this two or three times and keep the pace brisk.
- Ask the class two or three questions (e.g. *Can Lukas speak Polish?*) and elicit responses.

- Divide the class into pairs. Ask students to try to remember what languages people in the class can and can't speak.

> **One-to-one**
>
> Work with your student and do this as a pairwork exercise.
>
> Encourage your student to talk about languages that friends, family and colleagues speak.

B

- Look at the sentences with the whole class. Ask students if they think Paul and Judith are having the conversation face to face (*No, they are on the phone.*). What sentences show they are on the phone? (*This is Judith Preiss here. Paul, I'm calling about ...*)
- Help students to guess the meaning of any difficult phrases from the context (*I can't do, I can make, I can pick you up, say 10 o'clock*).
- Focus on the examples. Ask students to suggest the next sentence (*Hi, Judith*).
- Divide the class into pairs.
- Ask students to put the conversation into the correct order.

C ◀)) CD1.61

- Play the recording for students to check the answers.

> See audio script, Course Book page 161.

D

- Ask students to reread the dialogue in Exercise B (they may find it useful to rewrite it in the correct order first) and to look at the question with *can*.
- Ask them to each write three more questions based on the dialogue. Circulate, monitor and help where necessary.
- Students then work in pairs to ask and answer each other's questions. To make this more difficult, ask students to cover the dialogue to see if they can remember the answers.
- Have one or two pairs come to the front to ask and answer their questions for the class.

E ◀)) CD1.61

- Play the recording again and pause, then ask students to repeat each line of the conversation. Focus on pronunciation and intonation.
- Ask students to role-play the conversation with a partner.

LESSON NOTES

F

- Students work individually to complete the e-mail. Circulate, monitor and check.

- Go through the answers as a class and go over any areas that caused confusion.

> **1** can't **2** can **3** Friday **4** can **5** can
> **6** station **7** Can **8** can

G

- Divide the class into pairs. Less confident classes can prepare the questions and answers in same-role groups before doing the role play.

- Start the role play. Circulate and monitor. Help if necessary.

- Note that the prompts in the role cards are intentionally jumbled in order, so that students have to work out which response is required.

- If time allows, ask students to change roles and role-play again.

Reading: Business hotels

Students read about a hotel and ask and answer questions about the business facilities available.

A – B

- Books closed. Ask students to name some hotels that they know. Tell students about the kind of hotel you like to stay at on holiday / on business. Encourage students to say the type of hotel they like.

- Ask students what facilities they expect to find in a business hotel.

- Books open. Look at the facilities listed. Check students' understanding.

- Ask students to complete the exercise, comparing their ideas with a partner.

- Have a brief feedback session with the whole class.

C

- Focus on the photos. Ask students to describe what they see.

- Ask students what country they think the hotel is in. Get students to read the title and introductory paragraph to check (*Japan*).

- The idea is for students to scan the brochure information to find and underline the words which appear from Exercise A. It is not necessary for students to understand every word to complete the exercise.

- Ask students to call out the words they found.

> restaurants, health club, tennis courts,
> business centre

- Read the brochure again as a whole class. Where possible, help students guess the meaning of words from the context.

D

- Look at the example together. Elicit what a negative response would be (*No, you can't.*).

- Divide the class into pairs. Tell students to use the prompts to ask and answer questions about the Tokyo hotel.

- Circulate and monitor. Check that students are using *Yes, you can* and *No, you can't* to respond, rather than simply *yes* and *no*.

- Ask students if they think the Hilton Tokyo is a good business hotel. What facilities do they like? What facilities would they like to add to the hotel?

> 1 Yes, you can. All rooms have high-speed internet access.
>
> 2 No, you can't. The hotel doesn't have an outdoor pool, but it has an indoor pool.
>
> 3 Yes, you can. The hotel has two rooftop courts.
>
> 4 No, you can't. The Musashino serves Japanese food.
>
> 5 No, you can't. The biggest room is for 1,200 people.
>
> 6 Yes, you can. It's open 24 hours a day.
>
> 7 Yes you can. You can take the airport limousine direct to the hotel.

E

- Check that students know the meaning of *how far* and *how long*.

- Get students to read through the brochure again to find the information.

- Ask a student to read each question and briskly elicit the answers around the class.

> 1 a 10-minute walk
>
> 2 24 hours a day
>
> 3 about two hours

F

- Highlight the example and do item 2 together to demonstrate (*indoor pool*).

LESSON NOTES

- Ask students to complete the exercise individually.

- Get students to read the text again quickly, to check.

- Books closed. Say a word from the first column and ask students to complete the word partnership.

> 2 d   3 e   4 a   5 f   6 b

➡ Text bank (pages 138–139)

Language focus 2: *there is* / *there are*

This section looks at the positive, negative and question forms of *there is* / *there are*. Students practise the language and role-play a conversation.

- Read through the Language focus box together.

- Elicit the negative form of *there are* (*there aren't*).

- On the board write: *There aren't any shops in the area. Are there any meeting rooms?*

- Ask what word we add to the negative and question forms when we don't specify an exact amount (*any*). Don't spend too long on this point, as *some* / *any* are looked at on page 47.

- Divide the class into pairs. Give students five minutes to talk about things that are and aren't in the classroom using *there is*, *there isn't*, *there are* and *there aren't*.

- Elicit suggestions from the whole class.

- Ask students questions (e.g. *Is there a TV in the classroom? Are there any pictures?*). Encourage students to respond *Yes, there is*, *Yes, there are*, *No, there isn't* and *No, there aren't*.

A

- Look at the example and then do items 2 and 3 with the whole class (*Is there, There aren't*).

- Ask students to complete the exercise individually.

- Check the answers around the class.

> 2 **Is there** a problem with my ticket?
>
> 3 **There aren't** any aisle seats available.
>
> 4 **There is** a stopover in Frankfurt.
>
> 5 **Are there** any flights to Zurich tonight?
>
> 6 I'm afraid **there isn't** a flight to Warsaw this afternoon.
>
> 7 **There are** two cafés in the terminal.
>
> 8 **Are there** any buses from the airport to the city centre?

B

- Ask students to say some of the facilities at the Hilton Tokyo and write ideas on the board.

- Get students to read the text again quickly to check and add more information where necessary.

- Students can prepare the questions individually or in groups.

- Students work in pairs and ask and answer questions about the facilities.

C

- Books closed. Tell students they have a new job in a new city. What things do they want to know about the city? Brainstorm and write suggestions on the board.

- Books open. Read the information together. Highlight the example and elicit two or three more questions.

- Divide the class into pairs and start the role play.

- Monitor and help where needed.

Skills: Making bookings and checking arrangements

This section introduces the language needed to make bookings and check arrangements. Students listen to a dialogue and role-play a conversation between a hotel receptionist and a business traveller.

A 🔊 CD1.62

- Books closed. Tell students Simon is booking a hotel room. On the board, write two headings: *Simon* and *Receptionist*. Ask students what information Simon needs and what information the receptionist needs to book the room (e.g. *Simon: cost of room, is there a restaurant? Receptionist: single or double? number of nights? arrival time?*).

- Books open. Read the questions with the class and clarify any unfamiliar vocabulary.

- Pre-teach any words or phrases students may have difficulty with in the recording (such as *let me check*).

- Play the recording while students underline the correct answers.

- Play the recording again and pause to elicit the answers.

> 2 Wednesday   3 single   4 €120   5 two
> 6 six o'clock

- Ask students to turn to the audio script on page 161 and practise the conversation with a partner.

LESSON NOTES

B

- Students are going to role-play a telephone conversation booking a hotel room. Go through the phrases in the Useful language box. Help with pronunciation and clarify meaning where necessary.

- Divide the class into pairs.

- Tell students to use the prompts and the phrases in the Useful language box to role-play a telephone conversation. Less-confident classes may prefer to write notes first.

- Encourage students to sit back to back to simulate a telephone situation.

- If appropriate to your class, ask students what can make communication difficult on the phone (e.g. can't see the other person's face, the other person can speak too quickly). What things can they do to help communication (e.g. speak clearly, ask the other person to repeat if they don't understand, prepare information before the call)?

C

- Write *Receptionist* and *Caller* on the board. Go through the phrases in the Useful language box and ask students to identify useful phrases for booking a flight.

- Divide the class into pairs.

- Tell students to use the information on their role cards to role-play a telephone conversation. Give students a few moments to look at the information and prepare.

- Encourage students to sit back to back to simulate a telephone situation.

- If time allows, get students to change roles and practise the conversation again.

- ◎ Students can watch the phone call on the DVD-ROM.

⮕ Resource bank: Speaking (page 166)

CASE STUDY

The Gustav Conference Centre

A conference centre in Vienna, Austria, has requests for conference rooms from three companies. Students try to allocate available rooms while taking into account the guests' requirements.

Background

- Give students a few minutes to read the information in the *Background* section and table on page 43 and the information on page 140. Circulate and help where needed.

- Ask check questions (e.g. *How many people are in the group from Minnesota Chemicals?* (80) *How many seminar rooms does Elegant Ways Beauty Products need?* (two) *How long are JooC Designs at the conference?* (two days) etc.).

- Get students to read through the *Notes* and *Other requirements* sections. Pre-teach any unfamiliar vocabulary (e.g. *projector, screen, terrace, technical support*).

🔊 CD1.63

- Ask students to listen to the conversation and note down what the conference organiser from JooC Designs wants.

> She wants 30 more members of staff to attend the conference, giving a total of 65.

Task

- Read through the questions in the first part of the task with the class and check students understand.

- Ask students to work in pairs. They are going to role-play a conversation between the Manager and Assistant Manager at the conference centre.

- Encourage students to make notes about their decisions so that they can use them in the next part of the task.

- For the second part of the task, tell students that they are going to role-play a conversation between the Manager of the conference centre with the conference organiser for each company. They will take it in turns to play the Manager and each of the conference organisers.

- Get students to say how the Manager of the conference centre could start the call.

- Try to discourage students from writing their dialogues before doing the role play. Allow them to make brief notes if necessary.

- Get students to sit back to back and role-play the first conversation.

- Circulate, monitor and help if necessary.

- Ask one or two pairs to come to the front and act out one of the conversations.

- Now ask students to change roles and role-play the conversation with another conference organiser. Then students change roles again and role-play the call with the final conference organiser.

- Have a feedback session with the whole class. If pairs have allocated conference rooms differently, use this as a discussion point.

Writing

- Look at the Writing file on page 126 together.

- Tell students that they are receptionists at the conference centre. Ask students to suggest what a receptionist does in his/her job.

- Ask a student to read the instructions to the class. Draw attention to the information that students need to include in the e-mail.

- Encourage students to suggest an opening sentence and write it on the board (e.g. *I am writing concerning your conference room booking*).

- Choose a company and ask the class to help you write an e-mail on the board.

- Now ask students to choose another company and write an e-mail individually.

- Check which students have written to the same company and put them into same-company groups.

- Ask students to compare their e-mails.

- Collect in the e-mails and check any areas that need revision.

> **One-to-one**
>
> Read your e-mail to your student, omitting the company name.
>
> Ask your student to guess which company it is to. Now ask your student to read their e-mail in the same way and you guess the company.

➡️ Writing file (Course Book page 126)

➡️ Resource bank: Writing (page 192)

Food and entertaining

AT A GLANCE

	Classwork – Course Book	Further work
Lesson 1 *Each lesson (excluding case studies) is about 45–60 minutes. This does not include administration and time spent going through homework.*	**Starting up** Students talk about the kind of food they like and match dishes and countries. **Vocabulary: Eating out** Students look at food groups and different parts of a menu.	**Practice File** Vocabulary (page 20) **i-Glossary** (DVD-ROM)
Lesson 2	**Reading: Fast food in India** Students look at how fast-food chains changed their menus in order to be successful in India. **Language focus 1: *some/any*** Students correct mistakes using *some* and *any* and underline the correct words in a dialogue. **Listening: Entertaining clients** Students listen to an interview with Jeremy Keeley where he talks about business contacts and his favourite entertainment.	**Text bank** (pages 140–141) **Practice File** Language review (page 21) **Course Book Listening** (DVD-ROM) **Resource bank: Listening** (page 179)
Lesson 3	**Language focus 2: Countable and uncountable nouns** Students identify countable nouns and complete exercises using *a lot of, many* or *much*. **Skills: Making decisions** Students look at language for agreeing, disagreeing, giving opinions and making suggestions.	**Practice File** Language review (page 21) **Course Book Skills Dialogues** (DVD-ROM) **Resource bank: Speaking** (page 167)
Lesson 4 *Each case study is about 30 minutes to 1 hour.*	**Case study: Which restaurant?** Students decide which of three restaurants to choose to entertain four important overseas customers. **Writing** Students write an e-mail inviting a customer to dinner and giving details about the restaurant.	**Resource bank: Writing** (page 193) **Practice File** Writing (page 22)

For a fast route through the unit focusing mainly on speaking skills, just use the underlined sections.

For one-to-one situations, most parts of the unit lend themselves, with minimal adaptation, to use with individual students. Where this is not the case, alternative procedures are given.

BUSINESS BRIEF

Food can communicate complex messages about status, nationality and identity. The fashion for **eating out** in restaurants was adopted by the upper classes during the French Revolution. Many English words relating to eating out are adopted from the French (*hotel*, *café*, *menu*, *chef*, etc.), including *restaurant,* which was originally from the French verb meaning 'to restore'. Later, the migrations of the 20th century proved fertile ground for mingling cuisines, and a knowledge of the vast variety on offer is viewed as a mark of modern **cosmopolitan** taste.

Codes of eating vary from culture to culture. In one culture, it is polite to leave food on one's plate; in another, it shows lack of respect. An American will be amused to see a British person struggling to balance peas on the back, rather than the curve, of the fork. A European will retain the knife in one hand and the fork in the other throughout the meal. In contrast, an American will cut with the knife and fork and then lay the knife along the top of the plate and transfer the fork to their other hand to eat. The order in which food is served also differs from country to country. When eating out in Eastern countries, a variety of dishes can be served at the same time rather than dividing the meal into **courses**. The **diners** serve themselves by transferring small amounts of food from communal bowls onto their own plates. In Western restaurants, the food is served in individual portions, and the meal is generally divided into **starter**, **main course** and **dessert**.

Anthropologist Robin Fox believes that **'doing lunch'** has little to do with business and everything to do with status. He says, 'Just to be having business lunches marks one down as a success in the world of business.'* This was taken rather too much to heart by five bankers fired by a London investment firm for trying to write off on expenses a dinner bill of over £60,000. The traditional concept of a business lunch or dinner has broadened to encompass other meals. First there were breakfast meetings, followed by a trend in the USA to have meetings over afternoon tea. Whatever the context, it is important to check what etiquette is expected and what behaviour is acceptable. If in doubt, follow the lead of the host and allow them to guide you through the meal. Turn off mobile phones and be polite and attentive. It may be a free lunch, but remember that it is still business.

Read on

*Robin Fox: www.sirc.org/publik/foxfood.pdf *Food and eating: An anthropological perspective*

Tom Standage: *An Edible History of Humanity*, Atlantic Books, 2010

Carole Counihan and Penny Van Esterik: *Food and Culture: A Reader*, Routledge, second edition 2008

http://blog.simplyhired.co.uk/2011/01/business-lunch-etiquette.html
Etiquette tips for business lunches

LESSON NOTES

Warmer

- See how many meals the class can name in English (*breakfast, lunch, tea, dinner, supper*).

- On the board write:
  tea
  dinner
  breakfast
  supper
  lunch

- Ask the class to put the meals in the correct order (*breakfast, lunch, tea, dinner, supper*).

- Note that while *breakfast* and *lunch* always refer to the same meal, there can be regional variations in the use of *tea, dinner* and *supper* in different parts of the UK. All three terms can be used to describe the main evening meal, although traditionally the correct term is *dinner*, and this is the main word used when referring to eating out.

- Ask students what the main meal of the day is in their country. What time do they eat it? What time do they eat the other meals? Do they usually have lunch? How long is the normal lunch break in their country?

Overview

- Tell students that you are going to look at language for food and entertaining today. Ask them to look at the Overview section on page 44. Point to each heading and elicit or explain a little about each. Point to the sections you will be covering in this lesson, using the table on page 50 of this book as a guide.

Quotation

- Read the quotation with the class. Check students understand the meaning of *soul*. Ask students to say whether they agree with quotation.

- You might also like to pick up on the implication that conversation is as important as food. Ask students what happens in their own cultures – are conversations kept until after the meal is finished, or do they go on during the meal?

- Tell the class about a meal that you have had with friends, family or colleagues and say whether the food and conversation made it a good or bad experience. Ask them to think of meals they have had in restaurants with business colleagues, friends or family. What made it a good/bad experience, the conversation or the food?

Starting up

Students are introduced to dishes from different countries and talk about business entertainment in their own country.

A

- With the whole class, run through the countries in the box and ask the students to make adjectives from them. Discourage students from using *English* as the adjective for *the UK*. Keep this brisk.

> China – Chinese; Japan – Japanese; Thailand – Thai; India – Indian; Turkey – Turkish; Greece – Greek; Italy – Italian; France – French; Germany – German; Russia – Russian; Sweden – Swedish; the UK – British; Spain – Spanish; Mexico – Mexican

- Tell the class about the kind of food that you like.

- Ask students to tell a partner about the foods that they like.

- You may wish to tell students that with the more common types of foreign cuisine, the word *food* is often omitted when the context is clear: *I like Chinese, I love Italian*.

- Circulate and monitor.

B

- With the whole class, match the dishes and adjectives. Keep this brisk.

- Highlight the example sentence, then do item 2 together to demonstrate (*Snails are a French dish.*).

- Ask students to make sentences in pairs.

- Check the answers around the class.

> curry – Indian; snails – French; sushi – Japanese; spaghetti – Italian; goulash – Hungarian; burger – American; paella – Spanish; sweet-and-sour-chicken – Chinese; fajitas – Mexican

- Ask students if they think these are typical dishes for the countries listed. Are there any that students disagree with?

- Get students to call out any other typical dishes that they know (tell them not to say the country that the dish comes from yet).

- Write ideas on the board, pausing and asking students to help you spell the words.

- Ask the rest of the class to guess what country each dish comes from.

LESSON NOTES

C

- Read the three questions together. Check students understand *business breakfast* and *entertain*.

- In pairs, get students to answer the questions about their country. If you have a multilingual class, try to get students to work with a partner from a different country.

- Have a feedback session with the whole class.

Vocabulary: Eating out

Students look at vocabulary for talking about different sorts of food and parts of a menu.

A

- Run through the words in the box and check understanding. Elicit/explain the difference between seafood and fish (*Seafood can include creatures that live in the sea, including those that have shells, such as prawns and lobster. Fish can live in rivers, lakes or the sea and do not have shells.*).

- Highlight the example.

- Divide the class into pairs and tell students to choose the odd one out and explain their answer using a word from the box. Encourage the class to use dictionaries.

- Quickly ask five of the pairs to give the answers.

1 onion: It's a kind of vegetable. (The others are kinds of fish.)

2 apple: It's a kind of fruit. (The others are kinds of meat.)

3 trout: It's a kind of fish. (The others are kinds of vegetables.)

4 veal: It's a kind of meat. (The others are kinds of fruit.)

5 prawns: They're a kind of seafood. (The others are kinds of vegetables.)

B

- Books closed. Try to elicit the three parts of a menu (*starter, main course, dessert*).

- Books open. Quickly check students' understanding of the words in the box.

- Ask students to complete the exercise individually.

- Check the answers around the class.

Starter	Main course	Dessert
soup	steak	apple pie
pâté	grilled fish	ice cream
salad	roast duck	fruit
spring rolls	beef stew	chocolate mousse
prawn cocktail	pork	cheesecake
stuffed mushrooms	mutton	tiramisu

- You may wish to point out that *mutton* is the meat from an older sheep and elicit the word for meat from a young sheep (*lamb*).

- In some countries, the food items may not fall into these categories. See if students can add any more items to each category.

C

- Describe an unusual food that you have tried. Ask the class to guess which country you tried it in.

- Give students time to think of a dish that they have tried. They can make notes and write down useful vocabulary if they wish, but encourage them to use it for reference rather than read from the page. If students cannot think of an unusual food, they can describe a dish that they liked or didn't like.

- Ask students to work in pairs and describe the unusual food to their partner.

- Get two or three confident students to describe their food and get the class to guess the country/place where they tried the food.

D

- Do the exercise with the whole class.

1 menu   2 bill   3 check   4 receipt

- Ask students what they deduce from sentences 2 and 3 (*that* bill *is the BrE word and* check *is the AmE word for the same thing*).

- Books closed. Consolidate the vocabulary by saying: *It's the start of the meal, what do you ask for?* (the menu). *It's the end of the meal and you want to pay, what do you ask for?* (the bill / the check). *After you pay, you can ask for …?* (a receipt). Ask the class to spell the four words and write them on the board.

E 🔊 CD1.64

- Books closed. Play the first part of the recording and ask: *How many people are speaking?* (two) and *Where are they?* (in a restaurant).

LESSON NOTES

- Books open. Look at the dishes on the menu. Ask students which countries the main courses are from (*Italy, Spain* and *Japan*).

- Draw attention to the example. Play the first part of the recording again and pause to ask what the man orders as a starter (*snails*).

- Play the rest of the recording while students complete the exercise.

- Play it again for students to check.

> **1** snails (M); soup (W) **2** spaghetti (M); paella (W)
> **3** apple pie (M)

- Elicit how the man describes paella (*It's Spanish. It's a kind of rice dish. It's made with seafood.*).

- To extend the activity, ask the class to turn to the audio script on page 162. Play the conversation again while students read.

- Ask students to read the conversation with a partner, then to adapt the conversation, substituting their own choice of dishes.

F

- Read through the sentences together.

- Highlight the example and elicit which sentence students think comes next in the conversation (*e*).

- Get students to put the remaining sentences into the correct order.

- Ask students to compare answers with a partner.

> c, e, g, a, f, b, d, h

G CD1.65

- Play the recording while students check their answers.

- Ask students to read the dialogue with their partner.

- Play it again. Ask students which sentences are used to say *thanks* at the end of the meal (*Thanks very much. That was a lovely meal. I really enjoyed it.*). Ask which sentences are used when the person doesn't want anything else to eat (*No thanks. I'm full.*).

- What similar expressions do students have in their own language?

- Get students to dictate the conversation in the correct order while you write it on the board.

- Ask students to work in pairs and read the dialogue. Then ask students to practise the conversation again, recommending different dishes. They can use the menu in Exercise E or write their own menu.

H

- Tell students that they are going to role-play a conversation in a restaurant.

- Give students time to read their role cards. Explain that Student A starts the conversation.

- After students have completed the role play, they could write a menu with a starter, main course and dessert and role-play a similar conversation talking about other dishes.

◉ i-Glossary

Reading: Fast food in India

The article looks at the way that fast-food companies have adapted their menus in different countries to suit local tastes.

A

- Books closed. Write *fast food* and *fast-food restaurants* on the board and ask students to suggest types of fast food and any fast-food companies that they know. Write their suggestions under the correct heading. Ask students: *Do you like fast food?* Encourage them to say why / why not.

- Books open. Allow students to work in pairs for a few minutes to discuss the three questions, then briefly open up the discussion to the whole class.

B

- Write the question on the board. Encourage students to give their opinions. Write the opinions on the board.

- Ask students to read the article and see if it mentions their ideas.

> According to the article, it's important for international fast-food companies like McDonald's to adapt their food for Indian tastes. The article gives lots of practical examples of how they are changing their menus to be successful in the Indian market.

C

- You can choose to do this vocabulary exercise either before or after students have read the article in detail. Doing it before will help students to understand more on their first thorough reading; doing it afterwards will make the exercise easier, as students will have seen the words in context.

- Give students a few minutes to complete the exercise individually, then go over the answers together.

> **1** c **2** d **3** e **4** b **5** a

LESSON NOTES

D

- Read through the questions together to check understanding. Do the first question with the whole class.

- Ask students to answer the rest of the questions; you may prefer to let them do this individually then compare their answers with a partner, or to work in pairs.

- Check answers around the class.

---

1 College students, mothers and office workers

2 At least once a week (= always once, but sometimes more often)

3 Rs300 ($6.60)

4/5 a) McDonald's offers spicy and vegetarian dishes. It also offers Mutton and Chicken Maharaja Macs rather than the traditional beef products, because many Indians are Hindu and don't eat beef.

  b) In its chicken dishes, KFC uses Indian spices and cooking techniques because many Indians prefer spicy food.

  c) Pizza Hut has a mixture of Indian and international dishes and has more vegetarian toppings on its pizzas, because a lot of Indians (60%) are vegetarian, so don't eat meat.

E

- Remind students of the list of fast-food restaurants you wrote on the board in Exercise A. Invite them to add more examples of fast-food chains. Focus on one of the restaurants and ask students to suggest ways to improve the design or the menu. Write suggestions on the board.

- Ask students to work in pairs and choose another fast-food chain and discuss ways to improve it.

- To extend the activity, you could ask students to join with another pair who chose the same restaurant and compare improvements.

- Nominate two or three pairs to present their ideas to the class.

➡ Text bank (pages 140–141)

Language focus 1: *some/any*

Students look at *some/any* in positive and negative sentences and questions.

- Read through the Language focus box together and clarify where necessary.

- Focus on the use of *some* in positive statements and *any* in questions and negative statements.

- Point out that *some* can also be used for offers (*Would you like some cake?*), requests (*Could I have some cake, please?*) and suggestions (*What about some cake?*).

- You may also wish to tell your class that *Would you like …?* and *Could I have …?* are more polite than *Do you want …?* and *I want … .*

A

- Ask students to tick the correct sentences.

- Check around the class. Sentences 3, 5 and 6 are correct.

- Now, ask students to correct the remaining sentences.

- Check the answers together.

---

2 Could I have **some** more coffee, please?

3 ✓

4 There isn't **any** wine left.

5 ✓

6 ✓

B

- Ask students to read the dialogue and underline either *some* or *any* to complete the sentences in it.

- Check the answers together.

---

1 some 2 any 3 any 4 some 5 some

- In pairs, get students to practise the conversation.

- Choose a pair of confident students to read the conversation to the class.

Listening: Entertaining clients

Students listen to a two-part interview with Jeremy Keeley as he talks about how he entertains clients.

A 🔊 CD1.66

- Books closed. Write on the board: *Entertain business contacts.* Ask students to suggest places where they can entertain business contacts. Write suggestions on the board.

- Books open. Quickly read through the notes and ask students to suggest words to complete the sentences.

- Point to the picture of Jeremy Keeley and ask students if they remember hearing him speak in Unit 3 (page 23).

- Play the recording and ask students to listen to see if Jeremy mentions any of their ideas.

LESSON NOTES

- Play it again while students complete the notes.

- Nominate students to read out the completed sentences. Check answers with the class.

> **1** know **2** tell **3** talk **4** park **5** talked
> **6** important

- Ask students whether they like the way that Jeremy Keeley entertains clients.

B 🔊 CD1.67

- Play the first part of the recording and elicit whether the first statement is true or false (*true*). Do the same with the second and encourage students to correct the statement (*false: Don't take out a client you don't like.*).

- Play the final two statements and ask students to answer. Elicit answers around the class.

> **1** T
>
> **2** F (Don't take out a client you do not like.)
>
> **3** T
>
> **4** F (Don't spend too much money – it might embarrass the clients.)

C

- Ask students to work in pairs or small groups. Tell them that they are going to plan a meal for a mixed group of nationalities.

- Write on the board:
  location
  type of restaurant /at home
  type of food
  atmosphere

- Ask students to use the list to brainstorm ideas and discuss which would work best for a meal for a mixed-nationality group.

- Get groups to compare their ideas with another group.

- Have a brief feedback session with the whole class and encourage groups to explain their choices.

D 🔊 CD1.68

- Play the recording for students to compare their ideas with Jeremy's.

> Jeremy says get to know what they can and cannot eat and what they like. Ask them, don't assume. Plan it carefully and then relax.

- 🔘 Students can watch the interview with Jeremy Keeley on the DVD-ROM.

- ➡ Resource bank: Listening (page 179)

Language focus 2: Countable and uncountable nouns

Students identify countable and uncountable nouns, correct mistakes in sentences and complete an exercise using *a lot of, many* or *much*.

A

- Look at the Language focus box together. Clarify where necessary. Refer students to the Grammar reference for more information.

- As a general rule, we use *a lot of* in positive statements and in offers and requests. *Much* and *many* are often used in questions and negatives.

- In pairs, ask students to tick the countable nouns.

- With the class, go through the list and ask students to call out whether the noun is countable or uncountable.

> **Countable:** 1, 4, 5, 6, 8, 10, 12, 13, 16, 17, 18, 23

B

- Focus on the example. Do item 2 together to demonstrate. Ask students to correct the mistakes using *a lot of, many* or *much*. Point out that some sentences have more than one possible answer.

- Check answers around the class and spend time clarifying where necessary.

> **2** How **much** does it cost?
>
> **3** The restaurant hasn't got **many / a lot of** tables left.
>
> **4** I don't have **much / a lot of** time at the moment.
>
> **5** I drink **a lot of** coffee.
>
> **6** There aren't **many / a lot of** hotels in the city centre.
>
> **7** It costs **a lot of** money.
>
> **8** I don't want **much / a lot of** spaghetti. There's ice cream for dessert.

C

- Divide the class into pairs. Tell students to complete the questions with *many* or *much*.

- Check the answers with the whole class.

> **2** many **3** many **4** much **5** much **6** many
> **7** many **8** much

- Get the pairs to take turns to ask and answer the questions.

LESSON NOTES

Skills: Making decisions

This section introduces expressions for giving opinions, agreeing, disagreeing and making suggestions. Students take part in a role play where they discuss how to entertain a group of visitors.

A

- If students have already discussed different ways to entertain visitors during the listening on page 47, they can use this exercise as a brisk recap.

- Go through the activities and check that students understand. Ask students to discuss the question in pairs, then get feedback from the class.

- See if students can add any additional activities to the list.

- If suitable for your class, you could ask students to suggest activities which are *not* suitable to entertain a group of visitors.

B ◀)) CD1.69

- Play the recording and ask students to listen to see if the speakers mention any of their ideas.

- Play it again and pause to elicit whether the first statement is true or false (*false*). Ask students to correct the statement (*One person likes the idea of visiting a castle, the other wants to do something more interesting*.).

- Check the answers together.

> **1** F (Alex thinks it is a bad idea.)   **2** T   **3** T
> **4** F (It's for eight people on Wednesday.)

- You could say more statements and ask students to decide whether they are true or false (e.g. *Pierre's is always busy* (T), *The Grand Hotel isn't expensive* (F), *They don't have a menu for the Italian restaurant* (F), *They are going to meet at 8.30* (F), *They need to invite Jane Stirling, the Head of Marketing* (T)).

C ◀)) CD1.69

- Read through the extracts and encourage students to suggest words to complete the sentences.

- Play the recording while students check/complete the extracts.

- Get students to say the sentences. Encourage them to copy the intonation in the listening. Play the recording again if students need to check.

> **1** know; need   **2** agree; think; don't   **3** idea
> **4** could   **5** but   **6** about   **7** great

D

- Check students understand the four functions.

- Do this briskly with the whole class. Read the first part of the first extract (*I don't know about that*) and ask students to match it with a function (a–d).

> a) I think …; I also think …
>
> b) Yes, I agree; Good idea; that's a great idea
>
> c) I don't know about that; that's right, but …
>
> d) Why don't we …?; We could try …; How about …?

- Read through the Useful language box with the class and clarify where necessary.

E

- Divide the class into groups of three. If students need more support, get them to prepare in A, B and C groups.

- Give students time to read the information about their role.

- Circulate and help where necessary.

F

- In groups of three, students discuss their ideas.

- Each group decides on the best way to entertain the visitors.

- Ask each group to present their idea to the class. Encourage them to say why they think it is a good idea.

> **One-to-one**
>
> In one-to-one classes, you can take one of the roles. Use the information on pages 134 and 136.

◎ Students can watch the discussion on the DVD-ROM.

⇨ Resource bank: Speaking (page 167)

CASE STUDY

Which restaurant?

Students read information about three different restaurants in Sydney, Australia, and decide which is best to entertain four important customers.

Background

- Books closed. Ask students to name the three best restaurants in the area where you are. What type of food do they serve? Are they suitable for vegetarians? Are they expensive / popular / easy to get to? Do you need to book a table?

- Pre-teach any vocabulary that your class may need (*high-quality, access, atmosphere, portions, shore, bay*).

- Books open. Give students a few minutes to read through the information.

- Circulate and clarify where needed.

- Ask check questions such as: *Is the Kerala Sands a Chinese restaurant?* (No, it's an Indian restaurant.) *Where is it located?* (Five miles from the city centre.)

Task

- Divide the class into groups of four. Allocate or get each student to choose one of the role cards.

- Give students time to study the role cards individually and read the restaurant information again to decide which is best for their customer.

- Get students to discuss their choice with their group. Encourage students to give reasons why they prefer their chosen restaurant.

- Tell the groups that they must decide which restaurant is best for all four customers to visit together.

- Have a feedback session comparing the groups' opinions.

One-to-one

Allocate or get your student to choose a role card. You take another. Give your student time to read the restaurant information again to decide which is best for his or her customer. Then discuss the choice of restaurant with your student and decide which is best for both your customers. To extend, ask your student which restaurant they prefer for themselves. Which restaurant are they most and least likely to visit? Why?

Writing

- Ask students to turn to the Writing file on page 126.

- Choose one of the local restaurants students named at the beginning of the case study. Ask students to help you write an e-mail inviting a new teacher to dinner there.

- Elicit suggestions and write the e-mail on the board as the class dictates. Include the date, time and the name, location and type of restaurant. Clear the board.

- Ask students to write an e-mail to their customer.

- Divide the class into pairs, and ask students to compare and correct each other's e-mails.

- Circulate and monitor, helping where needed.

➡ Writing file (Course Book page 126)

➡ Resource bank: Writing (page 193)

UNIT 6 Buying and selling

AT A GLANCE

	Classwork – Course Book	Further work
Lesson 1 *Each lesson (excluding case studies) is about 45–60 minutes. This does not include administration and time spent going through homework.*	**Starting up** Students listen to three people talk about where and when they buy products. **Vocabulary 1: Choosing a product** Students find vocabulary in an advert for an electrical retailer and listen to a conversation between a buyer and seller. **Reading: A success story** Students read an article about Japanese clothes retailer, Uniqlo.	**Practice File** Vocabulary (page 24) **i-Glossary** (DVD-ROM) **Text bank** (pages 142–143)
Lesson 2	**Language focus 1: Past simple** Students complete a report on a sales trip using the past simple. **Vocabulary 2: Choosing a service** Students complete a leaflet for a car-hire company. **Listening: How to sell** Ros Pomeroy, a management consultant, gives advice about sales.	**Practice File** Language review (page 25) **i-Glossary** (DVD-ROM) **Course Book Listening** (DVD-ROM) **Resource bank: Listening** (page 180)
Lesson 3	**Language focus 2: Past time references** Students are introduced to expressions that refer to the past, such as *ago, last (week), for, on, from ... to, in* and *during*. **Skills: Describing a product** Students listen to an advertisement and complete the details. Then they role-play being the buyer and seller at a trade fair.	**Practice File** Language review (page 25) **Course Book Skills Presentations** (DVD-ROM) **Resource bank: Speaking** (page 168)
Lesson 4 *Each case study is about 30 minutes to 1 hour.*	**Case study: NP Innovations** NP Innovations is a group of stores in Seattle which sells gifts for the home, office and travel. Students listen to a discussion about products. Then they work in groups and describe products. **Writing** Students write an e-mail to the manufacturer of one of the products asking them to send a catalogue, price list and sample. They also ask questions about delivery dates.	**Resource bank: Writing** (page 194) **Practice File** Writing (page 27)

For a fast route through the unit focusing mainly on speaking skills, just use the underlined sections.

For one-to-one situations, most parts of the unit lend themselves, with minimal adaptation, to use with individual students. Where this is not the case, alternative procedures are given.

BUSINESS BRIEF

Things have come a long way since the days when peddlers went from door to door selling wares from a pack. Now advertisements pop up as text messages. Goods can be ordered by **mail order**. We can **compare prices, get quotes,** check if an item is **in stock** and **place an order** without moving away from our computer screen. In some ways, the methods of buying and selling have undergone a revolution, and in others, little has changed since the early 1900s when keywords in sales were *service* and *relationships*. A modern **sales force** uses a mixture of tried-and-tested techniques and new technology to **increase sales**. The foundation of modern **sales techniques** was developed in the 1950s and includes gaining the client's interest, building desire by showing product features or giving samples, increasing conviction by comparing the product with competitors or using statistics to highlight benefits and, finally, closing the deal.

One of the main strategies for building a solid **customer base** is through **relationship selling**. It costs more than five times as much to win a new customer as it does to maintain an existing client. So it makes sense to find ways to encourage **customer loyalty**. Most people react with suspicion to **hard-sell**, high-pressure techniques, even if they are genuinely interested in the product. Instead, relationship selling involves a low-pressure, **soft-sell** approach. The salesperson listens carefully to the needs of a client and works with them to find solutions tailored to their requirements. This involves maintaining regular contact and building trust by keeping promises and being accessible when a customer needs help. In addition to encouraging **repeat orders**, such an approach promotes **good service**. This encourages word-of-mouth **referrals** which can lead to additional sales. Where a real relationship exists between **client** and **supplier**, competitors find it more difficult to entice customers away with promises of lower prices or special deals.

Modern technology complements this approach. A **Customer Relationship Management system (CRM)** uses software to track interactions between the customer and the departments within the company which are supplying goods. Marketing, Sales and **Customer Services** can collate and access information about customers in order to address their needs quickly and efficiently. Another modern sales technique is called **high-probability selling**. This uses a detailed series of questions to focus efforts on clients who actively require the product or service that a company has to sell. This saves the clients time, and the **sales team** does not need to prepare a detailed **proposal** that is unlikely to be accepted by the potential customer. Sales techniques need to be adapted in accordance with each customer profile. The most effective techniques use technology to modernise traditional customer-care methods. The clients are encouraged to feel that they are more than just a signature on an order form.

Read on

Jill Konrath: *Snap Selling,* Portfolio Penguin, reprint edition 2012

Brian Tracy: *The Psychology of Selling*, Thomas Nelson, 2010

Geoffrey James: *How to Say it: Business-to-Business Selling*, Prentice Hall Press, 2010

Naomi Klein: *No Logo*, Fourth Estate, 10th edition 2010

Michel Chevalier, Gerald Mazzalovo: *Pro Logo*, Palgrave Macmillan, 2003

LESSON NOTES

Warmer

- Say: *I went online and bought some notebooks.*

- Point to a student and indicate that you want them to repeat what you said and add another product.

- Repeat with three other students, asking each to repeat everything listed before adding their own item.

- Divide the class into pairs or groups. Students repeat the activity. If a student forgets an item on the list, they drop out.

- After five minutes or so, ask students to stop. Find out who remembered the most items.

- Ask the class to call out some of the things on their lists. Write them on the board and elicit where you could buy the products.

Overview

- Tell students that they are going to study the language for buying and selling today.

- Ask students to look at the Overview section on page 52. Point to each heading and elicit or explain a little about each. Point to the sections you will be covering in this lesson, using the table on page 59 of this book as a guide.

Quotation

- Write the quotation on the board. Ask students what they know about J. Paul Getty (*A wealthy American industrialist, he founded the Getty oil company and was described as the richest living American in 1957. He is famous for his art collection which became the J. Paul Getty museum in Los Angeles, USA.*).

Starting up

Students listen and talk about what products people buy and when and how often they buy them.

A

- Tell the class about something that you have bought and say where you bought it.

- Ask students to tell their partner about something that they bought recently.

- Write on the board: *buy online.* Ask the class to call out things you can buy online and write suggestions on the board.

B ◀)) CD1.70–1.72

- Play the recordings all the way through and ask students how many people are speaking (*three*).

- Elicit or pre-teach any vocabulary your class may have a problem with (e.g. *January sales, electrical goods, discounts, bargain, department stores, download, convenient*).

- Play the recordings and pause to highlight the examples from the first speaker (*books, every two weeks*).

- Continue the recordings, pausing after each one to elicit the answers.

Speaker	Product	Place	How often
1	books	on the Internet	every two weeks
2	electrical goods	(big) department stores	once a year
3	music and movies	online	every week

C

- Focus on the words in the box and the example.

- Tell the class where and how often you buy the products that were mentioned in Exercise A.

- Divide the class into pairs and tell students to talk about where and how often they buy the products.

- Ask three or four students to tell the class about their partner (e.g. *He/She usually buys ...*).

D

- Still in their pairs, ask students to talk about two other products they buy.

- Ask a pair to tell you the products they chose and ask the class to guess how often the two students buy them.

E

- Still in pairs, ask students to say what things they prefer *not* to buy online.

- Open the discussion to the whole class. Write the products on the board and encourage students to say where they prefer to buy them and why.

Vocabulary 1: Choosing a product

Students look at vocabulary for buying and selling different products.

A

- Read the advert with the class.

- Ask: *What does the company sell?* (home cinema and audio equipment and TVs).

- Look at the example together. Do item 2 together to demonstrate (*low deposit*).

- In pairs, ask students to complete the exercise.

- Check the answers together.

LESSON NOTES

> **2** low deposit   **3** 12 monthly payments
> **4** free delivery   **5** interest-free credit

B

- Nominate students to read out each of the sentences.

- Ask students to call out whether the buyer or seller says them.

> **2** B   **3** B   **4** B   **5** B   **6** S   **7** S   **8** B

- If your class doesn't feel comfortable calling out the words, ask them to write *buyer* and *seller* on separate A4 sheets of paper. Continue as above, except students hold up the paper to indicate who says each sentence.

C 🔊 CD1.73

- Write the following on the board:
  a) *in a shop*
  b) *in an office*
  c) *on the phone*

- Play the recording and ask the class where the conversation is taking place (*on the phone*). Ask students if Karl Simpson is the buyer or the seller (*the buyer*).

- Go through the questions and possible answers with the class and clarify any unfamiliar vocabulary.

- Play the recording again. Pause to elicit the answer to the first question (*TX7*).

- Play the rest of the recording and ask students to underline the correct answers.

- Check the answers around the class.

> **1** TX7   **2** two years   **3** 15%   **4** over 50 units
> **5** yes

D

- Ensure students understand the six items (the first four occur in Exercise A; you may need to explain *a big discount* and *great after-sales service*).

- Ask students to work in pairs and rank the six items in order of importance.

- Bring the class together and ask pairs to call out their rankings. Does everyone agree? Where there are differences of opinion, ask students to explain their reasons.

- The context given for this discussion is for buying expensive items such as a computer, TV or car. Ask students if their answers would be different if the item were less expensive (e.g. a book or a briefcase).

◎ i-Glossary

Reading: A success story

Students read an article about Japanese clothing company Uniqlo.

A

- Ask students what the term *global companies* means (*companies that operate in many different countries around the world*).

- Ask students if they can think of any examples (e.g. Coca-Cola, Microsoft). Write their ideas on the board.

- Ask students which of the companies they named is most successful in their country. Ask them to say a little about the company (what it sells, where it is based, etc.).

- Write *Uniqlo* on the board and get students to say anything they know about the company. If they do not know the company, write:
  Does it sell a) cars, b) clothes, c) electrical goods?

- Get students to guess what type of products it sells (*b*). If they need more help, draw students' attention to the photo in Exercise C.

B

- Students do the matching exercise quickly. Encourage them to use dictionaries to help.

- Check answers around the class.

> **1** b   **2** e   **3** d   **4** f   **5** a   **6** c

C

- Ask students to scan the article quickly and underline the seven numbers. Write the numbers on the board.

- Say the numbers with the class. Ask students to explain what each one refers to.

- Check answers as a class.

> 1   the year when Yani started the first Uniqlo store
>
> 2   the year when Uniqlo closed most of its UK stores
>
> 3   the year Yani changed his strategy for international growth
>
> 4   the date of the opening of the first flagship store in New York
>
> 5   the date Yani hired German designer Jil Sander
>
> 6   Uniqlo's profits in 2010
>
> 7   the number of stores in Asia in 2010

- You may wish to point out that in the UK, a billion is 1,000,000,000,000 (i.e. a million millions), whereas in the USA, it is 1,000,000,000 (i.e. a thousand millions). However, given that this has the potential to cause confusion, the American definition is commonly used.

LESSON NOTES

LESSON NOTES

D

- Ask students to read the article more closely. Answer any questions they have about vocabulary, but encourage them to work out from the context any words they are unsure about.

- Ask students to do the exercise, then go through the answers as a class. Encourage students to correct the sentences that are false.

> 1 T
>
> 2 F (It had to close most of the shops because they were too small and in the wrong place.)
>
> 3 T
>
> 4 T
>
> 5 F (The clothes were for selected stores only.)
>
> 6 F (It opened 38 stores, increasing the total to 64.)

E

- Do this as a quick-fire class exercise, getting students to identify the missing verbs as quickly as possible.

> 1 grew   2 went up   3 increased

- Draw two arrows on the board ↗ and ↘. Ask students what the three verbs have in common (*They all describe increases / things that go up.*). Point out that two of them are irregular (*grow–grew–grown, go up–went up–gone up*).

- If you have a strong class, you could ask students if they can think of any verbs that describe the opposite, e.g. *decrease, go down*.

F

- Books closed. Ask students what factors they think contributed to Uniqlo's success, and whether these factors play a part in all business successes.

- Books open. Compare with the list in the Course Book. Are there other factors that they could add to this list?

- Ask students to work in pairs to rank the full list according to which factor they think contributes most to success.

- Get students to join with another pair and compare their rankings. Do they agree? Where there are differences, encourage students to explain why they have ranked the various factors in that way.

➡ Text bank (pages 142–143)

Language focus 1: Past simple

Students are introduced to regular and irregular forms of the past simple.

A 🔊 CD1.74

- Write the six verbs (*saved, delivered, launched, worked, decided, visited*) on the board and ask students to identify which tense they are (past simple).

- Explain that there are three ways of pronouncing the *-ed* ending, depending on the ending of the main verb.

- Play the recording several times, pausing after each group for students to repeat, focusing on the pronunciation of the ending (/d/, /t/ or /ɪd/). Students may have difficulty hearing the difference, especially when the ending is in an unstressed syllable.

B 🔊 CD1.75

- Tell students that they are going to hear nine different verbs, and that they need to match each verb with one of the endings in Exercise A.

- Play the recording, pausing after each verb and asking students which group it belongs to. Write the answers on the board.

> 1 advised, lived, opened
>
> 2 finished, missed, booked
>
> 3 started, wanted, invited

- Ask students if they can identify any patterns to the different pronunciations (*verb stems ending in* k, p, f, sh, ss *are in the* /t/ *group; verb stems ending in* g, b, v, s *are in the* /d/ *group; verb stems ending in* t *or* d *are in the* /ɪd/ *group*).

- Play the recording again and pause to allow students to repeat the verbs.

C

- Read through the Language focus box together and clarify where necessary. You may wish to refer students to the Grammar reference on page 150 and the list of irregular verbs on page 157.

- Tell students to look at the report on the sales trip. Highlight the example.

- Ask students to identify the regular verbs in the text (*visit, arrive, advise, introduce, ask*).

- In pairs, ask students to complete the report using the past simple form of the verbs. Don't hurry students; circulate, helping where necessary.

- Ask students to read sentences from the text. Check answers around the class.

> 2 arrived   3 met   4 made   5 advised
> 6 went   7 introduced   8 asked   9 gave   10 flew

LESSON NOTES

- With the whole class, ask students to put the regular verbs in the report into one of the pronunciation groups from Exercise A (/t/ *introduced, asked;* /d/ *advised, arrived;* /ɪd/ *visited*).

D

- Tell the class about a trip you made for business or pleasure. Encourage students to ask you questions to get more information.

- Give students time to prepare their ideas. Divide the class into pairs and ask them to tell their partner about a trip they made.

- Circulate and note any areas where students may need help with the past simple.

Vocabulary 2: Choosing a service

Students complete a leaflet for a car-hire company.

- Books closed. Ask students to name some car-hire firms in their town or country. Is it cheap or expensive to hire cars in their country? Is insurance expensive? Do car-hire companies offer special deals?

A

- Books open. Look at the leaflet together. Encourage students to use dictionaries to check unfamiliar vocabulary.

- Tell students to complete the leaflet using the words from the box.

- Check the answers together.

> **2** price   **3** Free   **4** discount   **5** period

- Ask students if they think Dart Car Hire is good value and to explain why or why not. How does the company compare to car-hire firms in the students' own country? What is similar? What is different?

B

- Tell students to complete the exercise individually.

- Check the answers together.

> **2** T   **3** T   **4** F (... *until the end of July.*)   **5** T
> **6** F (... *we e-mail you a detailed receipt.*)

C

- Students rewrite the false statements in pairs.

- Ask three pairs of students to read out their answers. Write them on the board and find out if everyone had the same answers.

> **4**   The offer is until the end of July.
> **6**   Gold Club members get their receipt by e-mail.

◎ i-Glossary

Listening: How to sell

The interview is in three parts. Students hear Ros Pomeroy, a management consultant, giving advice to salespeople.

A

- Write the two questions on the board.

- Ask students to work in pairs and discuss.

- Have a quick feedback session with the whole class.

B ◀)) CD1.76

- Read the answers with the whole class and ask students to guess what the missing words might be.

- Play the recording and ask students to listen to see if Ros Pomeroy mentions their ideas.

- Play it again and pause to complete the first gap together. Elicit the missing word (*patient*).

- Get students to listen to the rest of the recording and complete the exercise.

> **1** patient   **2** relationships   **3** understand
> **4** need   **5** want   **6** time   **7** wants   **8** listened

C ◀)) CD1.77

- Tell students that they are going to hear the second part of Ros's talk.

- Play the recording and pause to draw attention to the example. Play the rest while students complete the exercise.

- Ask students to compare answers with a partner, then play the recording again for them to check.

> **1** f   **2** c   **3** e   **4** a   **5** d   **6** b

- Depending on the time available, ask students to turn to the audio scripts on page 162. Play recordings 1.76 and 1.77 again as students read the audio scripts. Ask the class if they agree or disagree with Ros's ideas.

D ◀)) CD1.78

- Tell students that they are going to hear the third part of Ros's interview.

- This is a good opportunity to introduce students to note-taking. Tell students to listen for key words rather than try to write every word.

E

- Tell students about the best thing you ever bought. Encourage them to ask questions.

LESSON NOTES

- Divide the class into pairs and get students to discuss the question. To make it more of a dialogue, you could elicit the question to start the conversation (*What's the best thing you ever bought?*). Also encourage them to ask more questions to find out about the product.

- Ask two or three students to talk about what their partner bought (*He/She bought ...*).

- ◎ Students can watch the interview with Ros Pomeroy on the DVD-ROM.

- ➡ Resource bank: Listening (page 180)

Language focus 2: Past time references

Students are introduced to key past time references and use the language to write a short article.

A

- Go through the Language focus box together. Refer students to the Grammar reference on page 150 for more information.

- This article is a profile of a sales manager.

- Complete the first two items of the article with the whole class (*in*, *for*).

- Ask students to complete the exercise individually.

- Get students to compare their answers with a partner.

> 1 in   2 for   3 from   4 During   5 In   6 on
> 7 ago   8 Last

B 🔊 CD1.79

- Books closed. Write *Ikea* on the board and elicit any information that students know about the company. If students need prompts, ask: *What does it sell?* (furniture) and *What country did the company start in?* (Sweden). Ask students if they have visited an Ikea store and encourage them to say what they bought there.

- Books open. Read through the profile with the class. Play the recording and pause to draw students' attention to the example. Play the rest of the recording and ask students to complete the exercise with a partner.

- Play the recording again for students to check. Ask questions such as *What did he study at university?* (industrial design and marketing), *When did he work as a carpet salesman?* (1979).

> 2   industrial design and marketing
>
> 3   1979
>
> 4   1981
>
> 5   marketing
>
> 6   Country Manager
>
> 7   1991–1995
>
> 8   1995
>
> 9   Southern Europe and North America
>
> 10 1st September 2009

- The activity can be extended by asking students to work in pairs and write true and false statements using Mikael Ohlsson's profile. Get them to work with another pair. With books closed, get them to take turns reading their statements and saying whether it is true or false.

C – D

- Demonstrate the activity by making notes about your career on the board.

- Use the notes to describe your career. Ask students to make notes as you speak. Then get two or three students to read back some of the information about your career.

- Ask students to make notes about their own career. If you have pre-work students, they can use any part-time or voluntary work they have done, as well as including information about their studies. Alternatively, students can make up information about their ideal job.

- Divide the class into pairs. Ask students to take turns describing their career. Remind their partner to make notes including important dates and events.

- Circulate and monitor, noting any areas where students may need more practice.

E

- Read the instructions together and ask a student to read the example to the class.

- Ask the class to help you write a profile about your career using the information from Exercise C. Write the sentences on the board as students say them. Encourage the class to suggest past time references where appropriate. Correct any errors together.

- Then ask students to use their notes about their partner to write a short profile.

- Collect the profiles in to check and note any areas where students need more help.

LESSON NOTES

Skills: Describing a product

This section introduces useful language for describing a product. Students listen to an advertisement and complete product details and identify expressions from the Useful language box.

- The listening in this lesson is an advertisement for a new women's bag. To set the context, you may wish to bring in advertisements for products from magazines/newspapers, or record one or two advertisements from the TV.

- At the start of the lesson, you could get students to say which advertisements they like or dislike and identify what each one is selling.

- To round off the lesson, you could use the advertisements to revise the language in the Useful language box by asking students to describe some of the products and talk about the features and possible target market.

A ◄)) CD1.80

- Books closed. Ask students to suggest places where companies can advertise products (*on TV, radio, in magazines and newspapers, on the Internet*, etc.).

- Tell students that they are going to hear an advertisement. Play it and ask students to say what product is being advertised (*a bag*).

- Books open. Play the recording again and pause to elicit the target market (*smart, professional women*). Play the rest of the recording, pausing now and then to elicit information for the gaps.

- Encourage students to use this opportunity to check information (*How do you spell ...? Did she say ...?*).

> 1 professional 2 material 3 pockets
> 4 compartment 5 black 6 brown 7 75€
> 8 week

- Ask questions about the bag (e.g. *What is it made of? What are the features? What colours does it come in? How much is it? When do they deliver?*). Ask students to use their completed information to answer your questions.

B ◄)) CD1.80

- Read the Useful language box together and clarify meaning where necessary.

- Play the recording again while students tick the expressions they hear.

- Check answers around the class.

> It's stylish and fashionable.
>
> It's made of ...
>
> It comes in three colours.
>
> It weighs about half a kilo.
>
> It's lightweight.
>
> It's just 35 centimetres long.
>
> You can close it easily.
>
> It's just 75 euros.
>
> We'll deliver within a week.

- Point to an object in the class and ask: *What is it made of? How long/high/wide is it? How much do you think it cost?*

- If time allows, you could ask students to turn to the audio script on page 163 and read the advertisement together, copying the intonation in the recording. You could then ask students questions (e.g. *How many colours does it come in?* (three); *How much does it weigh?* (about half a kilo); *How much is postage and packaging?* (five euros)).

C

- Ask students if they have ever visited a trade fair. What do people do at a trade fair? (*try to sell products or services, get information about products or services, make contacts with people who work in the same industry*, etc.).

- Draw a lamp on the board and ask students to say what materials it could be made of, then encourage students to suggest questions (e.g. *How much does it cost? How high is it? What colours does it come in?*).

- Pre-teach vocabulary students will need (e.g. *model, bends, long-lasting batteries, bulbs*).

- Tell students that they are going to role-play a conversation between a salesperson for a lighting equipment company and a store manager who wants to buy some lighting.

- Divide the class into two groups (A and B). Ask Group A to look at their role cards and write the questions together. Ask Group B to look at the information on their role cards and predict what questions their partner will ask.

- Put students into A/B pairs and ask them to role-play the conversation. Circulate and monitor.

- If time allows, ask students to change roles and practise the conversation again.

- Books closed. Ask students what information they remember about the lamp.

◎ Students can watch the advert on the DVD-ROM.

⇥ Resource bank: Speaking (page 168)

CASE STUDY

NP Innovations

Students use information about products to role-play a conversation about which product a company should buy.

- Books closed. Write *Toys* on the board. Ask students to say what their favourite toys were when they were young. Tell students that they work for a company that sells gifts. Ask students to suggest some ideas for toys to sell.

Background

- Pre-teach any vocabulary that you think your class might have difficulty with.

- Read the *Background* paragraph aloud with students, clarifying where necessary.

◀)) CD1.81

- Read the three questions together. Ask students to work in pairs.

- Play the recording all the way through. Then play it again, pausing to answer the first question together.

- Play the rest of the recording, pausing to elicit answers.

---

1 The electronic tennis game brought a lot of people into the store and increased sales a lot.

2 Jim mentions the following products: skateboards; a robot; a space toy.

3 His reasons for each product are as follows:

- Skateboards are very popular. The market is growing fast. Young people will pay a lot for a skateboard which is different.

- He saw the robot at a toy fair and liked it.

- There was a lot of interest in the space toy at the toy fair.

- Books closed. Ask if students can remember the three products Jim mentioned and any details about the toys.

- Ask students how Jim and his manager want to advertise the product (*on television*).

- If time allows, ask students to work in pairs and read the audio script on page 163 together.

Task

- Divide the class into groups of three.

- Give students time to read the role cards and complete the table with information about their product.

- Encourage students to refer to the Useful language box on page 58.

- Get them to role-play the discussion, telling each other about their products and completing the chart. Then they discuss which product to buy. Encourage students to give reasons for their choice.

- Circulate and monitor.

- At the end of the conversation, groups present their decision to the class. Make notes for areas where students may need more practice.

One-to-one

Prepare useful phrases for two of the products with your student. You take one role card and your student takes another to role-play the conversation.

Writing

- Ask a student to read the instructions to the class.

- Work with the class to write an introduction to the e-mail on the board.

- Encourage students to suggest questions to ask the manufacturer.

- Circulate and monitor, helping where needed.

- To extend the activity, you could ask students to exchange e-mails and write a reply from the manufacturer, answering the questions (using the information in the role cards).

➡ Writing file (Course Book page 126)

➡ Resource bank: Writing (page 194)

Communication styles

Introduction

This *Working across cultures* unit focuses on different communication styles in China, Germany and the US. It requires students to think about the ways that their own culture compares with these countries and to explore similarities and differences.

A

- Write *China*, *Germany* and *the US* on the board and ask students to call out any information they know about each country (name of the leader, a famous company, a national dish, etc.).

- Ask students to work individually or in pairs and match each country to its description. Get students to check their answers on page 136 of the Course Book.

- Divide the class into groups and ask them to discuss question 2.

---

1   **1** Germany   **2** the US   **3** China

B 🔊 CD1.82

- Read through the statements with the class and clarify where necessary.

- Ask students to decide whether the statements are true or false and compare their ideas with a partner.

- Tell students that they are going to hear an expert on international communications.

- Play the recording so that students can check their answers.

- Ask them if they were surprised by any of the answers.

- Divide the class into pairs and ask them to discuss question 3.

- Have a feedback session with the class.

---

1   1   F (You should use a firm handshake.)

    2   F (They prefer direct eye contact.)

    3   T

    4   F (Their style is direct and informal.)

    5   T

    6   F (There are no special rules about business cards.)

C

- Books closed. Ask students if they have ever done business in Germany or visited Germany on holiday.

Write the headings on the board (*Greetings, Personal space, Communication style, Punctuality, Names and titles, Meetings*). Ask students to suggest words that they think might be used to describe business culture in Germany under each heading.

- Books open. Ask students to read the information about Germany. If any of your class is from Germany, you could ask them to read the guide and see if they agree with the information.

- Ask students to work in pairs and discuss the similarities and differences with their own country's business culture compared to Germany.

D 🔊 CD1.83

- Read the questions with the class and see if students can suggest answers to any of them.

- Play the first part of the recording and answer the first question together.

- Play the recording all the way through. Then play it again, pausing at relevant points to allow students to answer the questions.

- Check answers around the class.

---

1   At the beginning and end of the day

2   They do not want the other person to 'lose face'.

3   The Chinese style of communication is more indirect.

4   A good way is to study their body language, facial expressions and gestures.

5   b

6   By holding it in both hands with the Chinese translation on top

7   If you interrupt the Chinese person, they 'lose face'.

Task

- Go through the task with the whole class and make sure that they understand.

- Divide the class into groups and ask them to discuss the three questions.

- Give students time to read the information about the three countries again from Exercises A–D if necessary. Tell them they should think about language, what to take and which colleagues to talk to.

- Circulate and monitor.

- Ask each group to say where each person wants to work on their posting. Encourage students to give reasons for their choices.

Revision

4 Travel

Vocabulary

1 buy   2 book   3 queue   4 go through   5 watch
6 take   7 check in   8 do

There is / there are

1 is there   2 there isn't   3 there are   4 There's
5 Is there   6 Are there   7 there aren't
8 there are

Skills

A   1 R   2 R   3 C   4 C   5 R   6 C   7 R   8 C

B   1 c   2 b   3 h   4 f   5 a   6 d   7 e   8 g

5 Food and entertaining

Vocabulary

meat	fish	fruit	dessert	vegetable
beef	cod	apple	apple pie	aubergine
lamb	trout	grapes	cheesecake	onion
veal	tuna	peach	chocolate mousse	peas

some/any; many, much and *a lot of*

1 much   2 any   3 some   4 some   5 a lot of
6 many

Skills

A   1 d   2 a   3 e   4 b   5 f   6 c

B   1 exactly   2 know   3 right   4 point
    5 true   6 agree

6 Buying and selling

Vocabulary

1 All   2 a third   3 two chairs   4 no charge
5 doesn't cost   6 a small amount of

Past simple

1 graduated   2 did   3 offered   4 worked
5 decided   6 started   7 joined   8 became

Writing

Suggested answer

Lars Karlsson studied at Stockholm University
from 2003 to 2006. As part of his course, he did an
internship with a marketing firm. He graduated in
2006 with a degree in marketing. After graduation,
a company called JKKL Market Research offered
him a job as a researcher. He worked there from
2006 to 2009. During this time, he decided to start
his own small market-research company. In 2009,
he left JKKL and opened a small research company,
called Lars Karlsson Marketing. Two years ago, he
hired three researchers. His business is now very
successful.

Cultures 2: Communication styles

A   1 meet   2 nod   3 mean   4 Listen
    5 understand   6 notice   7 use   8 present
    9 show

B   1 Names and titles   2 Business cards
    3 Directness   4 Greetings

People

AT A GLANCE

	Classwork – Course Book	Further work
Lesson 1 *Each lesson (excluding case studies) is about 45–60 minutes. This does not include administration and time spent going through homework.*	<u>**Starting up**</u> Students answer a questionnaire about what sort of person they are. **Vocabulary: Describing people** Students look at adjectives to describe people's personalities. **Listening: Managing people** Ros Pomeroy, a management consultant, talks about the type of people she likes to work with.	**Practice File** Vocabulary (page 28) **i-Glossary** (DVD-ROM) **Course Book Listening** (DVD-ROM) **Resource bank: Listening** (page 181)
Lesson 2	**Language focus 1: Past simple: negatives and questions** Students focus on past simple negatives and questions and write questions using *Why, How long, What, When* and *Where*. **Reading: Andrea Jung** Students read an article about the businesswoman Andrea Jung, the Chief Executive of Avon Products. Students then answer questions about the article.	**Practice File** Language review (page 29) **Text bank** (pages 144–145)
Lesson 3	**Language focus 2: Question forms** Students look at *yes/no* questions and open questions in the context of an article about Steve Jobs. They complete a questionnaire and then listen to check answers. <u>**Skills: Dealing with problems**</u> Students listen to a conversation between an employee and a manager talking about a problem. Then they role-play a conversation negotiating a later starting time.	**Practice File** Language review (page 29) **Course Book Skills Discussion** (DVD-ROM) **Resource bank: Speaking** (page 169)
Lesson 4 *Each case study is about 30 minutes to 1 hour.*	<u>**Case study: Tell us about it**</u> A magazine has a message board on its website called Office Life, where people can write about their problems at work. **Writing** Students write a reply to one of the messages on the Office Life message board.	**Resource bank: Writing** (page 195) **Practice File** Writing (page 30)

For a fast route through the unit focusing mainly on speaking skills, just use the underlined sections.

For one-to-one situations, most parts of the unit lend themselves, with minimal adaptation, to use with individual students. Where this is not the case, alternative procedures are given.

BUSINESS BRIEF

What **characteristics** can help people to succeed in business and in life? A **positive attitude**, intelligence, **perseverance** and **self-discipline** all help. Are the personality traits that contribute to success or failure genetic? Or do we learn these characteristics as we grow up? Experts still disagree as to whether **nature** or **nurture** is more important.

Can personality and intelligence be measured? IQ and **psychometric** tests remain popular, and the latter are still used by many companies as part of the selection process. However, in recent years, the idea that only one type of intelligence exists has been criticised. Howard Gardner developed the theory of **multiple intelligences**. This said that people have a number of different types of intelligence that they possess to varying degrees. These are linguistic, musical, logical-mathematical, spatial, body-kinaesthetic, intrapersonal (e.g. insight) and interpersonal (e.g. social skills and the ability to understand and motivate other people). Gardner noted that teaching and learning should focus on the dominant intelligence of each person.

In business, it is important to recognise that not everyone perceives the world in the same way. This is particularly true when dealing with problems. A solution is more likely to be found if we can respect the fact that the other person may have an alternative viewpoint to our own. Explaining and exploring problems requires good **communication skills**. As well as the ability to explain problems and offer advice, successful resolution also requires the ability to actively listen. Some ways that we can employ active listening include:

- Give the person your full attention. It isn't possible to listen well when multitasking.
- Be aware of the person's body language as well as their words.
- Show that you are engaged with what the person says by nodding or adding brief verbal comments such as *go on*, *uh-huh*, *OK*, etc.
- Paraphrase or repeat back key information (*So what you're saying is ...*).
- Ask questions to clarify or gain more information.

Read on

http://www.mindtools.com
Includes useful information about communication, problem-solving and active listening

Howard Gardner: *Multiple Intelligences: The theory in practice*, Basic Books, third edition 2011

Daniel Nettle: *Personality. What makes you the way you are*, OUP Oxford, 2009

Alan Barker: *Improve your Communication Skills*, Kogan Press, second edition 2010

www.psychology.org
Includes a precis of theories connected to learning from a psychological perspective (search for 'Multiple intelligence theory' or 'Howard Gardner')

LESSON NOTES

Warmer

- The following activity will prepare the class for the language for describing people which they will look at later in the lesson.

- Say to the class: *The teacher's cat is an angry cat and his name is Albert.*

- Then say a word to describe the cat and a name beginning with B (e.g. *The teacher's cat is a boring cat and his name is Bob.*). You can write an example on the board to help students follow the model.

- Ask the class to call out suggestions for a word to describe the cat beginning with C and also a name beginning with C (e.g. *The teacher's cat is a calm cat and his name is Carlos.*). Allow students to use dictionaries if necessary. Write ideas on the board.

- Divide the class into pairs or small groups. Tell students that they are going to take turns to say a word to describe the cat and a name. They should follow alphabetical order, starting with D. Ask them to use full sentences like the model.

- As students become familiar with what they have to do, encourage the responses to be brisk.

- Have a feedback session where you say a letter and pairs/groups say what describing word/name they used. Ask students which letters were most difficult to find words and names for.

Overview

- Tell students that you are going to study language to talk about people.

- Ask students to look at the Overview section on page 66. Point to each heading and elicit or explain a little about each. Point to the sections you will be covering in this lesson, using the table on page 70 of this book as a guide.

Quotation

- The quotation is a play on words of the saying 'A person is only as good as the company they keep.' (In other words, you can judge someone by the people they know or socialise with.)

- Divide the class into pairs or small groups. Ask students to discuss what they think the quote means (*A company is only good if the people who work there are good.*). Do students agree or disagree with the quotation?

- Have a brief feedback session with the whole class.

Starting up

Students complete a quiz to see what sort of person they are. They then tell a new partner about the previous one. Underline that the quiz is for fun and is not a test.

A

- Quickly go through the questions and possible answers, checking students' understanding.

- Ask students to complete the quiz in pairs, noting their own and their partner's answers in the chart in the margin.

B

- Point to the first question and say: *I like to work in a team.* Ask the class to say the other possibilities (*I like to work alone, I like to work with a partner.*). Then ask students to transform the statements into the third person singular form (*He likes to work in a team, She likes to work alone, He likes to work with a partner.*).

- Nominate a student to read question 2 as a statement and elicit the alternatives around the class in both first and third persons.

- Ask students to work in pairs again, ensuring that they have a different partner than before.

- For each question, students should tell their new partner about their own and their previous partner's preferences, using the answers they noted in Exercise A.

- Circulate, monitor and help where necessary.

- After about 10 minutes, ask a few students to come to the front and give their statements to the whole class.

- Pause occasionally and open up discussion points with the whole class. For example: What are the differences between working at home, in the office and outside? Can students think of advantages and disadvantages to working in each place? Were there any options that nobody chose?

Vocabulary: Describing people

This section introduces adjectives to describe characteristics.

A

- Do the first one together as an example, then allow students to complete the matching task either individually or (for a less confident class) in pairs.

- Check the answers around the class.

> 1 h 2 a 3 b 4 j 5 g 6 c 7 f 8 d 9 i 10 e

- Can students add any other adjectives to the list?

- Ask students to think of some famous people. Choose one or two people and ask students to call out adjectives to describe them.

LESSON NOTES

- Books closed. Demonstrate how to play hangman using one of the adjectives. Divide the class into teams. Get students to play hangman using some of the adjectives in the list.

- Divide the class into A/B pairs. Ask Student As to open the Course Book and read one of the statements. Tell Student Bs to keep their books closed and try to remember the correct adjective. Then get students to reverse roles.

B

- Ask a student to read the first sentence.

- Ensure that students understand that the first sentence describes the missing adjective (*sociable*).

- Refer students to the list of adjectives in Exercise A and complete item 2 with the whole class (*punctual*).

- Get students to complete the rest of the exercise with a partner.

- Ask individual students to read out sentences from the report to check the answers.

> **2** punctual   **3** reliable   **4** hard-working
> **5** motivating/helpful   **6** creative

- Ask students if any of the adjectives describe themselves or their colleagues.

C

- Use the adjectives in Exercise A to tell the class about the characteristic you think is most important for a boss and a colleague in a team.

- Highlight the examples and give students a few minutes to think about the three characteristics they think are important for each role.

- Divide the class into pairs. Ask students to compare their ideas with a partner.

- ⊙ i-Glossary

Listening: Managing people

Students listen to a three-part interview with Ros Pomeroy, a management consultant. She talks about the people she likes to work with and gives examples of a good and bad management style. Students listen for gist and also for specific information.

A ◀)) CD2.1

- Pre-teach any vocabulary from the recording which you think might cause problems for students, such as *willing* and *give up*.

- Play the recording for students to get the gist of what Ros says.

- Play the recording again and ask students to tick the words she mentions from the list in Vocabulary Exercise A.

- Elicit answers around the class.

> creative, hard-working, reliable

B ◀)) CD2.2

- Remind students of the three words they thought were important for a boss (Vocabulary Exercise C). Ask students to use some of the words to say what a bad boss *isn't* (*He/She isn't hard-working*, etc.).

- Write these words from Vocabulary Exercise A on the board and ask students to say what the opposite word is (they can use a dictionary).
  hard-working (lazy)
  helpful (unhelpful)
  sociable (unsociable)
  reliable (unreliable)

- Tell students that they are going to hear Ros Pomeroy talk about a bad manager she worked with.

- Write the words *criticised* and *support* on the board.

- Play the recording and ask students to say what they think the words mean from context (*criticised – said negative things to someone, support – help or advise someone*).

- Read the questions and check students understand.

- Play the recording again and elicit answers.

> **1** Because the manager often criticised members of the team in front of others.
>
> **2** Because they knew that, if something went wrong, the manager would not support them.

- Ask students if they think the manager's actions were right or wrong.

C ◀)) CD2.3

- Books closed. On the board write *A good manager*. Ask students to suggest things that a good manager does.

- Play the recording and ask students to listen to see if any of their ideas are mentioned.

- Play the recording again and ask students to complete the words in the interview. Do the first one together to demonstrate (*task*).

- Play the recording a final time and pause to elicit the missing words.

> **1** task   **2** complete   **3** involved   **4** objective
> **5** results   **6** praise   **7** feedback

LESSON NOTES

LESSON NOTES

- Check that students understand the meaning of the missing words. Ask them to use dictionaries to clarify where necessary.

- Ask students if they agree with Ros Pomeroy's description of a good manager.

D

- Tell students about the type of people you like / don't like working with. Give reasons where possible.

- Ask students to think about the questions individually, then to discuss them in pairs.

- If it is not appropriate for students to have the discussion in class (for example if they feel uncomfortable discussing the subject with colleagues), you could ask students to complete the exercise in writing for homework.

- ◎ Students can watch the interview with Ros Pomeroy on the DVD-ROM.

- ➡ Resource bank: Listening (page 181)

Language focus 1: Past simple: negatives and questions

Students practise past simple negatives and questions by putting sentences in the correct order and finding mistakes in a message.

- Read through the Language focus box together. Elicit the uncontracted form of *didn't* (*did not*). Point out that we usually use contracted forms in speech and informal written communication (such as e-mails). In more formal documents (such as formal letters and reports), the uncontracted form is used.

A – B ◀)) CD2.4

- Books closed. Write these words on the board: *the deadlines /the projects /weren't /for /realistic.*

- Put the words in the correct order with the whole class.

- Books open. Ask students to look at the example to check.

- Divide the class into pairs. Ask students to complete the remaining items in the exercise with their partner.

- Circulate and monitor.

- Play the recording for students to check their answers.

> 2 Most people didn't leave the office until 8 p.m.
>
> 3 She wasn't a good manager.
>
> 4 Meetings didn't start on time.
>
> 5 She didn't know how to motivate the staff.

- Ask individual students to dictate the statements as you write them on the board.

- Spend some time clarifying any problems with word order.

C

- Focus on the mistake in the first line. Tell students that there is only one mistake in each line.

- Check answers around the class.

> 2 ~~I not~~ I didn't   3 ~~phoned~~ phone
> 4 ~~you not~~ you didn't

D

- Highlight the example and do item 2 of the exercise together.

- Tell students to complete the exercise individually.

- As they finish, get students to compare their answers with a partner.

> 2 were   3 did   4 did   5 was

E

- Read the extract with the class.

- Highlight the example.

- Tell students to complete the exercise individually. More than one question may sometimes be possible.

- Monitor and note any areas where students may need more help.

- Check answers around the class.

> **Suggested answers**
>
> Why did she leave Renault?
>
> How long was she at Renault? / How long did she stay at Renault?
>
> What did she study at university?
>
> When did she join Renault?
>
> When did she leave Renault?
>
> Where did she grow up?
>
> Where did she study?

- Get students to work in pairs and take turns asking the questions and answering them about Danielle.

F

- Encourage students to ask you questions about your past studies and jobs.

LESSON NOTES

- Divide the class into pairs. Give students a few minutes to write questions individually.

- Get students to ask and answer questions with their partner. Depending on your class, you could ask students to change partners two or three times.

- Circulate and note any areas that need further consolidation.

Reading: Andrea Jung

This article is about the businesswoman Andrea Jung, Chief Executive of Avon Products. Students exploit the text through true and false sentences and interview questions.

A

- Ask students how many famous businesswomen they can think of. If you think they will struggle with this, you could set them the task for homework and see how many they can come up with. If you have time, they could each select one and give a brief presentation on her at the start of the class.

- Brainstorm a list of qualities that students think are necessary to be a successful businessperson. Do they think this list is any different for women than it is for men? Do women need additional qualities to succeed? If so, why?

B

- Give students five minutes to scan the article and complete the profile. Be strict about the time limit – scanning for specific information is an important skill, and students should not be reading every word at this stage.

- Ask four students to give you the answers.

> **Suggested answer**
>
> **Born in:** Toronto, Canada
>
> **Grew up in:** Massachusetts, USA
>
> **Education:** Princeton University, USA
>
> **Appearance:** long black hair; always wears a pearl necklace
>
> **Company:** Avon Products (a global cosmetics company)
>
> **Professional achievements:** Became CEO of Avon in 1999.
>
> More than 12 years as CEO.
>
> On the boards of Apple and GE.

C

- Read paragraphs 1 and 2 with the class. Pause when you get to any words that students might find difficult and try to elicit a translation or meaning from the context.

- Tell students to take turns reading the remaining paragraphs with a partner.

- Ask students to underline any difficult words and have a short feedback session.

- Read the sentences, then ask students to read the article again and complete the exercise in their pairs.

- Check the answers around the class and ask students to correct the false statements.

> 1 F (It is a direct sales company. It sells door to door.)
>
> 2 T
>
> 3 T
>
> 4 F (Of the nine board members, four are women.)
>
> 5 F (She thinks teams with a mix of men and women make the best decisions.)
>
> 6 T

- You could follow this up by asking a few comprehension questions about the article, e.g. *How many countries does Avon sell cosmetics in?* (120); *Where was Andrea Jung born?* (Toronto); *When did she join Avon?* (1994).

D

- Ask students how many paragraphs there are in the text about Andrea Jung (*six*).

- Get a student to read the first item and ask students to look at paragraph 1 to find the word.

- Divide the class into pairs and ask them to complete the exercise. If your class is confident, you could ask them to compete to see which pair finds all the words first.

- Check answers around the class.

> 1 sales representatives   2 determination
> 3 quit   4 revenues   5 passion

- Books closed. Read out some of the definitions and see if students can remember the word that matches the meaning.

E

- Students work in pairs to come up with five questions they would like to ask Andrea Jung. Remind them that they are not writing questions whose answers are contained in the article, but questions that are prompted by the information in it, and they are not expected to know the answers.

- If students are struggling, reduce the number of questions to two and give them a few pointers by asking them whether they think Andrea finds it easy to balance home and work life, if she found it easy to get to the top of her profession.

LESSON NOTES

- Have a feedback session as a class and make a list of the best questions on the board.

- If you have a strong class, you could ask them to imagine what Andrea's answers might be and to role-play the interview.

➡ Text bank (pages 144–145)

Language focus 2: Question forms

Students review *yes/no* questions and question words.

- Read through the information in the Language focus box and clarify where necessary.

A

- Don't spend too long on this – it is really just a warmer for the following article.

- Students will probably know that Steve Jobs was one of the founders of Apple.

- Have a brief feedback session and write students' ideas on the board.

B

- Ask students to quickly read the article for gist. It is a short biography of Steve Jobs.

- Explain that the information required to fill the gaps in the article will be provided by the quiz on page 71, but that first they must complete the quiz questions.

- Go through the example with the class by looking at gap 1 in the article and asking students what information is missing (*Jobs's place of birth*). Then look at the quiz and the three possible answers to question 1, and ask students to formulate the relevant question.

- This is quite a complex process, so go through item 2 with the class too: identify that gap 2 in the article requires the name of the person he started Apple with; look at question 2 in the quiz and get students to supply the question that fits (*Who did he start Apple with?*).

- Students continue in pairs; circulate, monitor and help where necessary.

Suggested answers

1 Where was Steve Jobs born?

2 Who did Jobs start Apple with?

3 When did Apple introduce the famous Macintosh computer?

4 Why did Jobs leave Apple?

5 What did Pixar specialise in?

6 Who did Jobs marry?

7 How much did Apple pay for NeXT?

8 When did Steve Jobs resign as CEO of Apple?

9 How old was Steve Jobs when he died?

10 Who is Apple's new CEO?

11 How many people does Apple employ worldwide?

C 🔊 CD2.5

- Play the recording for students to check their questions. Point out that the version on the recording is not always the only possible answer (e.g. students may have used *When did the company introduce the Macintosh computer?*, *When did he leave Apple?*, etc.). Allow alternatives, providing the verb agreement and any use of the possessive is correct.

- Go through the answers as a class, focusing on the question forms and clarifying any problem areas.

D

- Students do the quiz, choosing from the multiple-choice answers. They may know some of the answers; others they will have to guess. If you prefer, they can do this in pairs.

- Students use their answers to complete the article in Exercise B. Do the first one together to demonstrate (*a) In California*).

- As students finish, ask them to compare their answers with a partner.

E 🔊 CD2.6

- Play the recording for students to check their answers.

- Ask students if any of the answers surprised them.

1 a 2 c 3 c 4 c 5 b 6 c 7 a 8 b 9 b
10 a 11 c

F

- Students work in pairs. Student A closes the Course Book and Student B chooses a question from the quiz. Can Student A remember the answer? They then swap roles.

- Allow students to help each other remember the answer if necessary, only opening the book as a last resort.

- Circulate, monitor and assist as necessary, focusing on the correct use of question forms.

G – H

- Write the prompts on the board and complete each one with information about yourself.

- Draw students' attention to the example in Exercise H and get two students to read it. Read out the first statement about you and get a confident student to respond. Ask the class to suggest follow-up questions.

LESSON NOTES

- Give students five minutes to complete the sentences in Exercise G with simple statements. Allow them to invent information if they want, as long as they can elaborate on it in Exercise H.

- Students work in pairs. They take it in turns to read out one of their sentences from Exercise G; their partner then asks as many questions as they can.

- Alternatively, ask students to work in small groups; each student reads out a sentence and each of the other members of the group has to ask a question about it.

- Circulate, monitor and assist as necessary, focusing on the correct use of question forms.

Skills: Dealing with problems

Students are introduced to key phrases for describing problems, responding and making suggestions.

A

- Read out the five suggestions and clarify any difficult vocabulary (e.g. *describe*, *in detail*).

- Give students five minutes to discuss in pairs which of the suggestions they agree with.

- Ask them to choose the one they agree with most and do a class poll. Is there a clear winner?

B 🔊 CD2.7

- Read the information and questions with the class.

- Play the recording twice.

- Check the answers around the class.

> 1 He wants the company to pay for his Spanish language lessons.
>
> 2 She suggests he should buy a self-study course.
>
> 3 No, but she tells him to bring her the receipt for his course.

C 🔊 CD2.7

- Play the recording again and ask students to complete the extracts.

- Check the answers together.

> 1 sorry   2 problem   3 possible   4 cheap
> 5 hard   6 pay   7 promise   8 receipt

- Play the recording one more time and focus on the words that are stressed in the conversation.

- Tell students to work in pairs. Ask them to turn to the audio script on page 164 and read the conversation together.

D

- Ask students to refer back to Exercise A to answer.

> Suggestions 1 and 3

E

- Ask students what time they start work/college. Do they like starting at this time? Would they prefer to start earlier/later?

- Students work in pairs to think of reasons why the office worker might want to start work later in the morning and why the manager might not agree.

- Spend time going over the phrases in the Useful language box.

- Divide the class into pairs. Give students time to read their role cards.

- You could put students into groups of office workers and managers to prepare their roles before having the conversation.

- After the role play, have a feedback session to discuss what pairs decided.

◎ Students can watch the discussion on the DVD-ROM.

➡ Resource bank: Speaking (page 169)

CASE STUDY

Tell us about it

A magazine has a message board on its website where people who have problems at work can leave messages. Students read the problems and discuss possible solutions.

Background

- Divide the class into pairs. Ask students to read the Background section together.

- Ask check questions (e.g. *What is 'Business Today'? What is the message board called? Do people discuss problems about home or work on the message board? What do the readers do?*).

- Ask students to read the questions about Susanna and Thomas and have a brief feedback session with the class.

🔊 CD2.8

- Play the recording. Ask students to say who Matthew has a problem with (*the project manager*). Ask: *What is Matthew's job?* (He works in customer relations for a medical insurance company.)

- Play the recording again; this time, students should make notes about the problem and summarise the project manager's mistakes.

- Ask students to compare their notes with a partner. Have a feedback session with the class to check students have all the information they need.

Task

- Read the instructions together.

- Divide the class into pairs.

- Ask students to quickly read through Susanna's and Thomas's problems again and also their notes about Matthew. Pairs then discuss what each person should do to solve their problem.

- Get students to join with another pair and discuss their ideas. The groups of four then agree on a decision for each case.

- Circulate and monitor.

- Have a feedback session with the whole class. What solutions did pairs choose? When they worked in groups of four, were they able to agree on a solution?

Writing

- Students can choose to reply to the message from Susanna, Thomas or Matthew.

- Get students to compare their reply with their partner from the task.

- Encourage students to talk about the similarities and differences in their e-mails.

- Circulate and help where needed.

➡ Writing file (Course Book page 126)

➡ Resource bank: Writing (page 195)

Advertising

AT A GLANCE

	Classwork – Course Book	Further work
Lesson 1 *Each lesson (excluding case studies) is about 45–60 minutes. This does not include administration and time spent going through homework.*	**Starting up** Students do an advertising quiz and talk about their favourite advert. **Vocabulary: Advertising and markets** Students listen to and repeat large numbers and look at adjectives to describe markets. **Reading: TV commercials** Students answer questions and match word partnerships from an article about Volkswagen's Black Beetle commercial.	**Practice File** Vocabulary (page 32) **i-Glossary** (DVD-ROM) **Text bank** (pages 146–147)
Lesson 2	**Language focus 1: Comparatives and superlatives** Students practise comparative and superlative forms of adjectives. **Listening: Good and bad advertising** Students listen to an interview with Liz Credé, an organisation development consultant, who gives examples of good and bad adverts.	**Practice File** Language review (page 33) **Resource bank: Listening** (page 182) **Course Book Listening** (DVD-ROM)
Lesson 3	**Language focus 2:** *much /a lot, a little / a bit* Students use the language to compare the advertising spend of a company and also to compare two pool tables. **Skills: Participating in discussions** Students listen to three owners of a chain of florists talking about new ways to advertise their business. Students then role-play a marketing meeting.	**Practice File** Language review (page 33) **Course Book Skills Dialogues** (DVD-ROM) **Resource bank: Speaking** (page 170)
Lesson 4 *Each case study is about 30 minutes to 1 hour.*	**Case study: Excelsior Chocolate Products** An international company is launching a new chocolate bar. Students discuss advertising information about the product. They then choose the product's name, slogan, price, target market, advertising and sales outlet. **Writing** Students write a short description of their plans for the launch of the new chocolate bar.	**Resource bank: Writing** (page 196) **Practice File** Writing (page 35)

For a fast route through the unit focusing mainly on speaking skills, just use the underlined sections.

For one-to-one situations, most parts of the unit lend themselves, with minimal adaptation, to use with individual students. Where this is not the case, alternative procedures are given.

BUSINESS BRIEF

BUSINESS BRIEF

If a company wants to sell a product or service successfully, it must identify the **target market**. There are many different types of market to choose from. The **mass market** aims to sell to as many people as possible, crossing age and income groups. In contrast, a **niche market** focuses on a narrowly defined group of customers. It often caters to a need that has been overlooked by those **suppliers** who cater for markets which deal in more mainstream products or services. Focusing on niche markets can be **cost-effective**, as marketing campaigns can aim budgets directly at potential customers, for example through advertising on local radio or in magazines targeting special-interest groups.

Two European countries lead the **luxury market**. Italy has 30 per cent of the market and France 25 per cent. Luxury product categories include art and antiques, cosmetics and fragrance, jewellery and cars. One of the most successful companies in this market is LVMH (Louis Vuitton, Moët Hennessey) with over 13 per cent of the global market for luxury goods.

Before a new product or service is **launched** on a particular market, it can be tried on a **focus group** to test whether people are likely to buy. A **product launch** is often followed (or sometimes preceded by) an **advertising campaign**. New technology has had an impact on the variety of **media** that brands now utilise. In recent years, there has been a sharp increase in the amount of advertising on the Internet and mobile devices, as well as on social networking sites. Despite this, more traditional advertising platforms such as the press and TV remain popular.

Some marketing campaigns may have direct, measurable aims such as boosting sales or increasing the company's **market share**. Others might have a different **strategy**, such as using the campaign to raise **brand awareness** or to create a new image in order to attract a new segment of the market.

Read on

Marian Burk Wood: *Essential Guide to Marketing Planning*, Financial Times/Prentice Hall, 2010

Winston Fletcher: *Advertising: A very short introduction*, OUP Oxford, 2010

Helen Powell et al.: *The Advertising Handbook*, Routledge, 2009

LESSON NOTES

Warmer

- Ask students to say some companies that are famous in their country.

- Write suggestions on the board and ask students to say what the companies make or do.

- Get students to talk about any adverts they have seen for the company. Where did they see or hear the advert (e.g. on TV or radio, in a magazine or newspaper, on the Internet)? Was it interesting?

- You could also bring in advertisements cut out from magazines and newspapers (or record some if you are able). Cover up the text and see if students can identify what the advert is selling.

- Ask students to work in groups and compare two adverts that are selling similar products or services. What are the similarities and differences between the two adverts? Which one do students prefer?

Overview

- Tell students that you are going to study language to talk about advertising.

- Ask students to look at the Overview section on page 74. Point to each heading and elicit or explain a little about each. Point to the sections you will be covering in this lesson, using the table on page 79 of this book as a guide.

Quotation

- Students may need some help with phrases such as *the number of ads you run* (the number of times an advert is shown on TV or in a magazine) and *the impression you make* (whether people remember the advert).

- Read the quotation together. Do students agree with William Bernbach?

Starting up

Students do an advertising quiz and talk about their favourite advert.

A

- Go through the questions with the class and clarify where necessary.

- Get students to answer the questions individually before working in pairs and comparing their answers with a partner. If students have different answers, encourage them to say why they think their answer is correct.

- Then ask pairs to turn to page 131 and check their answers.

- To make the exercise competitive, you could get students to answer the questions in small groups and award points for each correct answer.

| 1 c | 2 a | 3 b | 4 c | 5 b | 6 a | 7 b | 8 b | 9 b |

B

- Tell students about your favourite advert and say why you like it.

- Divide the class into pairs and get students to tell their partner about their favourite advert.

- Ask two or three students to describe the advert without saying what company or product it is for. Ask the rest of the class to guess the company/product.

Vocabulary: Advertising and markets

This section looks at how to say large numbers. It also introduces some key words and expressions for describing markets. Spend as much time as needed on the exercises. It is not necessary to rush through them.

A 🔊 CD2.9

- Play the recording. Get students to listen and repeat.

- In pairs, ask students to say the numbers again.

- Ask two or three students to write a large number or a percentage on the board and encourage the class to try to say the number.

B 🔊 CD2.10

- Ask the class to say the numbers in each sentence.

- Play the recording. Pause after each sentence and elicit the answer.

| **2** 13 | **3** 850,000 | **4** €900,000 | **5** 11.5 |
| **6** 2,100,000 |

C

- Ask students to complete the exercise and compare their answers with a partner. Encourage students to use a good dictionary to help.

- Check the answers around the class.

| 1 e | 2 a | 3 d | 4 b | 5 c |

D

- On the board, write the five types of market mentioned in Exercise C (*mass market*, *niche market*, *luxury market*, *export market*, *home market*).

- Divide the class into small groups.

- Give groups five minutes to think of one or more products to match each market.

- Have a feedback session with the whole class. Write suggestions on the board.

LESSON NOTES

E

- Look at the words in the box. Ask students to say any brands of these products that they know.

- Go through the ways to advertise products and clarify where necessary.

- Divide the class into pairs and ask them to discuss which is best for each product. If students prefer, they can use the products they discussed in Exercise D.

- Have a feedback session with the whole class. Encourage students to give reasons for their choices.

- To extend the activity, you could ask pairs to say which type of advertising they like most/least. Alternatively, pairs could number the ways of advertising in the order that they think are most likely to increase sales (1 = most likely, 10 = least likely).

 i-Glossary

Reading: TV commercials

Students read an article about Volkswagen's Black Beetle advert.

A

- Write *Volkswagen* on the board and ask students to say what the company makes. Write suggestions on the board.

- If you think your class will not know what a VW Beetle looks like, bring in a picture to show them.

- Divide the class into pairs and ask them to answer the questions, then open up the discussion to the whole class.

- Ask students to sugget other adjectives to describe a VW Beetle (e.g. *simple*, *small*, *sporty*).

B

- Read the questions together before students read the article.

- Ask students to read the article quickly and answer the questions.

- As a follow-up, ask students if they think this is a typical advertisement for a car.

- If students want to see the ad and/or a video about the making of the ad, direct them to http://www. youtube.com/watch?v=-NGN4J6F_vI and http:// www.youtube.com/watch?v=r1MHNIuQ920.

> 1 The photo is from the advert for the 2012 Beetle.
>
> 2 They wanted male drivers to see the advert.

C

- Ask students to read the article again carefully and answer the questions.

- Get students to compare with a partner before checking answers with the class.

> 1 An American   2 masculine
> 3 male and female   4 doesn't show   5 US
> 6 Shanghai

D

- Ask students to do the exercise, then read the article again to check.

- Check answers with the class.

> 1 c   2 a   3 b   4 f   5 e   6 d

E

- Complete the sentences about a TV advert that you like and tell the class about it.

- It might be useful to elicit more words to describe music (*loud*, *quiet*, *soft*, *rock*, *classical*, *instrumental*, etc.).

- Give students time to complete the sentences individually. Less confident students may prefer to write their sentences first. If so, encourage them to refer to their writing briefly rather than read each word out.

- Divide the class into pairs and ask them to tell their partner about the advertisement.

- If time allows, you could ask students to change partners and describe the advertisement again. Encourage them to add more details.

➡ Text bank (pages 146–147)

Language focus 1: Comparatives and superlatives

This section introduces comparative and superlative adjectives. Students do not usually have a problem grasping the concept of comparatives and superlatives. But you may need to spend some time focusing on details that students may omit (e.g. the use of *than* after comparatives, *the* before superlatives and the use of *more* or *most* with adjectives of two or more syllables).

- Books closed. Elicit some adjectives and write them on the board.

- Books open. Read through the Language focus box together.

- Refer students to the Grammar reference. Read and clarify where needed.

LESSON NOTES

- Point out that there are few irregular adjectives, so it is not a problem to learn them.

- Point to the adjectives on the board. Elicit whether they are short, long or irregular adjectives. Ask students to say the comparative and superlative form of each adjective.

- Write the examples from the Language focus box on the board. Point out the use of *than* after the comparative.

- You could also point out that short adjectives that end in a vowel followed by a consonant (e.g. *big*) double the last letter in the comparative and superlative (*bigger, the biggest*).

A 🔊 CD2.11

- This exercise focuses on comparative adjectives.

- Do the first one together to demonstrate.

- Ask students to complete the exercise individually and compare answers with a partner.

- Circulate and monitor. Note any areas where students need more practice, then play the recording for students to check their answers.

- Play it again and pause after each word to get students to repeat.

> **1** smaller **2** faster **3** slower **4** higher
> **5** worse **6** better **7** more competitive
> **8** more efficient **9** more interesting

B

- Look at the chart together and clarify if necessary.

- Do the first question together to demonstrate.

- Check the answers around the class. When students correct the false answers, encourage them to use a comparative in their answer.

> **1** F (The Mazda is a slower car than the Mini. / The Mini is a faster car than the Mazda.)
>
> **2** T
>
> **3** F (The Passat has better petrol consumption than the Mini. / The Mini has worse petrol consumption than the Passat.)
>
> **4** F (The Passat is more expensive than the Mazda./ The Mazda is cheaper than the Passat.)
>
> **5** T

- To extend the activity, you could divide the class into pairs and ask students to write two more questions about the cars, using comparative adjectives. Get pairs to join with another pair and ask their questions.

C

- Highlight the example and do item 2 together (*more powerful*). Remind students that they will use the comparative form in all the sentences.

- Tell students to complete the exercise individually.

- Circulate and help where necessary.

- As students finish, ask them to compare their answers with a partner.

- Check the answers by asking students to dictate the sentences as you write them on the board. Use this as an opportunity to clarify any problem areas.

> **2** more powerful **3** easier **4** cheaper; than
> **5** more spacious; than

D

- In this exercise, students use superlative adjectives. To prepare students, you could use the chart in Exercise B to ask questions (e.g. *Which car has the biggest engine?*, *Which car is the fastest?*, *Which is the most expensive?*).

- Revisit superlatives in the Grammar reference.

- Look at the example together.

- Ask students to complete the exercise individually.

- Check the answers around the class.

> **2** the best **3** the worst **4** the highest

E

- Nominate students to read out the information about Stefan, Sophie and Petra.

- Give students five minutes to read through the information about the cars again in Exercise B. Then ask them to choose the best car for each person. Ask students to think of reasons for their choices.

> **Suggested answers**
>
> Stefan: the Passat (space for the family)
>
> Sophie: the Mazda (fun) or Mini (easier parking)
>
> Petra: the Mini (smaller and cheaper than the Mazda)

F

- Ask a student to read out the example for the class.

- Divide the class into pairs. Ask students to take it in turns to explain their choices.

- To extend the activity, ask students to say which car they like best and to say why.

Listening: Good and bad advertising

Liz Credé, an organisation development consultant, talks about a bad advert, a good advert and what makes an advert effective. Students listen and answer questions and complete information.

A

- Read the questions together.

- Divide the class into pairs and ask students to discuss the questions.

- Have a brief feedback session with the whole class.

B 🔊 CD2.12

- Tell students they are going to hear an interview with a consultant. The interview is in three parts.

- Play the first part of the interview. Ask students to say which question in Exercise A she answers.

> Question 2

C 🔊 CD2.12

- Go over any words which you think your students may have problems with (*partner, unrealistic, goes on*).

- Ask students to listen again. Answer the first question together.

- Play it again and ask students to answer the other two questions.

- Elicit answers around the class.

> 1   Potato crisps
>
> 2   A man choosing whether he loves potato crisps more than his partner
>
> 3   It is unrealistic and it goes on for a long time.

D 🔊 CD2.13

- Read through the extract with the class and see if students can guess any of the words.

- Play the recording while students complete the extract.

- Play it again for students to check.

- Ask students to dictate the extract and write it on the board. Ask the class if they agree with Liz Credé's opinion.

> 1 effective   2 memorable   3 message
> 4 product   5 advert   6 modern

E

- Divide the class into pairs.

- Ask students to think of four ways to complete the sentence.

- Circulate and monitor, helping where necessary.

F 🔊 CD2.14

- Students listen to the final part of the recording and complete the sentence in Exercise E for Liz.

- Play the recording again and ask students to say what example she gives.

- Ask students to compare their answers with a partner, then check answers around the class.

> Adverts should not use claims or promises that do not seem to be delivered at home.
>
> Example: cleaning products which claim to remove stains but don't.

◎ Students can watch the interview with Liz Credé on the DVD-ROM.

➡ Resource bank: Listening (page 182)

Language focus 2: *much / a lot, a little / a bit*

Students learn some expressions used with comparative adjectives and use the information to complete exercises about a company's advertising budget over a two-year period. They also compare information about two pool tables.

- Give students a few moments to read through the Language focus box individually.

A – B

- Draw attention to the chart. Ask students for examples of print advertising (newspapers, magazines) and outdoor advertising (billboards).

- Elicit answers to the question. If students have any problems answering, write these three items on the board and ask students to say which one they think best describes the chart (*sentence b*):

a) *How much the advertising budget increased in 2012*

b) *How much of the advertising budget was spent on five types of advertising*

c) *The type of advertising that was most successful in 2010*

- Ask students what year the dark-blue information in the chart represents (*2011*).

- Complete the first item in Exercise B together.

LESSON NOTES

- Ask students to complete the rest of the exercise individually and compare answers with a partner.

- Check the answers around the class.

> **A** What Toptek spent its advertising budget on in 2010 and 2011
>
> **B** **1** TV (adverts/advertising) **2** much / a lot
> **3** a little / a bit **4** internet

C

- Ask a student to read the example to the class.

- Get students to complete the exercise individually and compare answers with a partner.

- Ask students to dictate information about points 2 and 3 and write the information on the board.

> **Suggested answers**
>
> **2** In 2010, Toptek spent about 32 per cent of its budget on print advertising. In 2011, the amount was a little / a bit lower.
>
> **3** In 2010, Toptek spent about five per cent of its budget on radio advertising. The amount was a little / a bit lower in 2011.

D

- Point to the photo. Ask students if they can play pool.

- Check students' understanding of *width*, *length*, *height* and *weight*. You could demonstrate by asking students to help you write the approximate dimensions and weight of a table in your classroom.

- Write on the board: *width*, *length*, *height*, *weight*, *price*.

- Ask students to suggest the comparative and superlative adjectives that we use with each word.

width	+	wider, widest
	–	narrower, the narrowest
length	+	longer, the longest
	–	shorter, the shortest
height	+	higher, the highest
	–	lower, the lowest
weight	+	heavier, the heaviest
	–	lighter, the lightest
price	+	more expensive, the most expensive
	–	cheaper, the cheapest

- Elicit or model how to say the dimensions for one of the tables.

- Highlight the example. Divide the class into pairs.

- Get students to use the information to talk about the two tables.

- Circulate and check that students are using *much*, *a lot*, *a little* and *a bit*.

> **Suggested answers**
>
> The Classic pool table is a little / a bit longer than the Trainer pool table.
>
> The Trainer pool table is a little / a bit lower than the Classic pool table.
>
> The Trainer pool table is much / a lot lighter than the Classic pool table.
>
> The Classic pool table is a lot / much more expensive than the Trainer pool table.

Skills: Participating in discussions

This section uses a recording with people talking about new ways to advertise their business to introduce useful phrases for agreeing, disagreeing, asking and giving opinions and making suggestions. Point out to the class that many of these phrases are used in meetings and negotiations and also in social situations.

A ◀)) CD2.15

- Books closed. Ask students in what situations people give flowers in their country. Where do they buy flowers?

- Books open. Read the instructions and check that students understand *wedding organisers*, *redesign* and *social networking sites*.

- Read the questions together and ask students to predict the answers.

- Play the first part of the recording and complete item 1 with the whole class.

- Play the rest of the recording. Ask students to complete the exercise individually and then compare their ideas with a partner.

- Play the recording again. Pause to check the answers around the class.

> **1** b **2** b **3** c **4** a

B ◀)) CD2.15

- Play the recording again. Ask students to complete the sentences.

- Check the answers around the class.

> **2** target **3** right **4** feel **5** like **6** starting

LESSON NOTES

- Look at the phrases together and check students' understanding.

C

- With the whole class, match the phrases from Exercise B to the language functions (a–e).

> **a)** 3, 5   **b)** 1   **c)** 4   **d)** 2, 5   **e)** 6

- Books closed. Write functions a)–e) on the board. Read out some of the phrases from the Useful language box and ask students to say which function each one matches.

- Books open. Go through the Useful language box with the class to check.

- Spend some time practising stress and intonation. Point out that students should try not to sound aggressive when disagreeing or giving an opinion.

D

- Books closed. Brainstorm brands of biscuit and write them on the board. Ask students to say how much some of the items cost and how the manufacturers advertise their products.

- Divide the class into groups of three.

- Tell students that they are taking part in a marketing meeting.

- Ask students to read the instructions. Elicit the aim of the meeting (*to discuss the name and price of a new biscuit and how to promote it*). Write the aim on the board. Tell students that this is the agenda for their meeting.

- Give students a few moments to read their role cards. Circulate and help where needed.

- Tell the groups that they have about 10 minutes to have their meeting.

- Encourage students to use phrases from the Useful language box.

- If the meetings are going well, be flexible about the time limit. Circulate and stop the meetings when the groups start to wind down.

- Have a feedback session with the whole class.

- Ask students to identify which phrases they found most useful. Tell the class to think about any meetings that they have at the moment or may have in the future and to learn the phrases that are most helpful to them.

◉ Students can watch the discussion on the DVD-ROM.

⇨ Resource bank: Speaking (page 170)

CASE STUDY

Excelsior Chocolate Products

Students have a meeting to discuss the launch of a new chocolate bar.

Background

- Books closed. Ask students if they can name any chocolate products and any companies that sell the products.

- Books open. Ask students to read the Background paragraph. Ask check questions such as: *Where is the company based? When are they launching the product? What is the marketing department making some decisions about at the moment?* etc.

🔊 CD2.16

- Tell students that they are going to hear a conversation with information about competitors' products. Before playing the recording, read through the three questions with the class. Then ask students to listen and make notes.

- See if students can use their notes to answer the questions. Play the recording again for students to check.

> 1 It was a good idea to use the film star; they chose some interesting places.
>
> 2 They have more money to spend.
>
> 3 They can advertise in all media.

- Ask students to read through the options about the new chocolate bar. Pre-teach or revise any vocabulary that you think your class may have a problem with.

Task

- Divide the class into small groups.

- Read the task instructions together. Highlight the points that the groups need to discuss.

- Tell groups that they are the marketing department and they have 20 minutes to complete items 1 and 2.

- Give each group a few minutes to present their ideas to the others.

- Students then work as one group to decide on the best launch plan from all the ideas on the table.

- Circulate and encourage students to use language from the unit where appropriate.

Writing

- Ask students to look at information about product launches in the Writing file. Read the information together.

- Ask students to remember the key decisions from their meetings (*slogan, a famous person to advertise their product (endorsements), TV advert* and *special events advertising,* etc.). Also ask students to think about what they chose to call the product.

- Ask students to write a short description of the planned product launch for the chocolate bar.

➡ Writing file (Course Book page 127)

➡ Resource bank: Writing (page 196)

AT A GLANCE

	Classwork – Course Book	Further work
Lesson 1 *Each lesson (excluding case studies) is about 45–60 minutes. This does not include administration and time spent going through homework.*	<u>**Starting up**</u> Students do a companies quiz, then talk about famous companies from their country. **Vocabulary: Describing companies** Students complete exercises to describe two companies, then complete a company profile. <u>**Listening: A favourite company**</u> A three-part interview with Jeremy Keeley, a specialist in change leadership, where he describes his favourite company.	**Practice File** Vocabulary (page 36) **i-Glossary** (DVD-ROM) **Resource bank: Listening** (page 183) **Course Book Listening** (DVD-ROM)
Lesson 2	**Language focus 1: Present continuous** Students look at the present continuous for temporary actions and things that are happening now. **Reading: Gamesa** Students read about Gamesa, a wind-energy business. They then answer questions and complete a fact file.	**Practice File** Language review (page 37) **Text bank** (pages 148–149)
Lesson 3	**Language focus 2: Present simple or present continuous** The tenses are compared and contrasted. Students then do exercises to find the correct tense before carrying out a role play showing someone around a company. <u>**Skills: Starting a presentation**</u> Students listen to the start of a presentation and use notes to introduce their own presentation.	**Practice File** Language review (page 37) **Course Book Skills Presentation** (DVD-ROM) **Resource bank: Speaking** (page 171)
Lesson 4 *Each case study is about 30 minutes to 1 hour.*	<u>**Case study: Presenting your company**</u> Students role-play introducing themselves and their company at a training course on giving presentations. **Writing** Students write a short profile about their company for the company website. They then use some of the information from their presentation in the case study.	**Resource bank: Writing** (page 197) **Practice File** Writing (page 38)

For a fast route through the unit focusing mainly on speaking skills, just use the underlined sections.

For one-to-one situations, most parts of the unit lend themselves, with minimal adaptation, to use with individual students. Where this is not the case, alternative procedures are given.

BUSINESS BRIEF

A company is an organisation that produces goods or services to make a profit. There are many different types.

A **small business** might become a **medium** or **large** business. If a company sells directly to the public, it is a **retail** business. A **wholesale** business sells goods in bulk to other companies. Some British companies have *Ltd* in their name. This stands for **limited company**. Here, **shareholders** only lose what they invested if the company goes **bankrupt**. A company with **PLC** after its name is a **public limited company** – its shares can be freely bought and sold. In contrast, a **private limited company** only passes shares to another person if other shareholders agree. A **conglomerate** consists of several companies that have joined together. A **multinational** or **transnational company** has **global operations** in many different countries.

Funding influences the type of ownership. Companies can be funded by **share capital** – money raised from **investors** who bought **shares**. It is owned by the **shareholders**, who elect a **board of directors** to make decisions and set **company policy**. **Venture capital companies** lend money to people to start a new business. Some projects which **venture capitalists** invest in may be **high risk** and unable to attract funding from elsewhere. If a person owns their own company without investors, they are a **sole proprietor**. When two or more people join together to start a company, they form a **partnership**. A company can be bought by another company in a **takeover**, which can be **friendly** or **hostile**.

Traditionally, a company board's main responsibility was to increase profits on behalf of the company's shareholders. In contrast, **business ethics** have been influenced by the idea of the **stakeholder,** which advocates that a firm also has an obligation to a wide range of people and groups, including shareholders, employees, suppliers, customers, government agencies, protest groups and the community in which the company operates.

Some factors which can contribute to a successful company include: effective **change management**, charismatic **leadership** with a commitment to **innovation** and improving **performance**, a **clear business strategy** as well as an easily identified **corporate identity** (so that the company name or products are recognised).

The ethics and actions of big companies have increasingly come under scrutiny. It will be interesting to monitor which qualities and values come to define the **corporate governance** and **company culture** of the most successful companies of the 21st century.

Read on

Richard Rumelt: *Good Strategy Bad Strategy: The difference and why it matters*, Profile Books, 2011

Daniel Kahneman: *Thinking Fast and Slow*, Allen Lane, 2011

Nitin Pangarkar, *High-Performance Companies: Successful strategies from the world's top achievers*, John Wiley & Sons, 2011

J.C. Collins: *How the Mighty Fall and Why Some Companies Never Give In*, Random House Business, 2009

Charles J. Fombrun, Cees Van Riel: *Fame and Fortune: How successful companies build winning reputations*, Financial Times/Prentice Hall, 2008

J.C. Collins, J.I. Porras: *Built to Last: Successful habits of visionary companies*, Random House Business, new edition 2005

LESSON NOTES

Warmer

- Think of a company. Don't tell the class what it is. Encourage students to ask you questions to discover the name of the company. Tell the class that you can only answer *yes* or *no*. The first student to guess correctly thinks of another company and answers questions from the class. Students can continue the activity in pairs or small groups.

- Alternatively, cut out the logos of a variety of well-known companies and stick them around the walls. Give students five minutes to work in pairs and identify which company each logo belongs to.

Overview

- Tell students that you are going to study language to talk about companies.

- Ask students to look at the Overview section on page 82. Point to each heading and elicit or explain a little about each. Point to the sections you will be covering in this lesson, using the table on page 88 of this book as a guide.

Quotation

- Get students to discuss the quotation in small groups. What do they think it means? Do they agree or disagree?

- Ask groups what sort of things a successful company needs to be skilled at. Some possible ideas include HR, marketing, sales, brand-building, management, customer relations, etc.

Starting up

Students complete a quiz about famous companies.

A

- Do question 1 together to demonstrate (*b*).

- Get students to complete the quiz individually, then to compare their answers with a partner.

- If students have access to a computer, they could check any questions that they are not sure of online before looking at the answers at the back of the book.

- Ask students to turn to page 131 for the answers.

1	b
2	b (It's Italian.)
3	a
4	b
5	a (over 2 million)
6	a (398,000m² in Everett, Washington)
7	b
8	c (It's based in Redmond, Washington.)
9	b (the VW Beetle, which sold 21.5 million units)
10	c (for the 4th year running in 2011, according to *Fortune* magazine)

- Ask the class if any of the information surprised them.

B

- If you have a multilingual class, ask students to think of a list individually. Monolingual classes could do this in pairs or small groups.

- Divide the class into pairs and ask students to compare their companies with a partner. Encourage students to ask questions about each other's list and to discuss similarities and differences.

> **One-to-one**
>
> You and your student can work individually to think of famous companies from your own countries. Ask your student to guess some of the companies on your list. Do the same with their list. Spend time talking about what the companies do or make. Discuss similarities and differences.

Vocabulary: Describing companies

This section looks at useful words and phrases to talk about what a company does, its workforce and products.

A

- Read the instructions with the whole class.

- Ask two students to read out the example sentences about Dalotek and Green Shoots.

- Get students to identify the pairs of sentences that describe similar things.

- Ask students to decide which sentences are about Dalotek and which are about Green Shoots.

- With the whole class, look at the second sentence for Dalotek (*sentence 2*) and match it with one for Green Shoots (*sentence 6*) to demonstrate how to do the exercise.

- Get students to compare answers with a partner.

- Ask students to call out the answers and write the sentences on the board.

> Dalotek: sentences 1, 2, 3, 4, 5, 12
>
> Green Shoots: sentences 6, 7, 8, 9, 10, 11

B

- You could get students to do this exercise individually or you could write the pairs of sentences on the board and ask students to come up and underline the verbs that mean the same.

LESSON NOTES

> 1/9: started, began
>
> 2/6: has a workforce of, employs
>
> 3/7: exports, sells some of its products abroad
>
> 4/8: manufactures, makes
>
> 5/11: introduces, launches
>
> 10/12: supplies, provides

C

- Ask students to quickly read the text and say what tense the verbs will use (*present simple*). Only the example sentence uses the past simple (*began*).

- Check students understand that they should complete the text using the verbs they underlined during Exercise B. Point out that sometimes more than one verb will be possible.

- Nominate individual students to read out sentences to check the answers.

> **2** makes/manufactures **3** exports/sells
> **4** employs / has a workforce of
> **5** has/employs **6** launches/introduces
> **7** supplies/provides **8** provides/supplies

D

- Ask students to use the profile in Exercise C as a model to write a profile of their own company. If students are not working, they can research some basic information about a well-known company.

- This task can be set for homework. Collect the profiles and check particularly for the correct use of verb tenses.

 i-Glossary

Listening: A favourite company

Students listen to Jeremy Keeley, a specialist in change leadership, talking about his favourite company. They complete notes about the company and answer questions.

A 🔊 CD2.17

- Books closed. Ask students to name three or four leaders of well-known companies. Ask students to say if they are good leaders. Encourage them to give reasons for their answer. Ask them to work in pairs and suggest things that a good leader does. Have a brief feedback session with the class.

- Books open. Play the first part of the interview. First, ask students to listen to see if Jeremy Keeley mentions any of their ideas about what a good leader does.

- Ask students to read the notes. See if they can remember any of the missing words. Play the recording again while students complete the notes.

- Check answers by asking students to dictate the completed bullet points while you write on the board.

> **1** look after **2** customers **3** needs
> **4** environment **5** need

- Ask students to read the notes again and say whether they agree with Jeremy's opinions.

B 🔊 CD2.18

- Ask students to read the four questions and check that they understand them. At this point, you may want to teach vocabulary such as *green energy* and *affordable housing*, and introduce expressions such as *(have a) big purpose* and *change things for the better*. Have a quick look at the audio script on page 165 to identify any terms that may cause your students problems.

- Play the second part of the interview, pausing after … *for people in the world for the better*. Ask students to answer the first question, either verbally or in writing. Continue, pausing the recording after each relevant piece of information. You may need to play the whole recording again for students to answer question 4.

- Check answers as a class. At this level, answers can be lifted verbatim from the recording rather than being paraphrased.

> **1** A company that has a big purpose, that wants to change things for people in the world for the better
>
> **2** Green energy, affordable housing for the poor or ways of feeding people
>
> **3** Strong leadership
>
> **4** a, b, c, e

C 🔊 CD2.19

- Write the names of the five companies on the board. Ask students which companies they have heard of. What do they think the companies are famous for?

- Play the final part of the interview. Ask students to listen to see if Jeremy mentions any of their ideas.

- Play it again and ask students to note what Jeremy says the companies are famous for. Have a feedback session with the class.

> **1** leadership **2** innovation and creativity
> **3** inventing new products
> **4** looking after people in the world
> **5** environmentally friendly

LESSON NOTES

- Ask students if they agree with Jeremy's ideas. Would they like to work for any of the companies he mentions?

D

- You could ask students to prepare this for homework or give them time to prepare individually in class.

- To demonstrate, tell the class about your favourite company and say why you like it.

- If students are having a problem thinking of a company, brainstorm the name of well-known companies and write them on the board.

- Divide the class into pairs and ask them to talk about their favourite company. You could ask more confident students to report back on what their partner said.

  ◎ Students can watch the interview with Jeremy Keeley on the DVD-ROM.

  ➡ Resource bank: Listening (page 183)

Language focus 1: Present continuous

This introduces the form of the present continuous. It focuses on its use for temporary actions and things that are happening now. Although some languages may have a similar form, they do not often use the present continuous in the same way as in English.

- Books closed. Write the following on the board.
  a) *Lydia writes for a business magazine.*
  b) *Lydia is writing an article about Toyota.*

- Ask the class to identify which sentence describes something that Lydia is doing at the moment (*b*) and which sentence describes something that she does most days (*a*).

- Point to sentence b. Underline *is*. Ask students to identify the verb (*be*) and highlight the *-ing* ending of the second verb.

- Books open. Give students a few moments to read through the Language focus box individually. Circulate and encourage students to ask for help if they need it.

- Write the following on the board: *Lydia is writing an article about BMW.*

- Ask students to form the question (*Is Lydia writing an article about BMW?*) and the negative (*Lydia isn't writing an article about BMW.*).

- Give students time to practise the use. Refer them to the Grammar reference on page 153 for more information.

A

- Highlight the example. Do item 2 together to demonstrate (*'s calling*).

- Ask students to complete the exercise individually. Remind them to use the contracted forms where possible.

- Elicit the answers and write them on the board.

> **2** 's calling   **3** 'm writing   **4** 're building
> **5** 're working   **6** isn't going   **7** is/are hiring

B

- Check students' understanding of the words in the box.

- Get two students to take turns to read the questions and responses in the example.

- Ask another student to read the questions again. Ask students to help you think of different responses this time (e.g. *I'm writing a report*, *They're building a new factory*.).

- You could give students a moment to think of more responses they might want to use.

- Divide the class into pairs. Ask students to take turns asking and answering the questions with their partner.

- Circulate and monitor. You could ask some of the pairs to repeat their questions/answers for the class.

- To extend the activity, you could ask students to suggest one or two more questions (e.g. *What are you working on in your English class at the moment? What's happening in your home?*) .

Reading: Gamesa

The article is about Gamesa, a wind-energy business. First students scan the article for information, then they read the article again carefully to complete a fact file about the company.

A

- Check that students understand what wind energy is. Point to the photograph and ask if they know the term *wind turbine*.

- Read the two questions as a class and clarify any problems with vocabulary (e.g. *clean form of energy, constant*).

- Divide the class into groups. Give groups five or 10 minutes to discuss the questions. If you are short of time, discuss the questions with the whole class and write ideas on the board.

- Have a brief feedback session. Ask students if they think wind energy is a good thing.

> **2** **Suggested answers**
>
> Advantages: safe; clean form of energy
>
> Disadvantages: wind not constant; noisy; ugly

LESSON NOTES

B

- Students do this vocabulary exercise before reading the article. Encourage students to use dictionaries and check answers as a class.

> **1** c   **2** e   **3** b   **4** a   **5** f   **6** d

- Check students understand the difference between *to install* and *to set up*.

C

- Ask students to read the article and elicit answers to the question. You could ask students to say what information in the text helped them to find the answer (lines 15–19).

> In international markets

D

- Ask students to scan the article quickly to find the information.
- Write the headings on the board and ask different students to come and complete the information.

> **2** Spanish   **3** wind turbines   **4** Latin America (especially Brazil)   **5** nearly 8,000   **6** 20   **7** 30
> **8** up by 26% to €1,297m   **9** up by 29%

E

- Write on the board *Brazil* and *India*. Tell students that they are going to read information about Gamesa in one of these countries.
- You may wish to divide the class into two groups (A and B) to prepare. Students will need to scan the short article on their role cards and complete the information.
- Circulate and monitor, helping where necessary.
- When students have completed their notes, divide the class into A/B pairs. Ask students to tell their partner about Gamesa in the country they read about.
- Encourage students to use their notes to compare similarities and differences in Gamesa's strategy in each country.
- Have a brief feedback session and ask students to tell you similarities and differences about Gamesa in India and Brazil. Write key ideas on the board.

Suggested notes for Brazil

Key events

July 2010 – opened first manufacturing plant in NE Brazil

Current projects

expanding its Camaçari plant

planning to use Brazil for developing markets of Argentina, Chile and Uruguay

Suggested notes for India

Key events

Feb 2010 – opened first manufacturing plant in Chennai, SE India

March 2010 – opened technology centre

Current projects

- setting up projects with university
- expanding its production capacity
- building new plants in Gujarat and Tamil Nadu

Similarities

- Entered the market in both countries by setting up a subsidiary.
- Manufactures the wind turbines for both markets locally.
- Is expanding its production facilities to meet increased local demand and to supply neighbouring countries.
- Is setting up a network of local suppliers.

Differences

- Brazil: plans to use subsidiary in São Paulo as a base for expanding activities in neighbouring countries.
- India: plans to develop India as a centre for R&D for the region.

F

- Do the first one together.
- Ask students to complete the exercise in A/B pairs.
- Check answers with the class.

> **1** c   **2** d   **3** a   **4** b   **5** f   **6** g   **7** h   **8** e

LESSON NOTES

- To extend the activity, ask students to close their books. Write some of the following sentences on the board and ask students to suggest what the missing word is (shown in brackets). Ask students to open their books and check the answers.

  They are installing new .... turbines at the moment. (wind)

  Are they opening a manufacturing .... in China? (plant)

  Where is your company's sales .... ? (office)

  How many companies are moving into the technology .... ? (centre)

  They want to enter the Asian .... to sell their products. (market)

  Is your company setting .... a subsidiary in Finland? (up)

  We need to improve the .... of our products. (quality)

  Are you recruiting more .... in your offices? (workers)

G

- Students can do this activity in class or for homework.

- Collect in the short texts and note any areas where students need more help.

➡ Text bank (pages 148–149)

Language focus 2: Present simple or present continuous

In this section, the two tenses are compared and contrasted to clarify their usage.

- Complete the rules in the Language focus box with the whole class (present simple, present continuous).

- Ask students to tell you how to form the present continuous (be + the -ing form of the verb).

A

- Read the instructions with the class.

- Highlight the examples and ask students to say which column they think currently should go in (present continuous).

- Divide the class into pairs and ask students to complete the exercise with their partner.

- Check the answers around the class.

> Present simple: always, every day, normally, usually
>
> Present continuous: at the moment, currently, now, this time, today

- Books closed. Read out some of the time expressions and ask students to say whether they are usually used with the present simple or the present continuous.

B

- Highlight the example. Do the second sentence in item 1 together to demonstrate (am staying).

- Ask students to complete the exercise individually.

- Elicit the answers and write them on the board.

> **1** stay; am staying   **2** is working; works
> **3** calls; is calling   **4** deal; am dealing
> **5** are taking; take   **6** use; are using

C

- Check if students know the company Pret A Manger. Ask what it sells (sandwiches and snacks).

- Check students know the verbs in brackets.

- Highlight the example and do item 2 with the whole class to demonstrate (sells).

- Ask students to complete the article individually, then to compare their answers with a partner.

- Circulate and help where needed.

- Check the answers around the class. Spend time clarifying where necessary.

> **2** sells   **3** give   **4** is doing   **5** operates
> **6** is planning   **7** has   **8** are growing
> **9** is opening   **10** is/are working

- Ask students to read the article again. Ask them to say what they think these words mean from context: homeless, outlet, global.

- Ask check questions such as: What do the shops do with unsold sandwiches? How many outlets does Pret have in the UK? Where is it planning to open new shops? What does Lewis PR want to do for Pret? etc.

D

- Read the instructions together.

- Divide the class into pairs.

- Give students a few minutes to read the information and write notes if necessary.

- Circulate and help with preparation where needed.

- Get students to do the role play.

- If your students are in work, ask them to draw a map of the building or department where they work.

- In different pairs, tell students to take it in turns to show each other round and explain what usually happens in each office or area and make up an activity that could be happening at the moment.

LESSON NOTES

Skills: Starting a presentation

Students are introduced to key phrases for starting a presentation, including greetings, introducing the topic and talking about the parts and aim of the presentation.

A ◀)) CD2.20

- Ask students if they have been to or given a presentation recently. What do they think makes a good presentation?

- Write the following on the board:
  Sales strategy
  Marketing strategy
  Buying strategy

- Play the recording all the way through. Ask students to identify the presentation topic (*marketing strategy*).

- Quickly run through the phrases (a–f). If students are unsure of the meaning, encourage them to listen to the recording, to hear the phrases in context.

- Play the recording again. Ask students to number the phrases in the order that they hear them.

- Check the answers around the class.

> **a)** 3 **b)** 5 **c)** 1 **d)** 6 **e)** 2 **f)** 4

- Go through the phrases again and clarify where necessary.

B ◀)) CD2.20

- Write the headings on the board. Play the recording again.

- With the whole class, match the items in Exercise A with the headings.

> **1** e **2** b **3** c **4** a, f **5** d

C

- Spend time going through the phrases in the Useful language box. Help with pronunciation and stress.

- Tell students that they are going to use the notes to prepare an introduction to a presentation.

- Divide the class into A/B pairs.

- Give students 10 minutes to read the notes and prepare. With less-confident classes, it may be helpful to divide the class into A and B groups to prepare together.

- Circulate and help where needed.

- Get students to make the presentation to their partner.

- ◎ Students can watch the presentation on the DVD-ROM.

- ⇥ Resource bank: Speaking (page 171)

CASE STUDY

Presenting your company

Students role-play introducing themselves and their company at the beginning of a training course.

Background

- Books closed. Tell students that they are on a training course. They are going to introduce themselves and their company to the other participants.

- Ask the class to call out the general information they think they need to include about themselves and their companies (e.g. *name, company name, job title, number of employees, products,* etc.).

- Write the information on the board and ask students to put it in the order that it would appear in their presentation.

- Books open. Give students a few minutes to read the background information.

🔊 CD2.21

- Ask students to read the four questions so that they know what to listen for.

- Play the recording, then ask students to volunteer the answers. Write them on the board.

---

1   To talk about the company and its plans for the future

2   New York

3   turnover: $50m, profit: $12.2m

4   To open at least 10 new stores on the West Coast

- If you have time, ask students to look at the audio script on page 165 and identify useful phrases for each stage of the presentation (e.g. **A** *Good morning, everyone. My name's …*; **B** *I'm going to talk about …*; **C** *My presentation is in three sections. Firstly, … Secondly … And finally …*; **D** *We own …; Our outlets sell …; Our main competitors are …*; **E** *Next year, we plan to …*).

Task

- Divide the class into groups of three and assign roles A, B and C. Tell students to read their company profiles. Circulate and help where needed.

- Tell students that they are going to prepare a presentation about themselves and their company. The presentation should last for about one minute.

- Go through the structure of the presentation with the class.

- Pre-teach *Does anyone have any questions?* Tell students to ask the group this as they end their presentation and to try to answer any questions.

- Encourage students to include phrases from the Useful language box on page 88, especially to talk about the aim and plan of their presentation.

- Give students 10–15 minutes to prepare their presentation.

- Get students to take turns to make their presentation to their group. While the rest of the group listens, ask them to note one or two questions to ask. Also ask students to note what they like and find interesting about each presentation.

- With the whole class, discuss how students prepare for presentations in their own language. What ideas do they have for preparing a presentation in English (e.g. *make a note of key words and phrases, think about what questions people could ask, record a practice presentation and listen to it in the car,* etc.)?

Writing

- Refer students to the Writing file. Read the company profile together.

- Tell students to write a short profile about their company from the case study, including some of the information from their presentation.

- Get students to compare their company profiles with another student who wrote about the same company.

- Collect in the profiles to check if any language points and vocabulary need to be revised.

- For homework, ask students to write another company profile. If they are in work, you could ask them to write a short profile about their own company. Otherwise, they could write one about one of the other companies from the case study or a famous company in their country.

⇨ Writing file (Course Book page 129)

⇨ Resource bank: Writing (page 197)

WORKING ACROSS CULTURES 3 Doing business Internationally

Introduction

This *Working across cultures* unit deals with aspects of doing business in France and Russia and looks at etiquette when invited into a person's home in Colombia.

A

- Books closed. Write *France* on the board and ask students to say any facts that they know about the country.

- Books open. Ask students to complete the exercise individually and then compare their answers with a partner.

- Have a feedback session with the whole class.

- To extend the activity, you could ask students to answer the questions (except question 4) about their own country.

> **1** F   **2** F   **3** T   **4** T   **5** F   **6** T

Task 1

🔊 CD2.22

- Go through the first question in the task with the whole class and make sure that they understand. Ask check questions such as: *What is Ryan Miller's job? What country is he working in? What is Sylvie Martin's job?*

- Write the four questions on the board and play the recording. Answer the first question together. Play the rest of the recording, pausing to elicit answers.

- Write on the board: *What didn't Ryan understand about French culture?* Play the recording again and ask students to make notes. If students need more help, they can read the audio script on page 165.

- Ask students to suggest answers and write ideas on the board.

> **1**   **1** Toulouse   **2** the first week of August
> **3** Paris   **4** No
>
> **2**   He didn't realise that:
> - many French people are on holiday in August
> - many French companies have their headquarters in Paris
> - you need to set up meetings some time in advance
> - you need to allow time to get to know people in business
> - further education is very important in France.

B

Task 2

🔊 CD2.23–2.25

- Ask students to name some cities in Russia. Ask if they would like to visit Russia. Encourage them to give reasons for their response.

- Tell students that they are going to hear three people talking about their business trips to Russia.

- Play the recordings and elicit which city each person visited.

- Play them again and get students to answer questions 2 and 3.

- Ask students to take notes on the key points. Play the recordings again two or three times until students feel they have all the information they need.

- Have a feedback session to share the information in students' notes. Ask students to suggest a tip for someone going on a business trip to Russia.

- Divide the class into pairs. Ask students to write more tips for someone visiting Russia on business. Get pairs to join together to make groups of four. Ask students to take it in turns to present their tips.

> **1**   **1** St Petersburg, Kazan, Moscow
> **2** The second speaker (Kazan)
> **3** The first speaker (St Petersburg)
>
> **3**   *Suggested answers*
> - Make appointments as far in advance as possible.
> - Confirm the meetings as soon as you arrive in Russia.
> - Avoid meetings in the first week of May.
> - Allow a lot of time for socialising and getting to know people.
> - Print out all documentation in both English and Russian.
> - Give a detailed presentation and be able to answer all technical questions.
> - Build up relationships.
> - Go to senior managers for decisions.
> - Allow Russians enough time to think about their answers.

C

- Read the information together. Ask check questions such as: *What is Susan Forbes's job? What is the subject of her workshop? Where was she invited to in Bogotá?*

- Ask individual students to read out the tips and check everyone understands. Do any of the tips surprise them?

Task 3

 CD2.26

- Tell students that they will hear Susan talk about her business trip in Bogotá.

- Write on the board: *What Susan did well* and *Mistakes Susan made*. Ask students to listen and make notes on the two topics.

- Play the recording twice while students make notes.

- Divide the class into small groups. Ask students to use their notes to discuss what Susan did well and the mistakes she made.

> 2 Did well: took gifts; talked about culture, history, soccer and literature
> Mistakes: arrived on time, asked her hosts to unwrap their gifts, asked about the gifts, made the first toast, refused an offer of coffee

D

- Read through the instructions and check students understand.

- Divide the class into small groups. Ask students to discuss the questions.

- Alternatively, you could ask students to do this exercise individually for homework. When students have completed it, they can use their notes to have the discussion in groups.

Revision

7 People

Vocabulary

Ahmed Adib: creative, hard-working, motivating, punctual, relaxed

Elizabet Martens: ambitious, helpful, practical, reliable, sociable

Past simple: negatives and questions

1 wasn't   2 didn't   3 Did   4 weren't   5 was
6 Were   7 Was   8 didn't   9 weren't   10 Did

Skills

1 need   2 do   3 'm   4 's   5 is   6 have
7 don't   8 'll   9 look   10 think

8 Advertising

Vocabulary

1   4,500

2   thirty-six thousand, five hundred and eighty-nine

3   839,230

4   one million, four hundred and thirty-three thousand, nine hundred

5   14.6%

6   two thousand, eight hundred and seventy

7   56,801

8   two hundred and seventeen thousand, four hundred and eighteen

9   5,284,566

10   ninety-eight point three per cent

Comparatives and superlatives

1 much   2 a little   3 more interesting
4 the most   5 lower   6 fewest
7 the most impressive

Writing

Sample answer

HairGlow and Sheen both performed well last year. HairGlow comes in a smaller bottle than Sheen, but it's more expensive. It's for a younger market (18–25) and is sold in hairdressers. Sheen is less expensive than HairGlow. Its target market is older (26–50) and it sells in supermarkets.

If we look at last year's sales figures, we can see that HairGlow's sales were much higher in the second quarter than in the first quarter. However, Sheen's sales were slightly lower in the second quarter.

Both companies have improved their year-on-year sales, but Sheen's sales have grown faster than HairGlow's.

9 Companies

Vocabulary

1 manufactures   2 supplies   3 produce
4 started   5 employs   6 exports   7 introduces

Present simple or present continuous

1 manufactures   2 exports   3 buy
4 are/'re making   5 need   6 are
7 are/'re planning   8 want   9 is/are doing
10 are/'re trying

Skills

1 to   2 about   3 in   4 of   5 of   6 about
7 of   8 of/about

Cultures 3: Doing business internationally

A   1 lots of different companies   2 don't focus
    3 is   4 Most   5 should   6 and not the best

B   1 Make   2 Confirm   3 Avoid   4 Plan
    5 Go   6 Allow

C   1 c   2 a   3 b   4 e   5 f   6 d

UNIT 10 Communication

AT A GLANCE

	Classwork – Course Book	Further work
Lesson 1 *Each lesson (excluding case studies) is about 45–60 minutes. This does not include administration and time spent going through homework.*	**Starting up** Students do a quiz about different methods of communication. **Vocabulary: Internal communication** Students complete a text about how people communicate at work. They then match words in the text to definitions. **Listening: Networking online** Ros Pomeroy, a management consultant, talks about social networking sites and communication skills.	**Practice File** Vocabulary (page 40) **i-Glossary** (DVD-ROM) **Resource bank: Listening** (page 184) **Course Book Listening** (DVD-ROM)
Lesson 2	**Language focus 1: Talking about future plans** Students look at the use of the present continuous for future arrangements and *going to* for future plans. **Reading: Communication technology at work** Students look at an article about Vittorio Colao, the CEO of Vodafone.	**Practice File** Language review (page 41) **Text bank** (pages 150–151)
Lesson 3	**Language focus 2:** *will* Students use *will* to complete exercises about future events and predictions. **Skills: Making arrangements** Students listen to four people making and changing arrangements by phone and role-play similar situations.	**Practice File** Language review (page 41) **Resource bank: Speaking** (page 172) **Course Book Skills Telephoning** (DVD-ROM)
Lesson 4 *Each case study is about 30 minutes to 1 hour.*	**Case study: Blakelock Engineering** A company has to cut its workforce. Students discuss who will have to leave and how to communicate the decision. **Writing** Students write an e-mail from the Managing Director of Blakelock Engineering to staff, arranging a meeting to discuss the present situation in the company.	**Resource bank: Writing** (page 198) **Practice File** Writing (page 42)

For a fast route through the unit focusing mainly on speaking skills, just use the underlined sections.

For one-to-one situations, most parts of the unit lend themselves, with minimal adaptation, to use with individual students. Where this is not the case, alternative procedures are given.

BUSINESS BRIEF

Communication skills are important on both an individual and a global basis. The success or failure of **interaction** can have an impact on relationships between people, companies and nations.

We often associate communication with **verbal** skills, where we rely on words to convey meaning. In many situations, **tone** can be as important as what it said. However, **non-verbal signals** such as **body language** and **gestures** can also be important.

During a normal day, we often employ our **interpersonal skills,** where we communicate with people in **face-to-face** conversations. Yet there is no doubt that technology has revolutionised communication. Internet technology and **mobile devices** mean that we are more **connected** than ever before. We can update colleagues, family and friends on what we do throughout the day and make new **virtual** friends. There are downsides to this. The line between work and leisure can become blurred when we can be contacted at any time, day or night. Some experts worry that using **the Web** to manage our relationships can contribute to a more egocentric society and increased isolation for the individual.

The **global economy** has come to rely on the constant exchange of up-to-the-minute information. **Information and communication technologies (ICTs)** have transformed the way that companies and employees communicate. The use of an **intranet** at work allows companies to use a private **network** for staff to communicate, and business increasingly relies on **electronic** communication between customers and suppliers.

Ultimately, successful communication, whether in person or through the use of technology, often involves an interchange of information. This can best be achieved by considering the message that needs to be delivered and selecting the most appropriate **medium** to communicate it. Both spoken and written communication should always strive to be both clear and polite. In the age of e-mail, social media and instant messaging, this can mean pausing to re-read the content before hitting the 'send' button.

Read on

Nicholas Christakis, James Fowler: *Connected: The amazing power of social networks and how they shape our lives,* HarperPress, 2011

Erik Qualman: *Socialnomics: How social media transforms the way we live and do business*, John Wiley & Sons, 2010.

John Adair: *Effective Communication: The most important management skill of all*, Pan, 2009

Nicky Stanton: *Mastering Communication*, Palgrave Macmillan, fifth edition 2009

John Kennedy, Dr Graham Lawler: *The Dynamics of Business Communication: How to communicate efficiently and effectively*, Studymates Ltd, 2009

BUSINESS BRIEF

LESSON NOTES

Warmer

- Write *face-to-face communication* on the board. Ask students to brainstorm different tools that we use to communicate when we can't use face-to-face communication (e.g. *pens, e-mails, the phone, texts,* etc.). Note their suggestions on the board.

- Then write the following on the board:
  Invite a client to lunch.
  Ask your boss for a promotion.
  Let your friend know that you're going to be 10 minutes late.

- Ask students to work in pairs and say how they would communicate in each of these situations (face to face or using one of the tools they suggested). Have a feedback session and encourage students to give reasons for their answers.

Overview

- Tell students that they are going to study language to talk about communication.

- Ask students to look at the Overview section on page 96. Point to each heading and elicit or explain a little about each. Point to the sections you will be covering in this lesson, using the table on page 100 of this book as a guide.

Quotation

- Tell students to read the quotation. Get them to discuss in small groups whether they agree or disagree. Ask groups to suggest reasons why it is important to listen.

- Have a feedback session and invite comments from different groups.

Starting up

In this section, students complete a quiz which helps them to consider various forms of communication.

- Go through the quiz with the class and clarify where necessary.

- Ask a student to read out the first question and answer for you. Ask students around the class to say which answer (a–c) applies to them.

- Get students to answer the rest of the questions individually. Circulate and monitor.

- Divide the class into pairs and ask students to compare their answers.

- Have a brief feedback session and ask pairs to share one or two similarities and differences that they discovered.

Vocabulary: Internal communication

This section uses a short text to introduce key terms for ways that employees communicate in the workplace.

A

- Divide the class into pairs and ask students to discuss ideas with their partner.

- Have a feedback session with the whole class to share ideas.

- Ask students to say which of the methods they have used recently.

B

- Look at the words in the box with the class and check understanding.

- Ask students to read through the text quickly and use the words to complete the information.

- Tell students not to worry about the words in red at the moment, they will be using these in Exercise C.

- Get students to compare their ideas with a partner before checking answers around the class.

> **1** print   **2** face to face   **3** workplace
> **4** electronic   **5** company intranet

C

- Read the definitions with the class and clarify where necessary.

- Do item 1 together to demonstrate (*download*).

- Ask students to complete the exercise with a partner.

- Check answers with the class.

> **1** download   **2** blog   **3** post, upload
> **4** channels   **5** wiki   **6** forums   **7** briefings

- Write the following words and phrases on the board: *regularly, occasionally, hardly ever, never.* Dictate the following:
  1   read magazines
  2   send text messages
  3   go on discussion forums
  4   send e-mails
  5   download photos

- Ask students to tell their partner how often they do these things (they can use the time references on the board or others that they know, e.g. *every day, twice a week, once a month,* etc.).

D

- Tell the class how you prefer to communicate with some of the people on the list and how they usually communicate with you.

LESSON NOTES

- Divide the class into pairs and ask students to say how they communicate with the people listed (they should choose the list that is most appropriate for their situation).

- Ask students to say what forms of communication they find most difficult to use or dislike. Encourage them to give reasons. You could ask them to suggest advice to help when they use communication they do not feel confident with.

◎ i-Glossary

Listening: Networking online
Students hear an interview in four parts with Ros Pomeroy, a management consultant.

A

- Say each of the sites and get students to say which they have heard of. Ask them to say anything they know about the sites. If you belong to any of the sites and have access to mobile technology / a computer, you could show them one to demonstrate.

- Divide the class into pairs and get them to say which they use.

- If you think your class may be uncomfortable saying which sites they use or would not use any of them, you could ask them to talk about someone they know who uses networking sites.

B ◀》 CD2.27

- Tell students that they are going to hear Ros Pomeroy talk about some of the social networking sites in Exercise A.

- Play the recording and ask students to tick the social networking sites that she mentions.

- Check answers together. Ask students to say what sort of networking site LinkedIn is (a specialist professional networking site).

> LinkedIn, specialist networking sites

C ◀》 CD2.28

- Write *advantages* and *disadvantages* on the board. Tell students they are going to hear the second part of Ros's interview.

- Check students understand how many advantages and disadvantages they need to note.

- Play the recording and pause to do the first advantage together. Play the rest of the recording while students make notes.

- Play the recording again and pause it at appropriate points to elicit answers.

> Advantages: keeping in touch with many people in her professional field; making contact with people who are interested in her work
>
> Disadvantage: people contacting her to sell things she is not interested in

D ◀》 CD2.29

- Tell students that Ros is going to talk about a good communicator that she knows. Ask students to suggest how Ros knows the person (family, friend, boss, client, colleague, etc.).

- Play the recording and ask students to say who the person is. Check students understand what an *ex-boss* is (*someone who Ros worked for in the past*).

> Her ex-boss (from 15 years ago)

E ◀》 CD2.29

- Play the recording again and do item 1 together.

- Play the rest of the recording and ask students to complete the text individually.

- Ask students to compare their answers with a partner.

- Play the recording a final time and pause it to elicit answers from the class.

> 1 passion 2 enthusiastic 3 subject
> 4 difference 5 spoke 6 important

F ◀》 CD2.30

- Read the instructions together and check students understand.

- Play the recording and pause to answer item 1 together.

- Play the rest of the recording and ask students to answer the questions individually.

- Ask students to check their answers with a partner. Play the recording again for students to check.

> 1 NM 2 L 3 L 4 NM 5 NL 6 NL 7 NM

G

- Tell the class about a good communicator you know. Describe the person and say why they are a good communicator. Ask the class to say any adjectives or phrases that you could use to describe someone who is a good communicator and write these on the board.

LESSON NOTES

- Divide the class into pairs and get them to answer the question.

- Circulate and monitor.

- ◎ Students can watch the interview with Ros Pomeroy on the DVD-ROM.

- ➡ Resource bank: Listening (page 184)

Language focus 1: Talking about future plans

Students look at the use of the present continuous and *going to* for talking about the future. They practise using these forms and then listen to Janine and Patrick talk about their plans for next year. Finally, students use the language to talk about their own plans.

- In English, talking about the future is based on levels of certainty (how sure we are that something is going to happen). This is not the case in most other languages, so spend some time helping students to focus on the concept, as well as on the form.

- Books closed. On the board, write: *I'm visiting my friends at the weekend.* Elicit the tense of the sentence (*present continuous*). Ask students if the sentence is talking about something that is happening at the moment or in the future (*in the future*).

- Remind students that you have previously looked at the present continuous to describe actions that are temporary or happening at the moment. Point out that it can also be used to talk about things that are happening in the future.

- Tell the class about things that you plan to do at the weekend.

- Books open. Give students a few minutes to read through the Language focus box individually and ask for help if they need it.

- Elicit what other way we can talk about the future (*going to*). Explain that we use both *going to* and the present continuous when we are sure we are going to do something. We have already made the decision and may have made firm plans and arrangements.

- Some students may want a firm distinction between when to use the present continuous and *going to*. If so, tell them that the present continuous can be used when we are very certain about doing something. But most English speakers use both ways of expressing the future interchangeably.

- Refer students to the Grammar reference for more information.

A – B

- On the board, write: *She is going to work next week.* Elicit the negative form (*She isn't going to work next week.*) and the question form (*Is she going to work next week?*).

- Divide the class into pairs and get students to complete the sentences in Exercise A and the text in Exercise B with a partner.

- Check the answers around the class and write them on the board. Spend as much time as needed demonstrating the form.

> **A** 1 Is; coming   2 is/'s travelling
> 3 is not / 's not / isn't coming
>
> **B** 2 He's arriving / He is arriving
> 3 I'm taking / I am taking
> 4 I'm not seeing / I am not seeing
> 5 I'm driving / I am driving

- Ask students to take turns reading the sentences with a partner.

C

- Tell students three things that you are doing next week. To make it more challenging, you could ask students to guess what arrangements you have next week.

- Give students a short time to prepare / look at their diaries.

- Divide the class into pairs and ask students to talk about their arrangements next week.

- You could ask stronger students to say what their partner is doing next week.

D

- Do the first one together with the class.

- Ask students to complete the exercise individually and check answers.

- Spend time clarifying where necessary.

> 1 are; going to   2 are/'re; going to
> 3 are/'re going to

E ◀)) CD2.31

- Read through the statements with the class and clarify where necessary.

- Highlight the example. Play the recording and pause to do item 2 together.

- Play the rest of the recording and briskly check answers with the class.

> 2 T   3 F (She's going to stay at home.)
> 4 F (He isn't going to change his job.)   5 T
> 6 F (He's going to sell his car and buy a motorbike.)

- Ask students to turn to pages 165–166 and read the audio script with a partner.

LESSON NOTES

F

- Ask the class to guess which plans are true for you.

- Tell students any other plans that you have for next week and next year.

- Ask students to look at the list again and tick the plans that are true for them.

- Encourage students to add four more plans to each of the lists.

- Circulate and help where needed.

G

- Divide the class into pairs.

- Get students to use the information from Exercise F to talk about their plans with their partner.

- You could ask two students to talk about their partner's plans for the future.

Reading: Communication technology at work

The article in this section is about Vittorio Colao, the CEO of Vodafone. Students practise scanning for specific information and reading for understanding.

A

- Books closed. Write on the board *mobile-phone companies*. Ask students to name some companies and write the names on the board. Get students to say which companies are most popular in their country.

- Books open. Nominate students to ask you the questions and answer them.

- Get students to answer the questions individually and then ask them to compare their answers with a partner.

B

- Ask students if they have heard of Vodafone and Vittorio Colao. Ask them to predict what he will say about his use of communication technology.

- Get students to read the article quickly. Have a brief feedback session where they say if he mentions any of their suggestions and if they find his use of communication technology surprising.

C

- Ask students to read the article again more closely and do the exercise individually.

- Check the answers around the class and clarify any vocabulary problems.

---

1 He has four mobile phones. He usually carries two or three with him.

2 a) business e-mails, swap SMS messages with colleagues

   b) for social contact and to access Facebook

3 In southern Europe (He says they always carry mobiles with them and use them all the time.)

4 He doesn't want to see the person he is talking to. He likes to take notes during phone calls.

5 a) project updates with colleagues

   b) sending messages to friends and seeing what they are doing

D

- Get students to work in pairs and find the words.

- Check answers with the class.

---

1 to swap   2 to access   3 disciplined   4 a fan

E

- Get students to ask you questions about your use of communication technology. Answer their questions. Encourage students to make comparisons between your use of technology and Mr Colao's.

- Give students a few moments to prepare questions to ask their partner.

- Divide the class into pairs and ask students to ask and answer the questions. Get students to compare their use to Mr Colao's.

- Have a brief feedback session and ask two or three students to talk about their partner's use of communication technology.

➡ Text bank (pages 150–151)

Language focus 2: *will*

Will is often the first future expression that students identify. The danger is that they will get into the habit of using it to talk about all future events. While it is important to encourage students to talk about the future in the correct way, don't let it become stressful. Give them lots of opportunity to practise and revise the language throughout the course.

- Read through the Language focus box together.

- Write the following on the board:
  a) *I'll get you a coffee.*
  b) *More people will use communication technology.*

- Ask students to identify which sentence is predicting a future event (*b*) and which is an offer (*a*).

LESSON NOTES

A

- Read the sentences with the class.

- Highlight the example. Ask students to say if sentence 2 is correct or not (*yes*). Do sentence 3 together.

- Ask students to do the remaining sentences with a partner, then check the answers and write the sentences on the board.

- Ask students to read the corrected sentences with their partner and say which predictions they agree with.

- Have a brief feedback session with the class.

---

2 *Correct*

3 As a result, it **will** not be easy for staff to have a good work–life balance.

4 I ~~will~~ think most companies **will** use social networking tools for internal communication.

5 *Correct*

6 As a result, managers **will not / won't** spend as much time travelling for work.

7 I **don't** think companies will use e-mail, except for external communication.

B

- Write on the board: *In 10 years, people won't use paper and pens in offices*. Ask students to say whether they agree with this prediction.

- In the same pairs as Exercise A, ask students to list three or four changes they think will happen in office communication.

- Get pairs to say their predictions. Write ideas on the board. Ask students to say which they think are most likely to happen.

C

- Talk about your plans for this month using some of the future time expressions in the exercise.

- Highlight the example. Do item 2 together to demonstrate (*tomorrow*).

- Get students to complete the exercise individually and then compare their answers with a partner.

- Check the answers around the class.

---

2 tomorrow   3 end of   4 the day after   5 July
6 time   7 in the next   8 five years'

- Write the following on the board:
  In two hours from now
  In three days' time
  Tomorrow morning

- Elicit ideas around the class about what students will be doing at these times.

- Divide the class into pairs.

- Ask students to write three future time expressions and show them to their partner. Their partner tries to think of things that they will be doing at those times.

D

- Get students to cover the offers (a–e). Ask them to read the statements (1–5) and suggest offers that they could make in these situations.

- Ask students to uncover the offers and do the first one together.

- Get students to complete the exercise individually and compare answers with a partner.

- Check answers with the class.

---

1 b   2 e   3 d   4 a   5 c

- Ask students to read the statements and offers with a partner.

- Get students to suggest two or three more statements and write them on the board. Ask students to suggest offers using *will*.

E

- Read the instructions together. Get a student to read the example to the class.

- Look at the second item on the list (*design the invitations*) and ask students to make the offer (*I'll design the invitations*) and to give a reason (e.g. *I enjoy art and I can do it on my computer*).

- Divide the class into groups. Ask them to offer to do things for the launch of the website.

- Circulate and monitor. Check that everyone has a chance to make an offer / give a reason.

- Have a brief feedback session. Ask each group to say who will do things for the launch and encourage them to say why.

Skills: Making arrangements

This section looks at key phrases for making arrangements. Students listen to four people making arrangements and use the language to role-play similar situations.

A 🔊 CD2.32–2.35

- Ask students what sort of arrangements they make in a normal week (e.g. *meeting friends*, *seeing colleagues and clients*, *attending English classes*, etc.).

- Go through the situations. Check students understand *existing*, *apologising* and *alternative*.

LESSON NOTES

- Tell the class that they will hear four people making arrangements by phone.
- Play the recordings and have students complete the exercise individually.
- Ask students to compare their answers with a partner and play the recordings again for students to check.
- Elicit answers around the class.

> 1 c   2 d   3 a   4 b

B 🔊 CD2.32–2.35

- Play the recordings again.
- Get students to listen and complete the exercise with a partner.
- Play the recordings again. Pause after each speaker to check the answers around the class.
- Check students understand the phrases.

> 2 later   3 fine   4 See   5 you   6 change
> 7 can't   8 missed   9 call

- Say the phrases and ask students to repeat them.
- Ask students to turn to the audio script on page 166.
- Get students to read the four conversations with a partner.

C

- Read through the Useful language box together.
- Model the phrases and ask students to repeat them.
- Divide the class into pairs.
- Read the instructions with the whole class and clarify where needed.
- Ask the class to suggest phrases that could be used in the first conversation.
- Choose a confident student to help you to demonstrate the first role play.
- Get students to role-play the three conversations.
- Circulate and monitor.
- If appropriate, ask three pairs to role-play one conversation each to the class.
- In a diary format, note on the board the things that you are doing next week. Ask students to do the same. In pairs, ask students to role-play a telephone call to make an arrangement to meet one day next week.

○ Students can watch the phone calls on the DVD-ROM.

⇒ Resource bank: Speaking (page 172)

CASE STUDY

Blakelock Engineering

A company needs to reduce the number of employees and communicate the decision to staff.

Background

- Get students to read the Background information. Ask check questions such as: *What problem does Blakelock Engineering have? What does the company need to do? What decisions does it need to make?*

🔊 CD2.36

- Play the recording and ask students to make notes about the three ways to decide who leaves the company.

- Play it again and pause to elicit answers.

- Ask students to work in pairs and think of any other ways they could decide.

- Have a brief feedback session to share ideas.

- Read the information in the *Arrangements for a meeting* box. Ask check questions such as: *When did Helen join Blakelock? Which department does she work in? Who does she want a meeting with? What does she want to find out? Does the Head of Human Resources want to meet her? What does he do?*

- Write on the board *Helen* and *Head of Human Resources*. Ask students to suggest how Helen could start the conversation. Ask them to suggest phrases each person could use.

- If you think students need support, ask those playing Helen to prepare together and those playing the Head of Human Resources to prepare together and think of an excuse.

- If students are confident, ask them to prepare the conversation in pairs. They can note a few phrases but do not need to write the whole conversation.

- Get students to work in A/B pairs and role-play the conversation.

- If time allows, get students to change roles and role-play again.

- Have a feedback session. Ask whether it was more difficult to be Helen or the Head of Human Resources. What excuse did the student playing Head of Human Resources use? Was the student playing Helen able to make him agree to a meeting?

Task

- Divide students into pairs. Tell them they are directors of the company and they will need to make decisions about what the company will do. Write on the board *Advantages* and *Disadvantages*. Get students to discuss the ways to choose who will leave the company and to list the advantages and disadvantages of each. Ask students to use their notes to decide which way is best.

- Then pairs decide how to communicate the decision to staff and shareholders. They also need to decide who will communicate the decision.

- Get students to join with another pair to make groups of four. Each pair should describe their solutions and compare their ideas.

- The groups then discuss how to help the employees who will leave the company.

- Open the discussion and ask groups to share their ideas on how to help employees.

Writing

- Write or dictate these questions:
  Who is the e-mail from?
  Who is it to?
  Why is the meeting happening?
  Who will be there?
  What date is it?
  What time is it?
  Where is it?

- Ask students to read the instructions and complete the information. Tell them they will need to decide the date, time and location.

- Refer students to the Writing file.

- Work together to think of ways to start the e-mail.

- Ask students to use the notes they made to write the e-mail.

- When they have finished writing, ask them to compare their e-mails with a partner.

➡ Writing file (Course Book page 126)

➡ Resource bank: Writing (page 198)

11 Cultures

AT A GLANCE

	Classwork – Course Book	Further work
Lesson 1 *Each lesson (excluding case studies) is about 45–60 minutes. This does not include administration and time spent going through homework.*	<u>**Starting up**</u> Students look at tips for visiting another country or doing business there. **Vocabulary: Company cultures** Students complete sentences about different company cultures. **Listening: Cultural mistakes** Students listen to six people talk about cultural mistakes they have made.	**Practice File** Vocabulary (page 44) **i-Glossary** (DVD-ROM) **Resource bank: Listening** (page 185) **Course Book Listening** (DVD-ROM)
Lesson 2	**Language focus 1: *should/shouldn't*** Students use *should* and *shouldn't* to give advice and make suggestions. **Reading: Cultural differences** Students read about different attitudes to business in Brazil and China.	**Practice File** Language review (page 45) **Text bank** (pages 152–153)
Lesson 3	**Language focus 2: *could/would*** Students look at *could* and *would* to make requests and offers. <u>**Skills: Identifying problems and agreeing action**</u> Students listen to a project manager talking to one of her team leaders about problems with an employee. Students role-play a similar problem.	**Practice File** Language review (page 45) **Course Book Skills Dialogues** (DVD-ROM) **Resource bank: Speaking** (page 173)
Lesson 4 *Each case study is about 30 minutes to 1 hour.*	<u>**Case study: The wind of change**</u> A new general manager of an international clothing company encounters problems when she wants to introduce new ideas. **Writing** Students write action minutes for the meeting they had in the case study.	**Resource bank: Writing** (page 199) **Practice File** Writing (page 46)

For a fast route through the unit focusing mainly on speaking skills, just use the underlined sections.

For one-to-one situations, most parts of the unit lend themselves, with minimal adaptation, to use with individual students. Where this is not the case, alternative procedures are given.

BUSINESS BRIEF

Companies which deal in the global marketplace need to be able to adapt to different business cultures. It is easier to make a good impression in our own culture than in another, where our knowledge of the language and rules of behaviour may be limited. Knowledge of the **protocol** and **etiquette** in the countries we do business with is essential. Protocol is adhering to the correct procedures and conduct in formal situations. This involves knowing the acceptable way to behave and includes formalities of **rank,** which denotes the level of a person's position in an organisation. Etiquette focuses on communicating in a respectful and polite way in accordance with the good manners and accepted norms of the culture.

When employees travel abroad on business, particularly on prolonged assignments, there can be a period of adjustment when they adapt to the local culture. If sufficient preparation has not been made, then the person may not be able to acclimatise to the loss of familiar **cultural cues**. These cues normally allow us to read gestures, body language and facial expressions and provide us with prompts that indicate how we should act in particular situations. If this is not possible, then **culture shock** may occur, leading to frustration and ineffective communication on both sides. To avoid this, some companies provide **cross-cultural training**. Staff are shown skills and strategies to help with cultural adjustment. These include factual information about the culture, negotiating across cultures, managing employees from different backgrounds, decision-making styles in different countries and differing attitudes to time and task management. A good course will also teach employees about their own culture and the preconceptions that others might have of them.

It helps to be aware that even the most basic forms of **non-verbal communication** are **culturally specific**. In most Western countries, people stand close enough to shake hands without moving forward. This is the **'comfort zone'**, which means that standing closer than this can make other people feel slightly uncomfortable. However, in Asian countries, people usually prefer to keep a greater distance, whereas in most of the Middle East and Latin America, the 'comfort zone' is much closer. In order not to cause offence, it is preferable not to back away. Similarly, maintaining **eye contact** is seen as a positive thing in the West and avoiding it can be interpreted as evasive. However, in South Korea, too much eye contact could be considered hostile or aggressive. Intermittent eye contact is acceptable in most parts of the world. A smile may be regarded as a universal gesture, but in Japan it can communicate that the person is uncomfortable or sad.

Cultural awareness may be complex, but companies can pay dearly if **intercultural** research has not been carried out. Nike Inc had to recall 38,000 basketball shoes because its swoosh design logo was considered offensive in some cultures. This example illustrates that even the largest companies can make cultural mistakes. Such errors can be costly in terms of both a company's money and its public image.

Read on

Geert Hofstede et al.: *Cultures and Organizations: Software of the mind*, McGraw-Hill Professional, third edition 2010

Fons Trompenaars, Charles Hampden-Turner: *Managing People Across Cultures*, Capstone, 2004

Terri Morrison, Wayne A. Conway: *Kiss, Bow or Shake Hands*, Adams Media Corporation, second edition 2006

Richard D. Lewis: *When Cultures Collide: Leading, teamworking and managing across the globe*, Nicholas Brealey Publishing, third edition 2005

Norine Dresser: *Multicultural Manners: Essential rules of etiquette for the 21st century*, John Wiley & Sons, 2005

LESSON NOTES

Warmer

- Ask the class to brainstorm countries that they have visited (or would like to visit) on holiday or business. Write suggestions on the board.

- In groups, ask students to compare the country they visited to their own country. If students have not travelled, ask them to talk about what they think will be the same or different.

Overview

- Tell students you are going to study language to talk about cultures.

- Ask students to look at the Overview section on page 104. Point to each heading and elicit or explain a little about each. Point to the sections you will be covering in this lesson, using the table on page 109 of this book as a guide.

Quotation

- Write the quotation on the board.

- Divide the class into small groups. Ask students what they understand by the quotation (*When I'm abroad, I want to experience new things, not the ones I can find at home.*). Do they agree or disagree with this view of travel?

- Feed back with the whole class and pool ideas.

Starting up

Students look at tips for visiting a different country and give advice about their own country.

A

- Divide the class into pairs.

- Highlight the example and do item 2 together to demonstrate (*money*).

- Get students to complete the exercise in their pairs.

- Check the answers around the class.

> **2** money   **3** hours   **4** date   **5** customs
> **6** language   **7** food   **8** clothes   **9** cards
> **10** gifts   **11** leaders

- Read through the tips with the whole class and clarify any difficult words.

B

- On the board write the headings: a) very useful, b) useful, c) not useful.

- Divide the class into small groups. Get students to decide which tips go in each category.

- Ask students to say why they found some tips very useful and some not useful.

- If students are happy to move around the room, you could try the following. Write the headings on A4 sheets of paper and attach them to the far left, far right and in the middle of a wall in the classroom. Ask individual students to stand up, read out one of the tips and move to the point along the wall that reflects their opinion about the advice.

C

- Get students to decide which tips are good advice for their country individually.

- Encourage students to add other ideas.

- Divide the class into pairs and ask students to compare advice.

- Circulate and monitor.

Vocabulary: Company cultures

This section looks at the different points that make up a company culture.

A

- Read the instructions aloud together and check that students understand the concept of company culture.

- Explain that some companies have a very formal culture (for example, some traditional banks) and others are more relaxed (such as some internet companies). The company culture can affect many areas of working life, such as what you call your boss (*Mr / Mrs ...* or first name) and how you dress (jeans or a suit) to meetings (big or small, formal or informal).

- Look at the example and complete item 2 (*uniforms*) with the whole class to demonstrate.

- Point out that one of the words or phrases in brackets is not used.

- Get students to complete the sentences with a partner.

- Check the answers around the class.

> **2** uniforms   **3** shift work   **4** flexitime
> **5** public holiday   **6** annual leave   **7** face to face
> **8** written report   **9** informal   **10** formal
> **11** family names   **12** job title

- Books closed. On the board, write three or four sentences from the exercise, including the gaps. Ask students to call out the correct words to complete the sentences.

- Ask students to note the vocabulary that is most useful to them in their vocabulary notebooks.

B

- Ask students to do the exercise individually and then discuss their ideas and reasons for them with a partner.

LESSON NOTES

- Divide the class into small groups and ask students to discuss the type of organisation that they would like to work for.

- Have a feedback session with the whole class.

C

- Allow students a few minutes to do the matching exercise, then check answers.

> 1 c   2 a   3 d   4 e   5 b

- Encourage students to write the key phrases in their notebooks.

D

- Ensure students understand the vocabulary from Exercise C, then allow five minutes for them to discuss and rank the characteristics.

- Conduct feedback as a whole class and compare rankings. Was there much variation?

E

- Divide the class into groups for the exercise. If possible, put students into groups with people who work for a different company.

- If students do not work, or if you think they might feel uncomfortable discussing the beliefs and values in their present organisation, you can ask them to talk about a company that they would like to work for or that they have worked for in the past.

- To extend the activity, you could ask students to brainstorm the names of well-known companies and write them on the board. Get groups to choose one of the companies and discuss what they think the company culture is like in that organisation.

◎ i-Glossary

Listening: Cultural mistakes

Students listen to people talking about cultural mistakes and answer questions about them.

A ◀)) CD2.37

- Tell students that they will hear John talking about a cultural mistake he made.

- Pre-teach any words your students may need (such as *Yemen*, *the Middle East*, *embarrassing*).

- Ask students what meal is talked about. Play the recording and elicit the answer (*dinner*).

- Read the questions together.

- Play the recording again. Ask students to answer the questions individually.

- Play the recording a final time and pause to elicit the answers.

> 2 a table
>
> 3 b (In some countries, it is better to avoid talking about people's possessions. They may think you want them.)

- Ask check questions such as: *Where were they having dinner? Why was John uncomfortable? How many times did his host offer John the table?*

B ◀)) CD2.38

- Play the recording twice, pausing the second time to check the answers about Cameron's story.

> 1 in France
>
> 2 c (In some countries, it is better to use family names at first. You may be invited to use first names later.)
>
> 3 They were not happy.

C ◀)) CD2.39

- Do the same with Susan's story.

> 1 Osaka (Japan)
>
> 2 Japanese sales staff
>
> 3 a (In Japan, it is not considered polite to pour your own drink.)
>
> 4 to pour drinks for the others

- Ask students to look at the audio scripts on page 166 and play all three recordings again as students read.

- Ask students what they would do in each situation. Focus on ideas rather than grammatical accuracy.

D ◀)) CD2.40–2.42

- Point to the three photos. Students will be familiar with Liz Credé, Jeremy Keeley and Ros Pomeroy from interviews in previous units.

- Play the first speaker and ask students to say who it is (Liz Credé).

- Pause the recording to highlight the example. With the whole class, identify the next piece of information to tick (*Liz thought a colleague was abrupt and rude*).

- Play the next two speakers and get students to do the rest of the exercise individually.

- Ask students to compare their answers with a partner.

LESSON NOTES

- Play the recordings again and pause after the relevant information to allow students to check their answers.

> 1 Jeremy   2 Liz   3 Jeremy   4 Ros   5 Ros   6 Liz

- Ask students if they have experienced similar cultural mistakes to the ones that Liz, Jeremy and Ros describe. What advice would they give about communicating by e-mail and making small talk in their country?

E

- Tell the class about any cultural mistakes that you have made. How did you feel?

- In pairs, ask students to think of other examples of cultural mistakes.

- Ask students if visitors to their country make cultural mistakes.

- ◎ Students can watch the interviews with Liz Credé, Jeremy Keeley and Ros Pomeroy on the DVD-ROM.

- ➡ Resource bank: Listening (page 185)

Language focus 1: *should/shouldn't*

Students look at *should/shouldn't* to give advice and to say that something is or isn't a good idea.

- Read through the Language focus box with students.

- Ask the class to listen and write down the following: *My friend is writing an important report. His boss wants him to finish it by next Monday. His boss says he can work on it at the weekend. But on Saturday my friend is going to a big family party. He is going to have a meeting with his boss tomorrow. What do you think he should do?*

- Ask students to read the problem back to you. Elicit advice around the class.

A

- Highlight the example.

- Get students to complete the exercise individually.

- Check the answers around the class and write them on the board. Clarify where needed.

> 2 should speak to our boss.   3 shouldn't be late.
> 4 should stay three days.
> 5 shouldn't buy an expensive computer system.

B

- Highlight the example and do item 2 together to demonstrate (*I don't think we should launch the new*

product now.). Tell students to use the form closest to the original sentence, as illustrated by the first and second items.

- Ask students to complete the exercise with a partner.

- Check the answers around the class. You may wish to elicit possible alternatives (e.g. *We shouldn't launch the new product now.*).

> 2 I don't think we should launch the new product now.
>
> 3 She should take customers to expensive restaurants.
>
> 4 We shouldn't take every customer complaint seriously.
>
> 5 I don't think staff should fly economy on every trip. / I think staff shouldn't fly economy on every trip

C

- Get two students to read the example to the class.

- Do the next sentence together to demonstrate the exercise (*You should take plenty of business cards.*).

- Get students to write sentences individually using *should* or *shouldn't*.

- Circulate and help if needed.

- Elicit the answers from the class.

> You should take plenty of business cards.
>
> You shouldn't arrange a lot of appointments on the same day.
>
> You shouldn't be late for appointments.
>
> You should write a short report after each meeting.
>
> You should keep all your receipts for travel and restaurants.

- Can students think of any other tips?

Reading: Cultural differences

Students read an article which talks about cultural differences between China and Brazil. They check information in a true/false exercise and discuss questions.

A

- Read the statements with the class. Divide the class into pairs. If you have a multicultural class, ask students from different backgrounds to work together initially.

113

LESSON NOTES

- Conduct a feedback session as a class. Ask students to say which statements they agreed and disagreed with. Encourage them to give reasons.

B

- Read the question with the class. Briefly ask students to suggest any differences they think the article will mention. Write ideas on the board.

- Get students to scan the article to see if any of their ideas are mentioned. Ask them to scan again to identify the two main causes of cultural misunderstanding between the two countries.

- Clarify any difficult vocabulary items (e.g. *trading partner*, *high inflation*).

Different ways of looking at:

- timing, e.g. starting times for meetings/events, how important it is to keep to schedules/ deadlines, etc.

- planning, e.g. when to do planning (planning or implementation stage), and how much detail is needed.

C

- Ask students to read the article again in more detail.

- Ask five students to read the statements and ensure students understand them.

- Allow them to work individually to decide whether each statement is true or false.

- Check answers around the class. Ask students to correct the false statements. Write the correct information on the board as students dictate.

1 F (China has replaced the US as Brazil's biggest trading partner.)

2 F (They learn the language, but also about Chinese business culture.)

3 F (There is also a lack of cultural understanding.)

4 T

5 F (They plan, but do most of the detailed planning as a project progresses, changing the plan when problems happen.)

- Ask students if any of the information in the article surprised them.

D

- Divide the class into pairs. Draw students' attention to paragraph 1. Ask them: *Was this a good start to the relationship between the Chinese and Brazilian businesspeople?*

- Get students to discuss the questions in pairs.

- Have a feedback session with the class. Ask students to say what the Brazilians could do differently next time and write suggestions on the board.

1 The Chinese were waiting for the Brazilians, who arrived late.

2 The Chinese probably felt irritated by the late arrival of the Brazilians. The Brazilians felt irritated by the traffic delay.

3 *Suggested answer*: Apologise if they arrive late and invite their Chinese guests to a meal.

- Ask students which attitudes to time are closer to their own country, the Chinese or the Brazilian. Do students expect meetings or events to start on time? How do they feel if they start late?

E

- Highlight the example and do item 2 together to demonstrate (*priority*).

- Students can do this individually and check answers with a partner. Alternatively, ask students to work with a partner and give a point to the pair which can find each word the quickest.

2 priority   3 issues   4 fail   5 (a) lack   6 deadline

F

- Choose one of the points and ask students to suggest advice. Write ideas on the board.

- Divide the class into pairs. If you have a multicultural class, ask students from the same backgrounds to work together initially.

- Get students to choose two or three of the points to give advice on.

- Ask students to join with another pair to present their ideas.

- Have a feedback session with the whole class. Write ideas on the board and encourage students to say whether they agree or disagree with the advice.

- Highlight any differences in the advice. This is a good opportunity to open the discussion to the fact that there is no right or wrong way to do these things, but that it is important to be aware of cultural differences.

➡ Text bank (pages 152–153)

LESSON NOTES

Language focus 2: *could/would*

Students look at requests using *could* and offers using *would*.

- Read the Language focus box together and answer any questions.

A

- Pre-teach any vocabulary your class may need (e.g. *fasten*, *seat belt*).

- On the board, write the headings *Flight attendant* and *Passenger*.

- Ask students to look at the sentences and find an example of something that the passenger says and an example of something the flight attendant says. Write the examples on the board.

- Ask students to complete the exercise with a partner.

- Check the answers around the class.

> See Exercise B below.

B

- Write the following on the board:
  a) *Could I have a cup of coffee, please?*
  b) *Would you like a cup of coffee?*

- Ask students to identify which is an offer (*b*) and which is a request (*a*).

- Do the exercise with the whole class.

> **1** P (request)   **2** F (offer)   **3** P (request)
> **4** F (offer)   **5** P (request)   **6** F (offer)
> **7** F (request)   **8** P (request)

- Ask students to identify what word the offers start with (*would*) and what word the requests start with (*could*).

C – **E** 🔊 CD2.43

- Read the instructions together.

- Highlight the example and the verbs in brackets. Do item 2 with the whole class to demonstrate. (*Could you recommend a good restaurant, please?*)

- Ask students to identify which sentences use *I* (1 and 5) and which use *you* (2, 3, 4, 6).

- Get students to complete the exercise individually.

- Circulate and monitor.

- Play the recording for students to check. Ask students to take turns saying the sentences.

- Play the recording again and ask students to practise the replies.

> **2** Could you recommend a good restaurant, please?
>
> **3** Could you say that again, please?
>
> **4** Could you copy this document for me, please?
>
> **5** Could I have my bill, please?
>
> **6** Could you call me a taxi, please?

- Point out that it is polite to add *please* to most requests.

- Get students to look at the audio script on page 166 and practise the dialogue with a partner.

- Can students think of any other things that they could request in a hotel?

F

- Ask two students to read the example to the class. Get them to suggest other things that the person may request.

- Divide the class into A/B groups to read the role cards and prepare the questions together.

- Circulate and monitor, helping where necessary.

- Ask students to work in A/B pairs and role-play the conversation.

- Choose one or two pairs to role-play the conversation to the class.

Skills: Identifying problems and agreeing action

This section features a recording about a foreign consultant. Students look at language for identifying problems and suggesting and agreeing action. A role play allows them to use the language in context.

A 🔊 CD2.44

- Read the instructions and the statements together and clarify any vocabulary that students are unsure of (e.g. *gets on well with, knowledge*).

- Play the recording and give students a moment to think about the statements.

- Play it again, pausing at the relevant points and asking students to respond to each statement. Confirm or correct the answers.

> **1** T   **2** T   **3** F (They respect him, but they don't really like him.)   **4** T   **5** F (She will have the meeting after she talks to Paul.)

LESSON NOTES

B 🔊 CD2.44

- See if students can complete any of the words before listening again.

- Play the recording and pause to complete the first word (*exactly*).

- Play the rest of the recording again for students to complete/check their answers.

- Play it a final time, pausing before the relevant words to elicit answers.

> **1** exactly **2** communicating **3** knowledge
> **4** best **5** advice

C

- Ask students to turn to the audio script on page 166. As a class, make a list on the board of the problems Tom has with Paul.

- Students then work in pairs to distil these problems into three pieces of advice. Encourage them to use *should/shouldn't*.

- Circulate, monitor and help if necessary.

- Ask each pair to read a piece of advice and write it on the board. Ask if any other pairs had the same advice expressed in a different way.

D

- Do this exercise quickly as a class.

- Encourage students to write the structures in their notebooks for future reference.

> **1** b **2** c **3** d **4** a

E

- Look through the Useful language box together.

- Write the following on the board:
  You are meeting an important customer in an hour. Your car won't start.

- Ask students to state the topic and suggest action using phrases from the Useful language box.

- Divide the class into pairs and allocate roles.

- Give students a few moments to read their role cards.

- Circulate and help students prepare where needed.

- Get students to role-play the conversation. Circulate and monitor.

- Ask pairs what action they agreed.

- ⊙ Students can watch the meeting on the DVD-ROM.

- ➡ Resource bank: Speaking (page 173)

CASE STUDY

The wind of change

A new general manager wants to introduce new ideas in an overseas branch of an international clothing company. She has problems convincing her manager about her ideas. Students role-play a meeting between senior staff.

Background

- Pre-teach any vocabulary that you think your students might need.

- Read the Background section with the class and ask check questions such as: *What is Kate's new job? What sort of company is it? What does she want to bring from the head office to the overseas branch?*

- Focus on the *Overseas branch culture now* column of the table. Read through it with the whole class.

- Ask students: *What would you change in the branch?* Get students to discuss ideas with a partner.

- Read the *Kate wants* column of the table together. Ask check questions such as: *Do staff use first names or family names at work at the moment? What are the working hours at the moment? What does Kate want to change about the working hours? How do employees dress at the office at the moment? How does Kate want staff to dress?*

- Ask students if they think the employees will like Kate's ideas. Ask students if they agree or disagree with them.

🔊 CD2.45

- Tell students that they will hear Kate talking to her manager at head office. Read the three questions and play the recording all the way through.

- Play the recording again and ask students to summarise why Kate wants to change the culture in the branch office (*She wants the style to be more relaxed and friendly to get more customers.*).

- Ask students to identify what problems Kate will face (*Staff don't want to change things.*) and what she will do at the meeting (*Present her proposals for change.*).

- Ask students whether Kate's boss is for or against changing things (*against*).

Task

- Divide students into groups of four and tell them to choose one of the roles. If there are only three students in a group, do not use the Finance Director's role card.

- Give students 10 minutes to look at their role cards and prepare for the meeting. Circulate and help students to prepare where needed.

- Ask students to identify the key points to discuss at the meeting and write the following on the board:
  Discuss Kate's ideas.
  What will we change?
  What will we keep the same?

- Get the groups to role-play the meeting.

- Circulate and monitor.

- Have a feedback session and find out what action each group agreed on.

One-to-one

Have a meeting between Kate and the Director of Human Resources, with you taking one of the roles. Note what you will keep the same and what you will change.

Then have a meeting between Kate and Stuart to discuss what was decided.

Writing

- Turn to the Writing file and look at the action minutes with the class.

- Highlight the style of the example.

- Ask students to identify the key decisions from their meeting.

- Circulate and help where needed.

- Divide students into their original groups for the case study.

- Ask them to compare minutes. Did they all see the meeting in the same way? What differences were there?

One-to-one

Ask students to write the minutes of the meeting between Kate and the Director of Human Resources.

➡ Writing file (Course Book page 128)

➡ Resource bank: Writing (page 199)

UNIT 12 Jobs

AT A GLANCE

	Classwork – Course Book	Further work
Lesson 1 *Each lesson (excluding case studies) is about 45–60 minutes. This does not include administration and time spent going through homework.*	<u>**Starting up**</u> Students discuss which jobs should get the highest salary and what aspects they would like or not like in a job. **Vocabulary: Skills and abilities** Students use verbs to complete a job advertisement. **Language focus 1: Present perfect** Students look at the use of the present perfect to talk about actions that continue from the past to the present.	**Practice File** Vocabulary (page 48) **i-Glossary** (DVD-ROM) **Practice File** Language review (page 49)
Lesson 2	**Listening: My ideal job** Liz Credé talks about her ideal job and gives advice to people starting work. **Reading: Professional networking sites** Students put headings in the correct place and answer questions about a profile on a professional networking site.	**Course Book Listening** (DVD-ROM) **Resource bank: Listening** (page 186) **Text bank** (pages 154–155)
Lesson 3	**Language focus 2: Past simple and present perfect** The tenses are compared and contrasted. Students complete a text using the correct form of the verb and look at time expressions that go with each tense. <u>**Skills: Interview skills**</u> Students look at interview tips, listen to an interview and role-play an interview situation.	**Practice File** Language review (page 49) **Course Book Skills Dialogues** (DVD-ROM) **Resource bank: Speaking** (page 174)
Lesson 4 *Each case study is about 30 minutes to 1 hour.*	<u>**Case study: Nelson & Harper Inc.**</u> The Vice-President of Human Resources of a multinational company interviews a candidate for a job. **Writing** Students write a letter to the successful candidate from the case-study interview.	**Resource bank: Writing** (page 200) **Practice File** Writing (page 50)

For a fast route through the unit focusing mainly on speaking skills, just use the underlined sections.

For one-to-one situations, most parts of the unit lend themselves, with minimal adaptation, to use with individual students. Where this is not the case, alternative procedures are given.

BUSINESS BRIEF

There are valuable skills that make job seekers attractive to employers:

- **Technical skills** – which include the specialist knowledge that will help them do the job.

- **Personal skills** – personality, attitudes, personal work habits and style. (Can they work under pressure? Can they work as a part of a team as well as unsupervised?)

- **Transferable skills** – the basic skills learned through everyday situations or previous **work experience** that can be usefully applied to a new **position**.

In the USA, the National Association of Colleges and Employers (NACE) carried out a survey and asked employers what skills and abilities a new graduate would need to be prepared for an **entry-level** job.

Seven top skills
1 interpersonal
2 teamwork
3 verbal communication
4 analytical
5 computer
6 written communication
7 leadership

The survey also found that work experience and academic qualifications were highly valued.

The findings suggest that employers want employees who can communicate effectively in speech and in writing (e.g. presentations and reports), who can interact well with colleagues or customers and who can work as part of a team.

The first steps of the **selection process** include filling out a job **application form** or sending a well-written **covering letter** and **CV (or resumé)**. The next hurdle is the interview. A survey noted that the five most common mistakes made during an interview were displaying little or no knowledge of the company, being unprepared to discuss career plans or goals, having limited enthusiasm, lack of eye contact and being unprepared to discuss skills or experience. Lack of **preparation** is a key mistake in any job interview. Most companies now have websites that include a company profile and product information which can be useful for background research.

The changing job market means that employers are increasingly choosing from an international **pool** of candidates. The employer may be in one country while the prospective employee is in a different country or even on a different continent. Applicants may find themselves taking part in a **virtual interview** via telephone, e-mail, video- or tele-conferencing. Traditional interview tips normally include advice to shake hands, maintain eye contact and dress appropriately. These cannot always be applied to telephone and e-mail interviews, where the interviewer will not know whether you are wearing your best suit or your pyjamas and will not be able to see when your gestures or facial expressions underline key information. However, the aim of the interview remains the same: to evaluate a potential employee's enthusiasm, motivation, skills and commitment.

Modern technology may allow an interview to take place in cyberspace, but the basics still apply: be informed and motivated and demonstrate that you are the best person for the job.

Read on

Jenny Rogers: *Job Interview Success: Be your own coach*, McGraw-Hill Professional, 2011

Corinne Mills: *You're Hired! How to write a brilliant CV*, Trotman, 2009

Jenny Ungless: *Career Ahead: The complete career handbook*, Raleo Publishing Ltd, 2008

Susan Hodgson: *The A–Z of Careers and Jobs*, Kogan Page, 2011

LESSON NOTES

Warmer

- Divide the class into small groups. Ask students to write a list of the five jobs that they think are most difficult to do.

- Have a brief feedback session. Ask the groups to explain why they chose certain jobs.

- Ask students if they would like to do any of the jobs on their lists. Ask them to explain why or why not.

Overview

- Tell students that they are going to study language to talk about jobs.

- Ask students to look at the Overview section on page 112. Point to each heading and elicit or explain a little about each. Point to the sections you will be covering in this lesson, using the table on page 118 of this book as a guide.

Quotation

- Write the quotation on the board.

- In groups, ask students to discuss what they think the quotation means and if they agree with it.

- Ask students to think of examples of jobs that they think are easy. Encourage them to think of tasks that a person doing this job would need to do. Ask them if they would like to do this job.

- If students are in work, ask them to identify something in their job that is easy and something that is difficult.

Starting up

This section gives students the opportunity to think about the theme of the unit and provides some speaking practice to get the lesson started.

A

- Quickly run through the list of jobs. Check students' understanding.

- Read the instructions together.

- Ask students to put the jobs in order of who *should* get the highest salary rather than who *does* get the highest salary in real life.

- Give students a few minutes to put the jobs in order.

- Ask the class to work in pairs or small groups and compare their lists.

- Encourage students to ask questions and to talk about their choices. It may be useful to remind them of or elicit the language for agreeing, disagreeing and asking for opinions from Unit 8 (page 80).

- Have a feedback session with the whole class. Highlight the differences and similarities.

B

- Now get students to put the jobs in an order that reflects the real salaries in their country.

- Divide the class into small groups. Ask students to compare their new lists.

- Encourage students to talk about any differences in the order compared to their original list.

- Have a brief feedback session with the whole class. You could write *Highest* and *Lowest* on the board and get groups to write their suggestions.

- If you have a multilingual class, compare differences and similarities in salaries in different countries.

C

- Go through the list and check students' understanding.

- Get students to do the exercise individually and then compare ideas with a partner.

- Circulate and monitor.

D

- Ask students to discuss this first in pairs or small groups, then with the whole class. Encourage students to justify their opinions.

Vocabulary: Skills and abilities

Students complete a job advertisement with key verbs. They then use the language to write about their present or past jobs.

A

- Books closed. On the board write *European Manager*. Ask the class to suggest some things that a person does in this job. What skills or experience would you need to get the job?

- Books open. Read the first part of the advertisement together. Ask students if they think this is a good salary for the job.

- Ask students to use a dictionary to look up the verbs and any other unfamiliar vocabulary.

- Highlight the example. Ask students to find a verb in the box that means the same as *start* in item 2 (*set up*).

- Get students to complete the exercise individually.

- Check the answers around the class.

> 2 set up   3 train   4 increase   5 develop
> 6 improve   7 cope with

- Ask the class if they think this is an interesting job. Would they apply for it?

LESSON NOTES

B

- Read the verbs in the box with the whole class and check students' understanding.

- Get students to complete the exercise individually and then compare their answers with a partner.

> 1 manage   2 plan   3 organise   4 deal with
> 5 motivate

C

- Tell the class about your present job or a past job using the verbs in Exercises A and B.

- Write some of your sentences on the board as an example.

- Ask students to use the verbs to write sentences about their own jobs. (If students are not working, they can write about a job they did in the past or a job they would like.)

- Circulate and monitor. Help where needed.

- Divide the class into pairs.

- Get students to talk about their present and past jobs using the sentences they have written.

 i-Glossary

Language focus 1: Present perfect

This section introduces the present perfect to talk about experiences and actions that continue from past to present. At this stage, it is not necessary to contrast the present perfect and the past simple tenses, as this will be looked at later in the unit.

- Write some sentences about yourself on the board (e.g. *I have lived here for ... . I have been a teacher for... .*).

- Point out that the action started in the past. Ask: *Am I still living here? Am I still a teacher?* Elicit *yes*.

- Tell students that we can use the present perfect to talk about actions that begin in the past and continue to the present.

- Focus on the form. Point out that the present perfect is formed using *have* or *has* + the past participle of the main verb.

- Now write on the board: *Have you ever worked in an office?*

- Ask if the question is interested in a specific time in the past or is asking a general question about experience (*about experience*).

- Highlight the form. Tell students that we use *ever* when we mean *at any time in the past*. Point out that it is not necessary to use *ever*. It is also possible to say: *Have you worked in an office?*

- Finally, elicit possible responses and write them on the board: *Yes, I have.* and *No, I haven't.*

- Ask a few more questions around the class (e.g. *Have you ever worked in a factory/shop/bank?*) and elicit responses.

- Use some of the negative responses as examples of the negative form (e.g. *I haven't worked in a shop.*).

- Give students a few minutes to read through the Language focus box individually. You could also draw their attention to the Grammar reference.

- Give students time to ask questions and clarify where needed.

A

- Highlight the example and do item 2 with the whole class (*haven't sent*).

- Ask students to complete the sentences individually.

- Circulate and help where needed.

- Get students to compare their answers in pairs.

- Get the class to dictate the sentences to you as you write them on the board.

> 2 have not / haven't sent   3 has/'s changed
> 4 has/'s been   5 have not / haven't had

- Go over any problem areas.

B

- Books closed. Ask students to suggest some topic areas and questions that you might hear in an interview.

- Books open. Ask students to read through the questions to see if they include any of their suggestions.

- Ask a student to read the first question and ask the class which response matches it (*e*).

- Get students to complete the exercise in pairs.

- Do not check answers yet, as this will be done in Exercise C.

C 🔊 CD2.46

- Play the recording while students check the answers in their pairs.

- Go through the answers with the whole class and clarify where needed.

> 1 e   2 c   3 b   4 a   5 d

- Ask students if they think the candidate gave good answers to the questions and to explain why or why not.

LESSON NOTES

C

- Highlight the example and do item 2 with the whole class (*have you used*).

- Ask students to complete the questions individually.

- Circulate and help where needed.

- Get students to compare their answers in pairs.

- Get the class to dictate the questions to you as you write them on the board.

> **2** have you used   **3** have you learnt/learned
> **4** have you had   **5** have you enjoyed
> **6** have you visited

- Go over any problem areas.

E

- Nominate students to ask you the first two or three questions and respond.

- Divide the class into pairs. Get students to take turns to ask and answer the questions.

- Circulate and monitor.

- Note any problem areas and spend time revising any necessary language points with the whole class.

Listening: My ideal job

Students listen to a three-part interview with Liz Credé, an organisation development consultant. They listen for gist and make notes and also listen for specific information.

A ◀)) CD2.47

- Write the two headings from the Course Book on the board and tell students that they are going to make notes.

- Play the recording all the way through. Play it again, pausing after Liz speaks about her job now and her job in the past.

- Divide the class into pairs and ask students to compare their notes with their partner.

- Circulate and monitor.

> **1** ideal job, leads a management consultancy of 35 consultants, enjoys working with all her colleagues does interesting work with a variety of clients, works long hours, it's rewarding, they have a good laugh
>
> **2** the company did not treat people well, did not involve people or get the best out of them, did not get on well with the manager

B ◀)) CD2.48

- Read the statements with the class. Ask students which they think are most likely to be true.

- Play the recording and pause to do the first one together.

- Play the rest of the interview and ask students to say which statements are true. Check answers around the class.

- Play it again and get students to correct the false information.

> **1** F (They come from her work as a consultant.)
>
> **2** T
>
> **3** T
>
> **4** F (She sometimes finds it hard to make decisions.)

C ◀)) CD2.49

- Books closed. Play the recording and ask: *Who is the advice for?* (young people starting work).

- Read the notes with the class. See if students can guess any of the missing words.

- Play the recording and pause to do the first one together (*opportunities*).

- Play the rest of the interview while students complete the notes.

- Get students to compare their answers with a partner. Play the interview a final time, pausing to elicit answers around the class.

> **1** opportunities   **2** learn   **3** listen
> **4** attention   **5** relationships   **6** interested

- Ask students if they agree with Liz's advice.

D

- Write these headings on the board: *Strengths and Weaknesses*, *People you work well with* and *Ideal job*.

- Divide the class into pairs.

- Ask students to discuss the questions with their partner; you may wish to set a time limit.

- Circulate and monitor.

- Have a feedback session with the class.

- ◎ Students can watch the interview with Liz Credé on the DVD-ROM.

➡ Resource bank: Listening (page 186)

LESSON NOTES

Reading: Professional networking sites

This section introduces the language and style of information used in CVs. The exercises give practice in skimming for gist and reading for specific information. The summary is then used as a model for students to write their own profile for a website.

A

- If you have access to a computer, you could introduce the topic by showing students a professional networking site such as LinkedIn or telling students about any professional networking sites you use.

- Read the questions together and check students understanding. Draw students' attention to the example in question 3.

- Divide the class into small groups. Give students five to 10 minutes to discuss the questions.

B

- Look at Helen Braoudakis's profile on a professional networking site with students. Ask them what sort of document might include similar information (*a CV*).

- Ask questions such as: *What is Helen's current job?* (Graduate Recruitment Manager) *How many people have recommended Helen on the site?* (10).

- Go through the words on page 115 and highlight the example.

- Ask students to complete the headings individually and compare their answers with a partner. Check answers around the class.

> **2** Professional summary   **3** Specialities
> **4** Work experience   **5** Education   **6** Interests

C

- Ask students to read Helen's profile again and complete the exercise individually.

- Nominate a student to read a sentence and ask the class if it is true or false.

- Ask the class to work together to correct the false statements.

> **1**   F (She did her Master's at Macquarie University in Sydney.)
>
> **2**   T
>
> **3**   F (In her first job at Gemini, she worked as a store manager.)
>
> **4**   T
>
> **5**   F (It is one of her roles in her current job with Deloitte.)
>
> **6**   F (As part of her job with ADM Consulting, she attended graduate recruitment events in SE Asia.)

D

- You may wish to ask students to do this for homework. Reassure students that their summary does not necessarily need to be as long as Helen's.

- To prepare, write *Experience*, *Qualifications*, *Skills* and *Personal qualities* on the board and encourage students to make notes for each heading.

- Get students to look through Helen's profile and note any useful words or phrases.

- Tell students that they can include voluntary work or holiday jobs if they do not have full-time work experience to include.

- Collect in the summaries and check for any areas that students need help with.

➡ Text bank (pages 154–155)

Language focus 2: Past simple and present perfect

In this section, students contrast the past simple and the present perfect and choose the correct tense to complete a text. They also look at time expressions that can be used with the present perfect.

- Give students a few moments to read through the Language focus box individually.

- Highlight the examples and write them on the board.

- Point out that a present perfect question may be answered in the past simple tense. Write this example on the board:
  'Have you had any experience working in a marketing department?'
  'Yes, I worked in a marketing department for two years and then I joined the sales department.'

- Refer students to the Grammar reference for further information.

A

- Look at the first item. Elicit why the present perfect (*have had*) is used here rather than the past simple (*The person's career started in the past and continues to the present*.).

- Do the next item with the whole class.

- Ask students to complete the rest of the exercise individually.

- Elicit the answers around the class, checking that students understand why each tense has been used.

- Items 8 and 9 illustrate that we can use the past simple to give further details once we have used the present perfect.

> **1** have had   **2** studied   **3** applied   **4** worked
> **5** came   **6** have been   **7** have done   **8** sold
> **9** taught   **10** have run

LESSON NOTES

B

- Write the start of the sentence on the board.
- Elicit what tense it is in (*present perfect*).
- Do the exercise with the whole class.

> this week; since Monday; for the last two weeks; today; recently

- Check that students understand that the other expressions (*last week/month, two weeks ago, yesterday*) wouldn't usually be used because they are located in a specific time in the past.
- Write this sentence beginning on the board: *I went to Rio … .*
- Elicit which expressions **cannot** be used to complete this past simple sentence (*since Monday, for the last two weeks*).

C

- Get two students to read the example.
- Write on the board: *Career*, *Projects*, *Places visited in last three years*.
- Give students time to prepare some information individually, if necessary.
- Divide the class into pairs and ask students to talk about the topics.
- Circulate and note any areas where students may need more help.

Skills: Interview skills

This section looks at interview tips. The listening exercise focuses on expressions used in different parts of an interview. Students use the language to role-play a job interview.

A – B

- Books closed. Ask students if they have ever had an interview for their studies or a job. Ask if the interview was formal or informal, long or short, etc. Ask how many people interviewed them and what sort of questions were asked. Have they ever interviewed someone?
- Books open. Go through the tips and check understanding.
- On the board, write the words *Interviewer* and *Candidate*.
- Ask students which is the person who is interviewed (*candidate*) and who is the person who does the interview (*interviewer*).
- Ask students to complete the exercise individually.
- Check ideas around the class.

- Divide students into pairs. Ask pairs to look at the list again and decide on the best two tips for interviewers and best two tips for candidates.
- Elicit students' choices around the class and write them on the board.
- Have a class feedback session. Which tips do the class think are most useful?

> For interviewers: tips 2, 4, 5, 7
> For candidates: tips 1, 3, 6, 8

- To extend the activity, you may wish to ask students to write their own list of tips with a partner (they can choose to write tips for the interviewer or the candidate).
- Ask pairs to join together to make groups of four.
- Get each pair to read their tips. The other pair decides whether they are for interviewers or candidates.

C ◀)) CD2.50

- Tell students that they are going to hear part of an interview.
- Pre-teach any vocabulary that you think your students may have problems with (e.g. *reputation*, *fluent*, *patient*).
- Read through the questions together.
- This is a long interview, so reassure students that they will hear it more than once.
- Play the interview all the way through and do the first question together.
- Play it again. Pause after relevant information to elicit answers.

> 1   She thinks it has an excellent reputation.
> 2   She's fluent in German and French.
> 3   People who work hard and are reliable.
> 4   Working as the Marketing Manager in an international company.

- Ask students whether they think the interview went well. Encourage them to give reasons.

D ◀)) CD2.50

- Read through the phrases in the Useful language box together.
- Ask students to say any expressions they remember hearing in the interview.
- Play the recording. Ask students to tick the expressions they hear.

LESSON NOTES

> The following expressions should be ticked:
>
> Do you have any special skills?
> What did you learn from your last job?
> I learned how to (work well in a team).
> What are your main interests?
> Where do you want to be in 10 years' time?

- Play the recording again. Ask students to repeat the expressions. Spend some time checking pronunciation and modelling the intonation of the questions.

- Tell students to turn to the audio script on page 167. Divide the class into pairs. Ask students to read the interview together.

- Then ask students to take turns asking each other the questions and answering about themselves.

E

- Books closed. Ask students what skills a manager in a sales office needs. What does the job involve?

- Books open. Read the instructions together.

- Divide the class into pairs and allocate roles.

- Give students a few minutes to read their role cards and make notes.

- Help with preparation where needed.

- Get students to role-play the interview.

- Circulate and monitor.

- Ask students to swap roles and role-play the interview again.

- Have a feedback session. Ask students which role they found easier and why. What things did they learn from being the interviewer? What did you learn from being the candidate?

- Students can watch the phone calls on the DVD-ROM.

- Resource bank: Speaking (page 174)

CASE STUDY

Nelson & Harper Inc.

Students role-play an interview for a position at a multinational company.

Background

- Books closed. Ask students to name some famous multinational companies that they know, and to name some of the departments that a multinational company might have.

- Give students a few minutes to read the first paragraph of the Background section. Pause and ask check questions such as: *Where is the company's head office? Where does it sell the products? What does it plan to do in the next five years? What type of position will staff be trained for?*

- Ask students to read the next part where the parts of the company are listed.

- Encourage students to say what skills might be required for a job in each area.

- Clarify where necessary.

◀)) CD2.51

- Tell students that they will hear a director of Nelson & Harper talking to the Vice-President of Human Resources. They are talking about the requirements for people who apply for a job with the company.

- Pre-teach any vocabulary or phrases your students may need (e.g. *values, honest, analyse*).

- Write the four headings on the board and ask students to make notes. Play the recording as many times as students need to complete their notes.

- Have a feedback session and ask students to summarise information under each heading. Write the information on the board.

- - Personal qualities: share our values, honest, open, reliable, sociable, friendly, have qualities as future leaders

  - Skills and abilities: good organisers, good at teamwork, be able to analyse and solve problems, computer skills, at least one foreign language

  - Experience: a minimum of three years' commercial or industrial experience

  - Interests: interests outside work

Task

- Divide the class into pairs. Get students to decide whether they will be interviewers or candidates. (If you think your class will have difficulty deciding, then allocate roles to students yourself.)

- Give students time to prepare for the interview. If they need more support, the interviewers and candidates can prepare in A/B groups.

- Ask students to role-play the interview.

- When all the interviews have finished, ask all the interviewers to work in a group and talk about the candidates' strengths/weaknesses. All the candidates work in a group and discuss which interview questions they thought were easy or difficult.

- If time allows, ask students to swap roles and role-play the interview again.

> **One-to-one**
>
> Take turns to be the interviewer and the candidate.
>
> Role-play the interview and ask your student to list the things that they thought went well in the interview and what they would change.

Writing

- Read the instructions together and check students understand what information they need to include.

- Tell students to turn to the Writing file for information about the format of letters.

- Highlight the opening of the letter.

- Circulate and monitor.

- Ask pairs to exchange letters with a partner and correct any mistakes.

- Discuss any language points that need clarification.

➡ Writing file (Course Book page 128)

➡ Resource bank: Writing (page 200)

WORKING ACROSS CULTURES 4

Team working

Introduction

This *Working across cultures* unit deals with attitudes to team working in Asian, northern European and southern European countries.

A

- First, ask students to consider the questions individually. Then divide the class into small groups to discuss the questions.

- If students have not worked in teams in their jobs, they can use experience of working as a team in sport or when doing a task with friends/family.

B

- Ask students to say the countries in the box with you. You could also ask students to say what continent each country is in.

- Divide the class into groups and ask students to discuss whether they think people prefer to work in teams or on their own.

- Have a feedback session with the whole class to share ideas. Tell students they will be able to check their answers when they do Exercise E.

C 🔊 CD2.52

- Tell students that they are going to hear a talk about attitudes to team working in different cultures. The talk will be in two parts.

- Read the statements with the class. Clarify where necessary. Ask students to say which statements they think are true.

- Play the recording. Pause to ask whether the first statement is true or false (*false*). Ask the class to dictate the correct statement to you.

- Play the rest of the recording. Ask students to complete the rest of the exercise individually.

- Get students to compare their answers with a partner and then play the recording again for them to check.

- Check answers with the class.

---

1   F (She mentions Indonesia, Japan, South Korea, Malaysia, Singapore and China.)

2   F (They are happier working towards team goals.)

3   F (They are naturally good team players, and it's not always necessary to spend a lot of time on team-building training sessions.)

4   T

5   T

D 🔊 CD2.53

- Read the questions with the class and check they understand.

- Play the second part of the talk and answer the first question together.

- Play the recording again and ask students to answer the remaining questions in pairs.

- Check answers with the class.

---

1   Southern Europe and northern Europe

2   Southern Europe: Portugal, Italy, Greece, Spain
    Northern Europe: Denmark, Norway, Sweden (and Finland, but see answer to 5)

3   Strong leaders

4   Without too much control

5   Finns prefer to work on their own.

E

- Divide the class into pairs. Students do Exercise B again, as they now have more information, and some of their original decisions may have changed.

- Have a feedback session to see if there were any changes in the choices students made the second time they did the exercise.

---

a) Indonesia, Japan, South Korea, Malaysia, Singapore, China, Sweden, Norway, Denmark

b) Portugal, Italy, Greece, Spain, Finland

F

- Students can complete this in class or for homework.

- Allow them to refer to the audio script on page 167.

- Ask students to compare their summary with a partner.

Task

- Go through the task with the whole class and make sure that they understand. Ask check questions such as: *What does the advertising agency want to increase? When did it hire the two British staff? Why can the company only keep one person?*

- Write on the board *Strengths* and *Weaknesses*.

- Divide the class into groups. Ask groups to read the profiles of the two British staff and write notes under the headings. Get students to use their notes to decide which member of staff to keep.

- Ask each group to say which member of staff they will keep. Encourage them to give reasons for their decision.

UNIT D Revision

10 Communication

Vocabulary

1 channels   2 print   3 face-to-face
4 briefings   5 workplace   6 electronic
7 intranet   8 blogs and wikis   9 post
10 upload   11 download

Talking about future plans; *will*

1 You have a meeting now, so you can't phone Dimitri. But don't worry, **I'll/will** do it.

2 What **is** Lance doing on Monday morning?

3 We **are/'re** meeting the legal team on Tuesday.

4 They're not going **to** attend the conference.

5 Mr Shen and Mr Lee **are** going to give a presentation together.

6 After we upgrade our network, computer security **will** not be a problem.

7 OK, then. **I'll/will** write an e-mail to Jean-Luc.

8 We're going **to** redesign our website next month.

Skills

1 c   2 a   3 e   4 f   5 d   6 b

11 Cultures

Vocabulary

1 casual Fridays   2 uniform   3 Shift work
4 flexitime   5 annual leave   6 part-time
7 public holiday   8 childcare   9 job title
10 informal   11 formal   12 social

could/would, should/shouldn't

1 Could   2 shouldn't   3 Would   4 Could
5 should   6 should   7 should   8 could

Writing

Sample answer

Dear Marcos

There are some things I'd like to talk to you about.

There's a problem with the 8.30–5.30 working day.

It's difficult for employees with children. I think we should introduce a flexitime system so that parents can start later. They could work a 9.30–6.30 day.

There's also a problem with office dress. Some people don't like wearing formal clothes all the time. I think we should have casual Fridays. This will allow staff to dress informally one day a week.

There's also a problem with communication. The problem is that staff say it's difficult to talk to you, and that they always have to use the phone or send e-mails. The best thing to do is to make time for more face-to-face communication. I think you should talk to people face-to-face every day.

Let me know if you want to talk about any of these issues.

Best regards,

12 Jobs

Vocabulary

1 motivate   2 cope with   3 train   4 set up
5 deal with   6 organise   7 manages   8 develop

Past simple and present perfect

1 studied   2 applied   3 got   4 has taken
5 has studied   6 has always enjoyed   7 has met
8 has been   9 has visited   10 asked
11 didn't apply   12 saw

Skills

1 What are you good at?

2 Do you have any special skills?

3 What did you learn from your last job?

4 What didn't you like about your last job?

5 What do you do in your free time?

6 What are your main interests?

7 What do you want to do in the future?

8 Where do you want to be in 10 years' time?

Writing

Suggested answers

1 People say that I am good at organising things.

2 My main strengths are writing and public speaking.

3 I learned to be efficient with my time.

4 Well, I had a problem with working too much overtime.

5 I really enjoy playing golf.

6 I spend a lot of time reading novels.

7 My main aim is to be successful and happy in my work.

8 I'd like to be working abroad in international marketing.

Cultures 4: Team working

A 1 like 2 natural and comfortable 3 before
   4 team work 5 good 6 isn't 7 often
   8 can often be 9 don't work 10 need to

B 1 Portugal 2 Malaysia 3 Indonesia

Text bank

TEACHER'S NOTES

Introduction

The Text bank contains articles relating to the units in the Course Book. These articles extend and develop the themes in those units. You can choose the articles that are of most interest to your students. They can be done in class or as homework. You have permission to make photocopies of these articles for your students.

Before you read

Before each article, there is an exercise to use as a warmer that allows students to focus on the vocabulary of the article and prepares them for it. This can be done in pairs or small groups, with each group then reporting its answers to the whole class.

Reading

If using the articles in class, it is a good idea to treat different sections in different ways, for example reading the first paragraph with the whole class, then getting students to work in pairs on the following paragraphs. If you are short of time, get different pairs to read different sections of the article simultaneously. You can circulate, monitor and give help where necessary. Students then report back to the whole group with a succinct summary and/or their answers to the questions for that section. A full answer key follows the articles.

Discussion

In the *Over to you* sections following each article, there are discussion points. These can be dealt with by the whole class, or the class can be divided, with different groups discussing different points. During discussion, circulate, monitor and give help where necessary. Students then report back to the whole class. Praise good language production and work on areas for improvement in the usual way.

Writing

The dicussion points can also form the basis for short pieces of written work. Students will find this easier if they have already discussed the points in class, but you can ask students to read the article and write about the discussion points as homework.

A NEW BUSINESS

Before you read

1 Answer these questions.

   a) What is the first thing you do when you go to work or college?

   b) What do you do at lunchtime?

2 Match the words (1–4) to the correct definitions (a–d).

   1 online — a) someone who works for the same company
   2 full-time — b) on the Internet
   3 web designer   c) working eight hours a day, five days a week
   4 colleague   d) someone who designs websites as a job

Reading

Read this article adapted from the *Financial Times* and answer the questions on the next page.

LEVEL OF DIFFICULTY ● ● ○

TEXT BANK

Business diary: Paul Trible, Paul Watson

as told to Vanessa Friedman

Paul Trible and Paul Watson are founders of Ledbury, a company that makes luxury shirts. Their company is in Richmond, USA.

5 The first thing they do every day when they get to work is check customer e-mails. They do about 95 per cent of their business online, selling about 4,500 shirts 10 a month. They sell 5 per cent of their shirts in the store in Richmond, Virginia.

The company has two full-time employees. They don't have 15 official meetings. They talk to each other. At lunchtime, they go to the shop to talk to customers.

They spend 25 per cent of the day on the phone with their web 20 designer. The website takes a lot of time and money.

To raise money ($300,000) to start the business, they asked 20 friends from their business school 25 to invest money. The friends also wear the shirts and introduce their colleagues to the company. For example, an investor who works in a large insurance company in 30 Houston wore their shirts, and in the past four months they got about 12 more customers from there.

1   **Match the questions (1–6) to the correct answers (a–f).**

1   What does the company make?   a)   check e-mails
2   Where is the company?   b)   their colleagues
3   What is the first thing Paul Trible and   c)   shirts
    Paul Watson do every day?
                                          d)   Richmond, USA
4   What do they do at lunchtime?   e)   talk to customers
5   How do they talk to their web designer? f)   on the phone
6   Who do friends introduce to the company?

2   **Complete these sentences about the article using *is, isn't, are* or *aren't*.**

a)   Paul Trible and Paul Watson *are* the founders of the company.
b)   Ledbury .... based in the USA.
c)   There .... 20 employees, there are two employees.
d)   Most of their customers .... online.
e)   There .... a meeting every day.

Over to you

Talk about a company that you know. Say:

- what it is called
- where it is based
- what it sells or makes
- who the founder or chief executive is
- how many employees there are.

THIS IS MY JOB

Before you read

1 Answer these questions about yourself.

a) What time does your day start?

b) Do you work best in the morning or in the afternoon? Why?

2 Use a dictionary to match the words (1–4) to the correct definitions (a–d).

1 administration   a) being alone or away from other people

2 solitude   b) things that interest you very much

3 maximising   c) making something as strong as possible

4 passions   d) doing paperwork and other things in the office

Reading

Read this article adapted from the *Financial Times* and answer the questions on the next page.

FT

LEVEL OF DIFFICULTY ● ● ○

Business diary: Johan Roets

as told to Jude Webber

Johan Roets is Head of Personal and Business Banking for the Americas at Standard Bank. He is based in Buenos Aires.

5   Johan says, "I don't really have a typical day. Sometimes I have a conference call with the executive committee at 3 a.m. – there is a five-hour time difference with 10 our head office in Johannesburg.

Usually, the Argentine day doesn't start until 10 a.m. or 11 a.m. I do my best thinking in the morning and my best 15 administration in the afternoon.

"I go to South Africa every couple of months. What I love about travel is the solitude to think and read. I don't 20 like meetings – they can be incredibly unproductive – and I try to avoid them. I sit on two boards and typically have six or eight meetings a week.

25   "The way I pay attention to things is to write them down. I buy notebooks and take them everywhere. I write whenever I can during the day, and I go 30 back and highlight important bits.

"I think the great secret in life – and business – is to focus on maximising your strengths, not improving your weaknesses. My 35 passions are business, technology and people."

1   **Decide whether these sentences about Johan Roets are true (T) or false (F).**

   a)   He works in a bank.   T

   b)   He is usually based in Argentina.

   c)   Every day is the same for Johan.

   d)   He often gets up late to make business calls.

   e)   He regularly travels to South Africa.

   f)   He has more than five meetings every week.

   g)   He never uses notebooks.

   h)   He has three main interests.

2   **Complete the sentences below using the words in the box.**

afternoon   five   six   ten   ~~three~~   two

   a)   Johan sometimes has a conference call at *three* o'clock in the morning.

   b)   There is a ....-hour time difference between Argentina and South Africa.

   c)   In Argentina, the working day usually starts at .... in the morning.

   d)   In the ...., he works on administration.

   e)   He usually goes to South Africa every .... months.

   f)   Johan usually has .... or eight meetings each week.

3 **Put these words in the correct order to make questions.**

   a)   get up? / What / time / you / do
        What time do you get up?

   b)   start / When / you / do / work?

   c)   meetings / have? / do you / How many

   d)   use / you / a notebook? / Do

   e)   to travel? / you / Do / like

Over to you

Discuss in pairs or small groups.

- Do you have a typical day?
- What are your interests?
- What do you like or dislike about travel?

TEXT BANK

A WORK PROBLEM

Before you read

1 How important are these things in a new job? Number them 1–5 (1 = very important, 5 = not important).

high salary

friendly colleagues

good job title

interesting projects

helpful manager

2 Use a dictionary to match the words (1–5) to their meanings (a–e).

1 disappointment   a) doing something in a hurry

2 colleagues   b) allow somebody to join or be part of something

3 hasty   c) giving someone a more important job in a company

4 promotion   d) feeling sad, because something is not as good as expected

5 accept   e) people who work for the same organisation

Reading

Read this article adapted from the *Financial Times* and answer the questions on the next page.

FT   LEVEL OF DIFFICULTY ● ● ○

Should I stay or should I go?

by Lucy Kellaway

The problem

"My new job is a great disappointment. My department is badly run, top management
5 don't seem to care, and my new colleagues are not very friendly. Now I hear that my old boss wants me back. I want to see if he is serious, but that might seem
10 like I am desperate to return to my old job. Besides, I don't want to be too hasty. I have worked in my new job for six months. After all, it takes time to be accepted into a
15 successful team."

Senior manager, male, mid-50s

The solution

Going back to an old employer is never a bad idea. You know
20 exactly what it is like to work for your old boss. You know that working there is comfortable, and sometimes comfort is a good thing.

25 You say your old boss is anxious to rehire you, but don't approach him yet. Wait and let him come to you. Try to negotiate a return with a lot more money and a
30 promotion.

But remember you've only been away for six months. I'm not sure that this is long enough to make a decision about the
35 new place.

Some organisations don't like outsiders; it takes a while before they accept them, and until then, they are pretty unfriendly.
40 Spend time working hard at your new job and be friendly. Then, if you decide to go back to your old job, you know that you tried.

1 What three things does the writer not like about his new job?

2 Decide whether these sentences are true (T) or false (F).

a) The person with the problem is a young woman. *F*

b) The writer is happy in his new job.

c) The writer's old boss wants him to return to his old job.

d) Lucy says that it is a good idea to make a decision immediately.

e) Trying to get a better salary for your old job is a good idea.

f) Six months is too soon to make a decision about the new job.

g) Lucy suggests it is a good idea to work hard and be friendly in the new job.

3 Complete the sentences below using the words in the box.

department   ~~negotiate~~   promotion   team

a) These products are expensive. Can we *negotiate* a better price?

b) Would they like to work on a new project, as part of an international
.... ?

c) Does she work in the Sales and Marketing .... ?

e) Do you want to stay in your present job, or do you want a .... ?

Over to you

1 Do you agree with Lucy's advice? Why? / Why not?

2 Choose the options in italics to make sentences that you agree with.

a) I think it's a good idea for him to *stay in /leave* his new job.

b) It *is /isn't* a good idea to return to his old job.

c) Six months *is /isn't* enough time to decide that a job is good or bad.

BUSINESS TRAVELLER

TEXT BANK

Before you read

1 Answer these questions.

Do you prefer to visit a city that has:

a) old buildings or new buildings?

b) good restaurants or interesting museums?

c) large, international hotels or small, independent places to stay?

2 Use a dictionary to match the words (1–6) to their meanings (a–f).

1 sightseeing   a) a market where you can buy lots of different products

2 schedule   b) something people have done for a long time and continue to do

3 unique   c) visiting famous or interesting places as a tourist

4 view   d) what you can see from a window

5 bazaar   e) something special, because there are no other things like it

6 tradition   f) a list of things to do at certain times of the day

Reading

Read this article adapted from the *Financial Times* and answer the questions on the next page.

FT

LEVEL OF DIFFICULTY ● ● ○

Istanbul guide: from the bazaar to the Bosphorus

by Andrew Finkel

1 *Where to stay*

If you are in Istanbul for sightseeing, then you could stay in Sultanahmet or find a small hotel away from the tourist areas.

However, this may not be the best option for the business traveller with a morning appointment on the far side of town. Traffic and distance can be a problem for those on a busy schedule. The challenge is to get the work done, but also find time to discover what makes Istanbul unique.

Many of the city's five-star hotels enjoy a view where you can see lights on the Bosphorus and passing ships.

2 ....

A visit to the grand bazaar can feel exotic. An afternoon at Hagia Sophia, once a Byzantine church, then a mosque and now a museum, is recommended. But some of the best sightseeing in Istanbul is done with a knife and fork.

3 ....

There are a large number of restaurants along the river. A Bosphorus meal is a great Istanbul tradition. A meal can include a cold *meze*, then a hot *hors d'œuvre*, followed by a perfectly cooked piece of fresh fish.

4 ....

Try to arrange your flights to avoid the rush hour, which in the evening can last until 9 p.m.

There is a metro line that takes 40 minutes from the European airport. But the last stop is not in the most convenient part of the old city, and the chances are that you will have to continue your journey by taxi.

Cabs from the airport are strictly controlled. All cabs in the city run on a meter and are reasonably priced. If you can reach your destination by ferry, it is the best way to see the city, and the boats run on time.

1 Match these headings (a–d) to the parts of the text (1–4).

a) How to travel around the city

b) What to see

c) Where to eat

d) Where to stay   *1*

2 Find these things in the article.

a) two religious buildings: c *h u r c h* , m *o s q u e*

b) two things you use to eat food: k _ _ _ _ , f _ _ _

c) two words for a car that you pay to take you somewhere: t _ _ _ , c _ _

d) two words for transport on water: f _ _ _ _ , b _ _ _

3 Decide whether these statements are true (T) or false (F).

a) Istanbul only has large hotels. *F*

b) The traffic in the city is bad sometimes.

c) Some of the expensive hotels have views of the river.

d) There are no restaurants near the river.

e) It's possible to take the metro to the airport.

f) Taxis in Istanbul are very expensive.

g) Travelling on the river is a good way to see Istanbul.

Over to you

Complete these sentences about your town or a town that you know.

• A good place to stay is .... It has a view of ....

• The best place to eat is .... You should try the ....

• An interesting place to visit is .... The best time to go is ....

• A good way to travel around is by .... or ....

TEXT BANK

FAST FOOD

Before you read

Answer these questions.

a) What is the most important meal of the day in your country?

b) Can you name three examples of fast food?

c) What dishes can you think of from these countries?
- China • the USA • India

Reading

Read this article adapted from the *Financial Times* and answer the questions on the next page.

FT

LEVEL OF DIFFICULTY ● ● ○

Yum plans to be the McDonald's of China

by Alan Rappeport

Yum! Brands, the operator of KFC, Pizza Hut and Taco Bell, plans to become the McDonald's of China. It is opening many fast-food restaurants over the next decade.

Its chief executive, David Novak, says that Yum plans to more than double its restaurants in China by 2020. It hopes to have 9,000 across the country in the best locations.

Yum is likely to earn about $900m in net income from its China business this year. It plans to build small restaurants in rail stations and airports.

It is already the leading international restaurant company in China, which is Yum's most successful market. But the company is trying to copy that success in India and other parts of Asia with more local dishes, extended hours and breakfast.

In two years, it expects to own 70 per cent of its restaurants in emerging markets and just 30 per cent in developed markets.

Currently, it owns 53 per cent of its restaurants in emerging market and 47 per cent in developed markets.

Executives call the brand's performance in the USA "disappointing" and "terrible". "It's been a big challenge in the US," Mr Novak said.

1 **Decide whether these sentences are true (T) or false (F).**

   a) Yum wants to sell KFC and Taco Bell. *F*

   b) In the next 10 years, Yum plans to increase its number of restaurants in China.

   c) It wants to build large restaurants in city centres.

   d) India is currently the company's most successful market.

   e) In Asia, Yum plans to increase the opening hours of its restaurants.

   f) The company's sales in the USA are very successful.

2 **Complete the sentences below using the figures in the box.**

2020   9,000 $900 million   53%   47%

   a) Yum wants to have *9,000* new restaurants in good locations.

   b) At the moment, ... of its restaurants are in emerging markets.

   c) By ...., it plans to double the number of restaurants.

   d) The amount of restaurants in developed markets is currently ....

   e) It is likely to earn .... from China this year.

3 **Complete the sentences below using the words in the box.**

decade   developed   dishes   double   earn   ~~emerging~~   executives

   a) Brazil, Russia, India and China are examples of *emerging* markets.

   b) In the next ...., we plan to open 12 more restaurants in Asia.

   c) How much does a chef ....?

   d) There are some interesting .... on the menu.

   e) We invest money in the tourist industry in traditional .... markets.

   f) Next week, there is a meeting for all the company ....

   g) The price of food is .... what it was in the past.

Over to you

Discuss in pairs or small groups.

- Do you think more fast-food restaurants are a good idea? Why? / Why not?
- What type of restaurant would you go to for these occasions?
   - an important business lunch
   - dinner with a friend
   - a family celebration

TEXT BANK

BUYING LUXURY BRANDS

Before you read

Answer these questions.

a) Think of the names of two luxury brands.

b) What are their products?

Reading

Read this article adapted from the *Financial Times* and answer the questions on the next page.

FT

LEVEL OF DIFFICULTY ● ● ○

Luxury brands and wealthy Chinese tourists

by Barney Jopson in New York

Ms Li is on a trip to New York. She is travelling with Affinity China, a luxury club that organises tours of New York.

5 But this isn't a business trip or a holiday. Ms Li and more than 80 other wealthy Chinese tourists are here to learn about luxury brands. Many Chinese consumers come 10 to the US and Europe to buy luxury goods. Prices are up to 50% lower than the price of some luxury goods at home.

Companies organise events to 15 show their products to Ms Li and the others in her group. Bergdorf Goodman, a department store, puts on a fashion show in their honour. "I liked it a lot. It was 20 my first fashion show," said Ms Li. She is the kind of person that luxury retailers want to meet. She is the co-founder of a recruitment agency in Shanghai.

25 Another luxury company that organises an event for the group is Mont Blanc, the pen maker. It puts a piano in the store and Lang Lang, the Chinese pianist, plays 30 for the group. Estée Lauder, the cosmetics brand, gives people in the Affinity China group samples of an expensive new eye cream.

Chinese travellers took 70 35 million overseas trips in 2011 and spent a total of $69bn, an increase of 25 per cent from the previous year. Coach, the handbag brand, says that 40 sometimes 15–20 per cent of its sales in New York, Las Vegas and Hawaii are from Chinese tourists.

1 **Decide whether these sentences are true (T) or false (F).**

a) Ms Li works for Affinity China. *F*

b) She is in New York on a business trip.

c) Some luxury products cost less in the US and Europe than in China.

d) Ms Li has been to a lot of fashion shows.

e) Mont Blanc is a company that makes pianos.

f) Chinese travellers spent 25% more in 2011 than in 2010.

g) Coach is a company that sells trips to Hawaii.

2 **Complete the sentences below using the words in the box.**

brand	~~fashion~~ goods price retailers sample

a) The designers have a *fashion* show every year, to show buyers their new clothing range.

b) What .... of perfume would you like to buy?

c) Could you tell me the .... of this jacket, please?

d) Try a free .... of our new chocolate before you buy.

e) Some customers buy luxury .... on the Internet.

f) They sell the magazine at supermarkets, newsagents and other ....

Over to you

Discuss in pairs or small groups.

- Why do you think the companies in the article organise such events?
- Would you like to go to any of the events? Why? / Why not?

TEXT BANK

A FAMILY BUSINESS

Before you read

Answer this question.

Is it a good idea for family members to work together? Why? / Why not?

Reading

Read this article adapted from the *Financial Times* and answer the questions on the next page.

FT

LEVEL OF DIFFICULTY ● ● ●

TEXT BANK

The next generation of a business empire

by Rachel Sanderson

Alessandro Benetton became the Executive Vice-Chairman of the Italian clothing company Benetton in 2007. He is the second son of Luciano Benetton, the founder of the business empire which now operates in 120 countries.

His wife is Deborah Compagnoni, three-time Olympic gold medallist and one of Italy's greatest ski champions. They have three children.

Alessandro Benetton is a graduate of Harvard Business School. He enjoys dangerous sports, which he describes as "the fun of life".

The company began in Ponzabno, Veneto, in Italy and today is the town's largest employer. It also funds schools, culture events and spectacular sports facilities.

Mr Benetton speaks quietly and is relaxed. He has three brothers. Before he joined the family clothing business, he was an entrepreneur. Following Harvard, where he studied with management guru Michael Porter, he spent a year working as an analyst at Goldman Sachs.

In 1992, Mr Benetton founded a private equity business called 21 Investimenti. He was chairman of Benetton's Formula One team for a decade. The team won two world drivers' championships with Michael Schumacher at the wheel.

1 Complete Alessandro Benetton's CV using the words in the box.

analyst   chairman   founded   ~~Harvard~~   married   sports   three

Alessandro Benetton: CV

Education: BSc in economics, Boston University; MBA, **a)** *Harvard* Business School

Career:

1988–89: b) .... in global finance department at Goldman Sachs

1989–98: c) .... of Benetton Formula One team

1992: d) .... private equity firm 21 Investimenti

1998: appointed to the board of Benetton, as well as family investment businesses Edizione and Autogrill 2007: became Executive Vice-Chairman, Benetton

2012: became Chairman, Benetton

Family: e) .... to Deborah Compagni, three-time Olympic gold medallist for Alpine skiing; **f)** .... children

Personal interests: dangerous **g)** ....

2 Decide whether these sentences are true (T) or false (F). Correct the false ones.

a) Alessandro Benetton founded a company called Benetton.

 F (Alessandro Benetton didn't found the company. His father, Luciano Benetton, founded the company.)

b) Benetton is in 12 countries.

c) His wife is a ski champion.

d) They have five children.

e) Alessandro Benetton likes dangerous sports.

f) Benetton began in India.

g) The company gives money to schools, culture and sports events.

h) Alessandro has two brothers.

i) He was chairman of the Formula One team for 15 years.

Over to you

1 Discuss in pairs or small groups.

Is it a good idea for people in a family business to get experience working outside the company?

2 Find out information about another family business and write a short description of it.

ADVERTISING ON THE INTERNET

Before you read

1 Answer this question.

Which of these places do you think is best to advertise a new film? Why?

• newspapers • magazines • radio • TV • cinemas • the Internet

2 Match the words (1–7) to the correct definitions (a–g).

1	annual	a)	all of something
2	the Web	b)	successful
3	social media	c)	when people know the name of your product or company
4	brand awareness	d)	happening once a year
5	hit	e)	Internet communication such as Facebook or Twitter
6	entire	f)	advertisement
7	ad	g)	the Internet

Reading

Read this article adapted from the *Financial Times* and answer the questions on the next page.

FT

LEVEL OF DIFFICULTY ● ● ○

Social media sites are a hit for ads

by David Gelles

The Super Bowl is the biggest annual advertising event in the world. It is an American football championship game that is played
5 every year and it is watched on television by millions of Americans. This year, 30-second advertising slots cost as much as $3.5m.
10   Many companies are using the Web and social media to make the most out of their big moment. Some companies released their ad online. Others
15 showed a teaser, a short extract from the advertisement. Some showed a longer version of the advertisement online. Many companies are using Twitter and
20 Facebook.

The campaigns are mainly designed to build brand awareness. Last year, Volkswagen in the US had the hit commercial
25 of the Super Bowl with its Star Wars-themed advertisement. This year, it released a teaser advertisement featuring a chorus of dogs dressed as Star Wars
30 characters. Then Volkswagen pre-released its entire ad. "At more than $3m for 30 seconds, it makes sense to get the most for your dollar," says Mr Mahoney, Chief
35 Product and Marketing Officer for Volkswagen in the US.

1 Decide whether these sentences are true (T) or false (F).

a) The advertisements last 30 seconds. T

b) A lot of companies use the Internet to show their advertisements.

c) Not many companies use Facebook or Twitter.

d) Last year, Volkswagen's Super Bowl commercial was not popular.

e) Volkswagen showed a short extract from its advertisement before showing the whole ad.

f) Mr Mahoney works for Honda.

2 Use these prompts to make questions. Then answer the questions.

a) What / the Super Bowl? *What is the Super Bowl? – an American football championship game*

b) How much / cost / advertise during the Super Bowl?

c) How long / the advertising slots?

d) What animals / in the Volkswagen advertisement?

Over to you

Discuss in pairs or small groups.

- Think of a popular sporting event. What types of company advertise at it?
- Do you look at advertisements on the Internet? Do you find them useful or annoying?

TEXT BANK

A JOINT VENTURE

Before you read

1 Answer these questions.

   a) What hot drinks do you like during the day?

   b) Where do you usually buy them?

2 Choose the correct option in italics to make true sentences. Use a dictionary if necessary.

   a) When two different companies work together, it is a *joint* /*double* venture.

   b) Another word for a drink is a *beverage* /*dish*.

   c) A shop that sells products from one manufacturer is *a studio* /*an outlet*.

   d) The money that a business earns from sales is its *salary* /*revenue*.

   e) The groups of customers or countries that you sell to are your *market* /*store*.

   f) A *catering* /*production* company provides food and drink for people at social or business events.

Reading

Read this article adapted from the *Financial Times* and answer the questions on the next page.

FT

LEVEL OF DIFFICULTY ● ● ○

Starbucks plans $80m Indian joint venture

by James Crabtree in Mumbai, James Fontanella-Khan in New Delhi and Barney Jopson in New York

Starbucks is bringing coffee shops to one of the world's greatest tea-loving nations. It plans an $80m Indian joint venture with Tata
5 Global Beverages.

   The first outlet will open in Mumbai or Delhi by September. Starbucks already has 544 stores in China. By the end of the year,
10 it could have as many as 50 stores in India.

Starbucks has more than 12,000 stores in North America. The Americas region – including a
15 few hundred stores in Canada and Latin America – accounts for three-quarters of its revenue.

   John Culver, President of Starbucks China and Asia Pacific,
20 said: "We think India can be one of our largest markets outside the US." The company has more than 17,000 stores in 55 countries.

The Indian venture is also likely
25 to see Starbucks products sold through other parts of the wider Tata group. The Tata group is one of India's most famous companies. It includes Taj Hotels
30 and TajSATS, an airline catering business.

1 Match the numbers (1–6) to the information they refer to (a–f).

1 $80m
2 544
3 50
4 12,000
5 17,000
6 55

a) Starbucks stores in North America
b) number of countries Starbucks has stores in
c) Starbucks stores in China
d) cost of the joint venture between Starbucks and Tata
e) planned stores in India by end of year
f) number of Starbucks stores worldwide

2 Choose the correct word (a–c) to make true sentences.

1 Starbucks hopes to open its first Indian store .... September.
   a) by   b) at   c) on

2 Starbucks .... has stores in China.
   a) usually   b) already   c) always

3 By the .... of the year, it could have 50 stores in India.
   a) beginning   b) end   c) after

4 The company has .... than 17,000 outlets around the world.
   a) only   b) less   c) more

Over to you

Discuss in pairs or small groups.

- Do you know any other companies that have worked together in a joint venture?
- Do you think it is a good idea for different companies to work together?

E-MAIL AND OVERTIME

Before you read

1 Answer this question.

Should employees get paid extra money to do these things? Why? / Why not?

- work weekends
- take documents home to read in the evening
- stay late to finish a project
- make phone calls to clients on the journey to or from work

2 Match the words (1–7) with their meanings (a–g). Use a dictionary if necessary.

1	after-hours	a)	stop something happening
2	overtime payment	b)	employing people
3	hiring	c)	money for additional time worked
4	productivity	d)	after a business usually closes
5	deadline	e)	someone who finds it impossible to stop working
6	workaholic	f)	how much work is completed in a fixed amount of time
7	prevent	g)	the time by which a task needs to be completed

Reading

Read this article adapted from the *Financial Times* and answer the questions on the next page.

FT

LEVEL OF DIFFICULTY ● ● ●

E-mail after hours? That's overtime

by Joe Leahy

Brazil has a new law introducing overtime payments for after-hours office e-mails and telephone calls. Workers approve, but businesses are angry. The cost of hiring people is already expensive. Some people think that it will be difficult to carry out the law.

Claudia Sakuraba, owner of Carnaval Store, a costume shop in São Paulo with four employees, says: "What about when you send an e-mail and because of problems with the Internet providers in Brazil, it doesn't arrive straight away? Or you send a text message early in the morning and for some reason, they don't get it until the evening? It's not clear how this is all going to work."

But what if this law actually improves productivity? Everyone knows that it is possible to waste time. A deadline can help people to work more efficiently.

Some people say that in São Paulo, the main things to do are to work, eat and spend the weekend in shopping centres.

Many employers and employees spend hours answering e-mail or working on the phone. Workaholics spend time sending and receiving office-related emails. Probably half of these are not really necessary.

Brazil's law encourages employers to prevent people working after hours when it is not necessary. If a company wants them to be available 24/7, it must pay them.

1 **Decide whether these sentences are true (T) or false (F).**

   a) Brazil has a law where workers must pay employers money to use e-mail. *F*

   b) It is expensive to employ people in Brazil.

   c) E-mail and texts always arrive immediately.

   d) There are shopping centres in São Paulo.

   e) All the e-mails that people send and receive are necessary.

   f) If employers want workers to be available all day, they need to pay them.

2 **Complete the sentences below using the words in the box.**

cost̶	half	laws	message	time	weekend

   a) How much does it *cost* to send a text?

   b) Different countries have different .... about how long employees can work each day.

   c) We can't have the meeting today, because .... the team is ill.

   d) What are you doing at the ....?

   e) He doesn't like to waste .... playing computer games.

   f) I'll send you a text .... when I arrive at the station.

Over to you

Discuss in pairs or small groups.

Is it a good idea to pay people overtime for sending and receiving texts and e-mails after work hours? Think of the advantages and disadvantages for
a) employees b) employers.

AVOID MISUNDERSTANDINGS

Before you read

Answer these questions.

a) Which things should you research about a country before you visit?

b) When you meet someone for the first time, do you do any of these things?

- bow • shake hands • exchange business cards • kiss

Reading

Read this article adapted from the *Financial Times* and answer the questions on the next page.

FT

LEVEL OF DIFFICULTY ● ● ○

Getting it right: doing business abroad

by Natasha Stidder

Good etiquette is important when you do business abroad. It is essential to research local customs, to avoid misunderstandings. Here
5 are some examples:

Japan
- Smiles can express joy or displeasure.
- Give gifts with both hands and
10 do not give gifts in odd numbers (bad luck).

China
- Exchange business cards using both hands.
15 - The following gifts should be avoided: clocks, umbrellas, white flowers and handkerchiefs – these signify tears or death.

India
20 - Business cards should be given and received with the right hand.
- Avoid wrapping gifts in black or white – these are believed to
25 bring bad luck.

Middle East
- Handshakes can last a long time. Do not be surprised if your host leads you by the
30 hand.
- Do not be surprised if people interrupt meetings with phone calls or walk in unexpectedly.

US
35 - Expect people to multi-task in meetings, for example checking and sending e-mails.
- In meetings, it is not unusual for people to
40 disagree – sometimes loudly.

1 Which countries do these statements refer to?

a) It's impolite to give a business card with your left hand. India

b) A smile can show that someone is pleased or not pleased.

c) Handshakes are not quick.

d) Don't give your host a gift of white flowers.

e) People may express their opinion in a loud way.

2 Complete the questions with words from the article. Then answer the questions.

a) Is good e t i q u e t t e important when you meet new business contacts?

b) How often do you go a _ _ _ _ d on business or on holiday?

c) What is a good g _ _ t to give your host when you visit?

d) Do you usually e _ _ _ _ _ _ e business cards at the start or end of a meeting?

e) What numbers or colours are good l _ _k in your country?

f) Would you i _ _ _ _ _ _ _ t a meeting to talk on your phone?

g) Is it a good idea to m _ _ _i – t _ _ k, or is it better to do one thing at a time?

h) When you d _ _ _ _ _ e with someone's opinion, do you tell them?

Over to you

Prepare notes for a short talk about local customs, using the topics below. You can talk about your own country or another country that you know.

- What to do when you meet someone for the first time
- Giving and receiving business cards
- Giving gifts
- What not to do in meetings

MORE PEOPLE BECOME SELF-EMPLOYED

Before you read

1 Answer these questions.

a) Is it easier or more difficult to get a job now than in the past?

b) Would you like to work for yourself?

2 Choose the best options in italics to make true sentences.

a) You don't work for an employer when you are *an employee /* (*self-employed.*)

b) When you work for some of the day or week, you work *full-time /part-time*.

c) Someone who doesn't have a job is *unemployed /hired*.

d) People who work for pay are in *employment /retirement*.

e) Something that is increasing is *falling /rising*.

f) A skilled worker, for example an electrician or plumber, is a *tradesperson /trader*.

g) A time that is bad for the economy and business is called a *recession /boom*.

h) A formal way to ask about jobs is 'What is your *occupy /occupation*?'

Reading

Read this article adapted from the *Financial Times* and answer the questions on the next page.

FT

LEVEL OF DIFFICULTY ● ● ○

Large growth in self-employment

by Brian Groom

There has been an increase in self-employment. It isn't because people want to become entrepreneurs. Instead, it is the result of people doing part-time odd jobs to avoid unemployment.

In the UK, the number of self-employed people has risen by 300,000 since spring 2008 to 4.14 million – the highest since records began in 1992. This represents 14.2 per cent of all employment. Over the same period, the number of employees in work has fallen by 700,000.

But the new self-employed are likely to take a job with an employer if they could find one. Most economists expect unemployment to carry on rising over the coming months.

Usually self-employed people are skilled tradespeople, managers or professionals working long hours in their job. But since the recession, the number of self-employed has increased. These people are from a wider range of backgrounds and occupations, including many 'handymen' without skills. They do whatever work is available.

As a general group, two-thirds of self-employed people work more than 30 hours a week. However, things are different for people who have become self-employed since 2008, where almost nine in 10 work fewer than 30 hours. In addition, around a quarter of self-employed people work in construction.

1 Decide whether these sentences are true (T) or false (F).

a) More people are becoming self-employed because they want to be entrepreneurs. *F*

b) People are choosing self-employed jobs because they don't want to be without a job.

c) There has been an increase in self-employed workers since 2008.

d) Most new self-employed workers don't want to work for an employer.

e) Experts think that unemployment will fall in the next few months.

f) Some of the new self-employed aren't skilled workers.

g) Most of the new self-employed work more than 30 hours a week.

h) Nearly 25% of self-employed people work in the building trade.

2 Complete this table with verbs used in the article.

Infinitive	Past simple	Past participle
want	a) *wanted*	wanted
fall	fell	b)
c)	was/were	been
rise	rose	d)
e)	increased	increased
work	f)	worked

3 Complete these sentences with the past simple or the present perfect form of the verb in brackets.

a) The number of skilled workers *has increased* (*increase*) by 15%.

b) He .... (*work*) here since last July.

c) Unemployment............... (*fall*) last month.

d) When she was at university, she .... (*want*) to be a lawyer.

e) They .... (*not go*) to Dubai before.

f) The number of jobs in IT .... (*rise*) by 5% since 2010.

g) I .... (*take*) the documents to the accountant yesterday afternoon.

Over to you

Discuss in pairs or small groups.

- What are your ideal working hours?

- Which of these jobs are suitable for self-employment?

  scientist   police officer   accountant   designer   teacher   firefighter
  secretary   dentist   carpenter   banker   sales assistant   waiter
  doctor   writer

TEXT BANK KEY

Unit 1

Before you read 2

2 c   3 d   4 a

1 2 d   3 a   4 e   5 f   6 b

2 b) is   c) aren't   d) are   e) isn't

Unit 2

Before you read 2

2 a   3 c   4 b

1 b) T   c) F   d) F   e) T   f) T   g) F   h) T

2 b) five   c) ten   d) afternoon   e) two   f) six

3 b) When do you start work?

c) How many meetings do you have?

d) Do you use a notebook?

e) Do you like to travel?

Unit 3

Before you read 2

2 e   3 a   4 c   5 b

1 The department is badly run; management don't care; colleagues are not friendly.

2 b) F   c) T   d) F   e) T   f) T   g) T

3 b) team   c) department   d) promotion

Unit 4

Before you read 2

2 f   3 e   4 d   5 a   6 b

1 2 b   3 c   4 a

2 b) knife, fork   c) taxi, cab   d) ferry, boat

3 b) T   c) T   d) F   e) T   f) F   g) T

Unit 5

1 b) T   c) F   d) F   e) T   f) F

2 b) 53%   c) 2020   d) 47%   e) $900 million

3 b) decade   c) earn   d) dishes   e) developed
f) executives   g) double

Unit 6

1 b) F   c) T   d) F   e) F   f) T   g) F

2 b) brand   c) price   d) sample   e) goods
f) retailers

Unit 7

1 b) analyst   c) chairman   d) founded   e) married
f) three   g) sports

2 b) F (Benetton isn't in 12 countries. It is in 120 countries.)

c) T

d) F (They don't have five children. They have three children.)

e) T

f) F (Benetton didn't begin in India. It began in Italy.)

g) T

h) F (He doesn't have two brothers. He has three brothers.)

i) F (He wasn't chairman of the Formula One team for 15 years. He was chairman of the team for 10 years.)

Unit 8

Before you read 2

2 g   3 e   4 c   5 b   6 a   7 f

1 b) T   c) F   d) F   e) T   f) F

2 b) How much does it cost to advertise during the Super Bowl? ($3.5 *million for a* 30-*second commercial*)

c) How long are the advertising slots? (*30 seconds*)

d) What animals are in the Volkswagen advertisement? (*dogs*)

Unit 9

Before you read 2

b) beverage   c) an outlet   d) revenue   e) market
f) catering

1 2 c   3 e   4 a   5 f   6 b

2 2 b   3 b   4 c

Unit 10

Before you read 2

2 c   3 b   4 f   5 g   6 e   7 a

1 b) T   c) F   d) T   e) F   f) T

2 b) laws   c) half   d) weekend   e) time
f) message

Unit 11

1 b) Japan   c) Middle East   d) China   e) US

2 b) abroad   c) gift   d) exchange   e) luck
f) interrupt   g) multi-task   h) disagree

Unit 12

Before you read 2

b) part-time   c) unemployed   d) employment
e) rising   f) tradesperson   g) recession
h) occupation

1 b) T   c) T   d) F   e) F   f) T   g) T   h) T

2 b) fallen   c) be   d) risen   e) increase
f) worked

3 b) has worked   c) fell   d) wanted
e) haven't been   f) has risen   g) took

Resource bank

Introduction

These Resource bank activities are designed to extend and develop the material in the Course Book. The Resource bank contains exercises and activities relating to:

Speaking

Each speaking unit begins with a language exercise that takes up and extends the language points from the Course Book unit, then applies this language in one or more activities. The speaking units are best done in the classroom. You have permission to photocopy the Resource bank pages in this book. In some units, you will give each student a copy of the whole page. In others, there are role cards which need to be cut out and given to participants with particular roles. These activities are indicated in the unit-specific notes that follow.

Listening

Students listen again to the interviews from the Listening sections in the Course Book, and do further activities on comprehension and language development. These activities can be done in the classroom, but they have been designed in a way that makes it easy for students to do them on their own as homework. Make photocopies for the students. Follow up in the next lesson by getting students to talk about any difficulties that they had. You could play the recording again in the classroom to help resolve problems if necessary.

Writing

A model answer is given for the writing task at the end of each case study in the Course Book. There are then two extra writing activities. These can all be done as homework. Again, make photocopies for the students. After correcting the writing exercises in class, go over the key points that have been causing problems.

Resource bank: Speaking

General notes

The language exercise at the beginning of each Speaking unit in the Resource bank can be used to revise language from the main Course Book unit, especially if you did the Skills section in another lesson. In any case, point out the connection with the Course Book Skills material. These language exercises are designed to prepare students for the role plays that follow, and in many cases can be done in a few minutes as a way of focusing students on the activity that will follow.

A typical two-person role play might last five or 10 minutes, followed by five minutes of praise and correction. An animated group discussion might last longer than you planned: in this case, drop one of your other planned activities and do it another time, rather than try to cram it in before the end of the lesson. If you then have five or 10 minutes left over, you can always go over some language points from the lesson again or, better still, get students to say what they were. One way of doing this is to ask them what they've written in their notebooks during the lesson.

Revising and revisiting

Feel free to do an activity more than once. After one run-through, praise strong points, and then work on three or four things that need correcting or improving. Then you can get the students to change roles and do the activity again, or the parts of the activity where these points come up. Obviously, there will come a time when interest wanes, but the usual tendency in language teaching is not to revisit things enough, rather than the reverse.

Fluency and accuracy

Concentrate on different things in different activities. In some role plays and discussions, you may want to focus on fluency, with students interacting as spontaneously as possible. In others, you will want to concentrate on accuracy, with students working on getting specific forms correct. Rather than expect students to get everything correct, you could pick out, say, three or four forms that you want them to get right and focus on these.

Clear instructions

Be sure to give complete instructions before getting students to start. In role plays, be very clear about who has which role, and give students time to absorb the information they need. Sometimes there are role cards that you hand out. The activities where this happens are indicated in the notes that follow.

Parallel and public performances (PPP)

In pair work or small-group situations, get all pairs to do the activity at the same time. Go round the class and listen. When they have finished, praise strong points and deal with three or four problems that you have heard, especially problems that more than one group have been having. Then get individual groups to give public performances so that the whole class can listen. The performers should pay particular attention to these three or four points.

One-to-one

The pair activities can be done one-to-one, with you taking one of the roles. The activity can be done a second time, reversing the roles and getting the student to integrate your suggestions for improvement.

Unit 1 Introductions

 A

- This relates to the language for introductions and asking questions in Unit 1. Get students to do this exercise individually to prepare for the role play.

- Check answers with the class. You could ask students to read the dialogue with a partner.

> 1 What is your name?   2 How do you do.
> 3 Where are you from?   4 Are you Italian?
> 5 What do you do   6 Where are you staying?
> 7 What's your hotel like?   8 Nice talking to you

B

- Divide the class into pairs (A and B).

- Read the instructions with the whole class. Make sure students understand what they have to do.

- Assign roles and tell students to look at the information cards.

- Help with pronunciation if needed.

- Get students to stand up and begin the role play (Conversation 1).

- Circulate and monitor. Note any points for praise and correction. Work on any points that need improving, getting students to say the correct form.

- Get one or two of the pairs to do their role play for the whole class.

- As students finish ask them to change roles and repeat the role play for Conversation 2.

> **One-to-one**
> You take one of the roles in the conversation.

Unit 2 Work and leisure

A

- This exercise allows students to revise the language for talking about work and leisure from Unit 2. They will use similar phrases about themselves to answer the questions in Exercise B.

- Students can do this individually or in pairs.

- Do the example. Do item 2 together to demonstrate (*He isn't keen on concerts.*).

- Circulate and monitor. Note any points for correction and spend some time noting the correct sentences on the board with the whole class. Say the sentences together.

> 2 keen   3 into   4 enjoy   5 doesn't   6 quite
> 7 isn't   8 at   9 always   10 week

B

- Divide the class into pairs. Ask students to write the questions individually.

- Ask students to add two more questions to the list. If they need help, suggest ideas from the box below.

- Circulate and check the answers around the class. Make sure students understand what the questions mean by asking one or two questions to individual students.

- Work on any points that need correction.

- Get students to ask and answer the questions with their partner.

- Ask students to tell the class some things about their partner using the information they have found out.

> 1 Which day are you busy during the week?
>
> 2 What time do you get up?
>
> 3 What do you like about your company or college?
>
> 4 What do you do in your free time?
>
> 5 How often do you travel abroad?
>
> 6 How often do you buy a newspaper?
>
> 7 When do you study English?

Unit 3 Problems

A

- This reminds students of the language used to talk about problems from Unit 3. Do the exercise with the whole class.

- Ask students to suggest other possible responses to use in each situation.

> 1 e   2 a   3 b   4 f   5 c   6 d

B

- There are two telephone role plays. Students can do one or both role plays depending on the time available. The role plays are linked; in the first, Student A asks about products and places an order; in the second, there is a problem with the order.

- Divide the class into pairs. Give a role card to each student.

- Tell students they can use their real names or they can invent names.

- Phrases for starting a telephone call are given on page 27 of the Course Book. Elicit phrases for starting the first telephone call and write them on the board:

  This is Grove Electrical supplies. (How can I help?)

  Hello. I want to buy some photocopiers.

  What model do you want?

  Do you have any model ...?

- Check that Student A knows that they should write down the order number that Student B says.

- Get students to sit back to back to simulate the telephone calls or, if practical, get them to use real telephones.

- Start the first role play. Circulate and monitor.

- Then get students to do the second role play. Elicit phrases for the second call.

- Circulate and help where necessary. Note down any good use of language or areas that might need more work and have a feedback session at the end of the role play.

- Get a few pairs to do their role play for the whole class.

- You could ask students to change roles and do the role play again.

Unit 4 Travel

A

- Exercises A and B allow students to revise some of the language used in Unit 4.

- Start by telling students about a hotel that you know and get them to ask questions about the facilities: *Does it have a restaurant?*, etc.

- Ask students to complete the information about the Globe Hotel and check answers with a partner.

- Check the answers around the class. Spend some time eliciting questions to ask the hotel about the information: *Do you have a single room with a shower?*, etc.

> **1** business **2** shower **3** Double **4** internet
> **5** non **6** park

B

- Ask students to read through the information and prepare questions. If your class needs more support, divide the class into two groups and get Group A and Group B to read the information and prepare questions together.

- Divide the class into A/B pairs. As this is a telephone role play, ask students to sit back to back.

- Elicit phrases that students should use if they do not understand information (*Could you repeat that, please?*, *Could you spell that, please?*). Tell students that they can use an imaginary name and e-mail address when asked.

- Circulate and monitor. Note examples of good language or areas where students need more practice. Share these in a feedback session.

- Get students to change roles and redo the role play, incorporating any points from the feedback session.

Unit 5 Food and entertaining

A

- This revises the functional language from Unit 5. Highlight the example and do question 2 together.

- Ask students to complete the exercise and compare answers with a partner. Check answers around the class. Spend some time on *some, any, much, many* and *a lot of* if necessary.

- Write the name of a restaurant that you know on the board. Get students to ask you questions about the restaurant (location, dishes, parking, cost, etc.).

> **2** a lot of **3** any **4** much **5** a lot of **6** any
> **7** some **8** many

B

- Draw students' attention to the example question. Do the next question together (*Is there any parking?*).

- Divide the class into pairs and ask students to prepare their questions individually. Circulate and help where necessary.

- Ask students to take turns asking and answering the questions. Ask students to complete the information about the restaurants. Check answers with the class.

C

- Divide the class into groups of between four and six.

- Read the information about the task with the class and check students understand.

- Ask students to discuss which restaurant is best for the group.

- Give groups a few minutes to make a decision and ask each one to say why they chose their restaurant.

- To extend the activity, you could ask students to role-play booking a table at the restaurant. They could then write a menu for the restaurant and role-play ordering their meal.

Unit 6 Buying and selling

A

- This revises the functional language from Unit 6.

- Do this as a quick-fire activity with the whole class.

- Get students to suggest questions to ask about the product (*Who is it aimed at? What colours does it come in? What does it weigh? How wide is it? What is the delivery time?*).

- Ask students to work in pairs and take turns to say the product description.

> **2** aimed **3** made **4** weighs **5** wide **6** colours
> **7** design **8** close **9** costs **10** postage
> **11** deliver

B

- Divide the class into pairs. Refer students to the Useful language box on page 58 of the Course Book. Give each student a product information card and form.

- Give students time to read their product description. Circulate, help and encourage.

- Tell students to take it in turns to present their product to their partner. Their partner listens and underlines the correct word or phrase on the product information form.

- Circulate and monitor. Note down language points for praise and correction afterwards, especially in relation to the language for describing a product.

- Bring the class together. Highlight good language points and delivery style. Practise any language points that need improving, getting students to provide the correct forms where possible.

- Ask pairs to check the information on their form with their partner.

- As an extension, you could ask students to use the notes on their partner's talk to write up a full description of the product.

Unit 7 People

A

- This activity revises the functional language from Unit 7.

- Ask students to do the exercise in pairs. Circulate, monitor and assist if necessary.

- Go through the answers with the whole class.

- Ask students to practise the dialogue in pairs.

Lisa: I **really need** an assistant to work on this sales and marketing project.

Ravi: I'm sorry, but the **problem** is that we can't employ any extra staff.

Lisa: It would be really helpful **to/for** me. I can't finish on time on my own.

Ravi: **Why** didn't you tell me that you had a problem with the project?

Lisa: I didn't realise there was so much work. So, can I have **an** assistant?

Ravi: I'm sorry, it's **just not** possible. Why don't you give some of the work to sales?

Lisa: OK, I'll think **about** it.

Ravi: I think you should **speak** to the Sales Manager. I can call him for you.

Lisa: OK, thanks. That's a **good idea.**

B

- Explain the background to the role play. Get two students to read the example.

- Hand out role cards. Give students time to prepare. You could ask all the Project Managers to prepare in one group and all the Project Directors to prepare in another. Circulate and assist if necessary.

- Once they have got the idea, get students to role-play the conversation in pairs.

- Circulate and monitor. Note down language points for praise and correction afterwards, especially in relation to the language of negotiations and dealing with problems.

- Bring the class together. Praise strong language points and work on half a dozen points that need improving, getting students to say the correct forms.

- Get students to change roles and redo the role play, incorporating the correct forms you have suggested.

Unit 8 Advertising

A

- This reminds students of the language used to participate in discussions.

- Get students to do this exercise in pairs, then check the phrases in the Useful language box on page 80 of the Course Book.

> **1** c **2** a **3** b **4** d **5** b **6** a **7** d **8** c

B

- Ask students to name some popular brands of shampoo. Ask: *Where is it sold? How much is it? What is the target market? Does the company advertise the product? Where?*

- Divide the class into small groups. Check that students understand the role play.

- Negotiate with the class how long they need to have the meeting and set a time limit.

- Explain that everyone in the group should contribute ideas. Ask students to suggest phrases for asking for an opinion (*What do you think?, What's your opinion?*).

- When the groups are ready, begin the meeting. Circulate and monitor.

- You could ask students to write up their ideas for homework.

C

- Give groups time to prepare a short presentation to talk about their ideas.

- Ask each group to find another group to work with.

- Groups take it in turns to present their ideas to each other. After each presentation, encourage the group that was listening to give an opinion, ask a question or make a suggestion.

One-to-one

You take part in the discussion. You could also write the names of two other (imaginary) participants on the board. Note two or three ideas in bullet points for each one. This will give the student ideas to agree or disagree with.

Unit 9 Companies

A

- This exercise relates to the language for starting a presentation in Unit 9 and will help students prepare for the role play in Exercise B.

- Do this as a quick-fire activity with the whole class.

- Ask a student to read the class the completed introduction.

- You may wish to refer students to the Useful language box on page 88 of the Course Book and ask them to suggest other phrases to replace those that Nadim uses in his talk.

1 good to see you all   **2** subject of my presentation
3 three sections   **4** Secondly   **5** finally
6 By the end of my talk

B

- Read the instructions with the whole class.

- Divide the class into pairs. Give each student a set of notes and a checklist.

- Give students time to prepare their presentations. Circulate and assist if necessary.

- Ask Student A to introduce their talk and Student B to complete their checklist while they listen to the presentation.

- Then ask Student B to introduce their talk while Student A completes the checklist.

- Circulate and monitor. Note down language points for praise and correction afterwards, especially in relation to presentations.

- Bring the class together. Praise strong language points and work on the main points that need improving, getting students to say the correct forms.

- Ask students to use their checklists to give their partner feedback about the talk.

Unit 10 Communication

A

- This reminds students of the language used to make arrangements from Unit 10.

- Do this as a quick-fire activity with the class.

- Refer students to the Useful language box on page 102 and invite them to suggest alternative phrases where appropriate.

- Ask two students to read the conversation to the class.

- Tell the class that one of the callers discovers that they have a problem with Wednesday at 2.30. Ask students to suggest phrases for a telephone call to apologise and suggest a different time. Write their ideas on the board.

a 6   **b** 5   **c** 2   **d** 4   **e** 1   **f** 7   **g** 3

B

- Explain the situation. Divide the class into pairs and hand out the diaries. Ask students to look at their diary and note what times they are free next week.

- Ask a student to read the example, making sure they insert their name in the gap. Ask students to suggest other phrases to start the call.

- Get students to sit back to back to simulate the telephone calls and begin the role play.

- Circulate and monitor. Note language points for praise and correction afterwards, especially in the language used for telephone calls.

- Praise strong language points and work on a few points that need improving, getting students to say the correct forms.

- Get one or two pairs to do their role play for the whole class, incorporating your corrections.

C

- Explain the second situation and check students understand.

- Ask students to suggest phrases to start the call. Then start the role play.

- Circulate and monitor, and note any language points for praise and correction afterwards.

- Bring the class together and ask students to say the day and time of their new appointment.

- You could then personalise the role play by asking students to use their real diaries and to role-play making an appointment with their partner next week.

One-to-one

You take one of the roles in the telephone role play.

Unit 11 Cultures

- This reminds students of the language used to identify problems and agree action.

- Get students to do this exercise in pairs. Ask students to suggest one more phrase for each heading.

- Check the phrases in the Useful language box on page 110 of the Course Book.

> Opening: 3, 7
>
> Stating the topic: 4, 8
>
> Suggesting action: 1, 6
>
> Responding to suggestions: 2, 5

B

- Divide students into groups of four.

- Read Sam Rowland's e-mail together. Clarify where necessary.

- Read the instructions with the whole class.

- Write the following on the board:

  Write list of problems.

  Suggest solutions.

  Agree two most important actions.

- Tell students that this is what they should discuss. You could also remind them of the language for participating in discussions from page 80 of the Course Book.

- Agree on a time limit for the discussion. When groups are ready, begin the discussion.

- Circulate and monitor. Note down language points for praise and correction afterwards.

- Ask groups for the outcome of their discussion. What solutions do they suggest?

C

- Ask students to work in pairs. You could remind them of the language for identifying problems and agreeing action from page 110 of the Course Book.

- Allocate roles and give students time to prepare.

- Start the role play. Circulate and monitor.

- Ask one of the pairs to role-play the conversation to the class.

Unit 12 Jobs

- Do this exercise quickly with the whole class. This reminds students of the functional language used during interviews.

- You could also ask students to suggest alternative ways to ask the questions. Refer students to page 118 to check.

- Then ask them to ask and answer the questions with a partner. They can use the answers in the exercise or use real/invented information.

> **2** a **3** d **4** f **5** c **6** b

B

- Explain the situation. Hand out the role cards. Ask students to prepare the questions in same-role groups.

- Make sure that students understand that they have to choose answers for some of the responses, but they can also formulate their own responses if they prefer.

- The interviewer should also think of one more question to ask the candidate (before asking for questions). Tell the candidate to respond to the question in the best way they can.

- Circulate and assist students in preparing if necessary.

- Divide students into A/B pairs.

- Start the role play.

- Circulate and monitor. Note down language points for praise and correction afterwards, especially in relation to the language used for participating in interviews.

- When pairs have finished, praise strong language points and work on the main points that need improving, getting students to say the correct forms.

- Ask students to change roles with their partner and redo the activity, incorporating the improvements.

Introductions

EXCHANGING INFORMATION

A Two people at a conference have a conversation in the coffee break. Put the words in italics in the correct order to complete the conversation.

1 Hi, I'm Carlos. *your /What /name? /is*

2 I'm Jian. *do /How /you /do.*

3 Pleased to meet you, Jian. *from? /you /Where /are*

4 Shanghai. *Italian? /you /Are*

5 No, I'm Spanish. *do /you /do, /What* Jian?

6 I'm a marketing manager. *are /staying? /you /Where*

7 I'm staying at the Continental. It's near the conference centre. *your /hotel /What's /like?*

8 It's OK. Ah, here are my colleagues. *talking /Nice /you, /to* Jian.

B Work in pairs. You are at a conference. Read the information on the cards. Role-play Conversation 1. Student A starts. Then swap roles and role-play Conversation 2.

Student A	**Student B**
● Introduce yourself to Student B. *Hi, I'm …*	● Respond to Student A's introduction. *Nice to meet you.	How do you do.	Pleased to meet you.*
● Ask questions to find out Student B's name/nationality and where they are staying.	● Ask questions to find out if Student A is English and what their hotel is like.
● Ask Student B to spell any difficult words. *Can you spell that, please?*	

Conversation 1

Student A	**Student B**
Name: Jay Guryev	Name: Sam Bernard
Job title: Sales Director	Job title: Production Manager
From: Kazan, Russia	From: Lyon, France
Hotel: The Europa (small hotel in the city centre)	Hotel: The Washington (large hotel near the airport)

Conversation 2

Student A	**Student B**
Name: Jo Verma	Name: Chris Peck
Job title: Sales Manager	Job title: IT Manager
From: Delhi, India	From: Hanover, Germany
Hotel: The Merlin (large hotel near the conference centre)	Hotel: The Metropole (small hotel near the station)

RESOURCE BANK – Speaking

Work and leisure

TALKING ABOUT WORK AND LEISURE

A Complete the sentences below using the words from the box.

> always   at   doesn't   enjoy   ~~interested~~   into   isn't   keen   quite   week

1 Are you *interested* in sport?

2 He isn't .... on concerts.

3 I'm really .... computer games.

4 Do you .... learning languages?

5 He .... like football or rugby.

6 They .... like classical music.

7 She .... interested in the cinema.

8 We never work .... the weekend.

9 Do they .... watch TV in the evening?

10 I usually go to the gym three times a ....

B Work in pairs. Use the prompts below to make questions to ask your partner. Add two more question to the list. Take turns to ask the questions. Present the information to the class.

This is (Jorge/Lisa). He/She likes ...

He/She is/isn't keen on ...

He/She sometimes/often/always/never ...

Student A	Student B
1 What do / at the weekend?	1 What do / in the evenings?
2 What music / like?	2 What sport / like?
3 What sport / don't like?	3 What music / don't like?
4 How often / eat in restaurants?	4 How often / go to cinema?
5 When / usually / go on holiday?	5 How often / go on holiday?
6 When start / work (or college)	6 When finish / work (or college)?
7 How many hours a week / work?	7 How many hours a week / study English?
8 What do / at work (or in your studies)?	8 What do / at work (or in your studies)?
9	9 ....
10	10 ....

TELEPHONING: A PROBLEM WITH AN ORDER

A Match the sentences on the left (1–6) to the correct responses (a–f).

1 Hello, this is Green Stationery Supplies.
2 When do you deliver?
3 Do you have any blue paper?
4 What's your order number, please?
5 I have a problem with my order.
6 The camera is the wrong model.

a) Tuesday morning and Friday afternoon.
b) No, but we have some green paper.
c) I'm sorry to hear that. What's the problem?
d) Sorry about that. I can send you the correct model tomorrow.
e) Hello, I want to buy some envelopes, please.
f) It's JLN928.

B Work in pairs. Role-play two telephone conversations.

Student A	Student B
Call 1	**Call 1**
You are the Purchasing Manager. Phone Grove Electrical Supplies and find out if the sales assistant has the items on this list.	You are the Sales Assistant for Grove Electrical supplies. A customer calls to ask about products. Answer customer's questions.

Student A — Call 1 (continued)

List
- two photocopiers, model GY883
- five printers, model 97DG4

You can order different models if necessary.

Place your order. Write down the order number. Ask the sales assistant what day they deliver.

Student B — Call 1 (continued)

Product list	Number available
Photocopier model GY883	1
Photocopier model LS422	1
Printer model 67DG4	0
Printer model 97DJ2	10

Give the customer this order number: HXZ509224

You deliver on Wednesday morning.

Call 2

Student A

You are the Purchasing Manager. There are some problems with your order (see below). Call the Sales Assistant at Grove Electrical supplies. Give your order number. Explain the problem and say what you want to happen.

Problem

The two photocopiers are the wrong model. They are model XW361.

There are three printers, not five.

Student B

You are the Sales Assistant. You get a telephone call from a customer. Ask for the order number. Listen, apologise for the problem, then try to solve it.

Possible solution

Offer to replace the wrong models. Advise when the additional printers will be delivered.

Travel

MAKING BOOKINGS AND CHECKING ARRANGEMENTS

A Complete the information below about the Globe Hotel using the words from the box.

> business   double   internet   non   park   shower

The Globe Hotel

Perfect for .... [1] travellers and family holidays.

Single room with .... [2] €97

.... [3] room with bath   €135

All our rooms have cable TV and .... [4] access.

Please note all rooms are .... [5] -smoking.

Facilities

- restaurant
- conference rooms
- swimming pool
- car .... [6]
- gym
- room service

We accept Visa and Mastercard.

B Work in pairs. Use the information in Exercise A to role-play a telephone conversation to book a hotel room.

Student A

You are the hotel receptionist. Use the information about the Globe Hotel in Exercise A to answer Student B's questions.

You need the following information. Write it down and ask questions to check it is correct:

- Name and e-mail address?
- Date arriving?
- Credit-card details?
- Time expected to arrive?

Student B

You want to book a room at the Globe Hotel. Phone the hotel and ask for:

- single room with bath or shower
- four nights from Monday 17th

You also need the following information:

- price per night?
- internet access?
- swimming pool?
- possible to pay by American Express or Mastercard? (your credit card number is 4298 5237 233976)

Food and entertaining

MAKING DECISIONS

A Choose the best word or phrase to complete each of these sentences.

1 How *(many)*/*much* tables are there in the restaurant?

2 There are *much* /*a lot of* cafés in the city centre.

3 Are there *some* /*any* fish dishes on the menu?

4 How *much* /*many* does it cost?

5 Are there *a lot of* /*much* fast-food restaurants in the town?

6 They don't have *some* /*any* music or entertainment.

7 This restaurant does *some* /*any* interesting desserts.

8 They don't have *many* /*much* vegetarian dishes.

B Work in pairs. Ask and answer questions to complete the information about the two restaurants.

Student A: *Where is the Garden Restaurant?*

Student B: *It's in the city centre.*

Student A	**Student B**
Ask Student B about the Garden Restaurant.	Answer Student A's questions about the Garden Restaurant.
The Garden Restaurant	***The Garden Restaurant***
Location:	Location: in the city centre
Parking:	Parking: no car park
Number of tables:	Number of tables: 40
Music or entertainment:	Music or entertainment: classical piano
Starters:	Starters: a selection of vegetarian dishes
Main course: .... dishes	Main course: meat and fish dishes
Cost per person:	Cost per person: €30
Answer Student B's questions about the Emerald Restaurant.	Ask Student A about the Emerald Restaurant.
The Emerald Restaurant	***The Emerald Restaurant***
Location: 3km from the city centre	Location: ....
Parking: large car park behind the restaurant	Parking: ....
Number of tables: 80	Number of tables: ....
Music or entertainment: jazz band and dancing after 10 p.m.	Music or entertainment: .... after 10 p.m.
Starters: special fish dishes	Starters: special .... dishes
Main course: meat and vegetarian dishes.	Main course: meat and .... dishes
Cost per person: €45	Cost per person: ....

C Work in groups. You are planning a celebration dinner for friends. Use the information in Exercise B to talk about the two restaurants and decide which to choose.

Number of people: 15 (seven like dancing, five like quiet restaurants, four are vegetarians, seven like fish, six are driving to the restaurant)

RESOURCE BANK – Speaking

Buying and selling

DESCRIBING A PRODUCT

A Complete the product description below using the words from the box.

> aimed   close   colours   costs   deliver   design
> made   postage   ~~product~~   weighs   wide

> This is our best-selling *product* ¹. It's .... ² at people who travel on
> business. It's .... ³ of steel and leather and .... ⁴ about half a kilo. It's
> just 56 centimetres long and 40 centimetres .... ⁵. It comes in three stylish
> .... ⁶: orange, blue and black. It's a unique .... ⁷ and you can open and
> .... ⁸ it easily. It .... ⁹ just €89. The price includes .... ¹⁰ and
> packaging, and we can .... ¹¹ within five days.

B Work in pairs. Take turns to describe your product to your partner. Listen to your partner's description and write the model number and then choose the correct word in italics to complete the product description.

Student A	Student B
Product information	**Product information**
Vigo exercise bike, model GS559J	***Wanda computer desk, model XT766Y***
Target market: busy professionals	Target market: students and people who work from home
Made of: plastic and steel	Made of: wood and steel
Weighs: 8 kilos	Weighs: 12 kilos
Dimensions: 150 centimetres high, 170 centimetres long	Dimensions: 95 centimetres long, 53 centimetres wide
Colours: white, silver	Colours: brown, black
Features: easy to use and has a 10-year guarantee	Features: stylish and practical design
Price: €320 (+ €20 postage and packaging)	Price: €412 (includes postage and packaging)
Delivery: 2 weeks	Delivery: 10 days

Product information form	**Product information form**
Wanda computer desk, model	***Vigo exercise bike, model*** ....
Target market: *families /students /offices* and people who work from home	Target market: *busy professionals /companies / gyms*
Made of: *wood and steel /plastic and aluminium / plastic and steel*	Made of: *wood and steel /plastic and aluminium / plastic and steel*
Weighs: *12 kilos / 18 kilos / 20 kilos*	Weighs: *6 kilos /8 kilos /11 kilos*
Dimensions: *95cm long x 53cm high /95cm long x 53cm wide /95cm wide x 53cm high*	Dimensions: *150cm high x 170cm long /170cm high x 150cm long /15cm high x 190cm long*
Colours: *brown, black /green, black /brown, grey*	Colours: *yellow, silver /white, green /white, silver*
Features: *small /fashionable /stylish and practical design*	Features: easy to use and has a *5 /10 /20*-year guarantee
Price: *€42 / €412 / €4,012* (includes postage and packaging)	Price: *€230 /€320 /€3,200* (+ €20 postage and packaging)
Delivery: 10 *hours /days /weeks*	Delivery: two *days /weeks /months*

RESOURCE BANK – Speaking

UNIT 7 People

NEGOTIATING: DEALING WITH PROBLEMS

A Correct one mistake in each line of the dialogue.

Lisa: I need really an assistant to work on this sales and marketing project.

Ravi: I'm sorry, but the problems is that we can't employ any extra staff.

Lisa: It would be really helpful by me. I can't finish on time on my own.

Ravi: When didn't you tell me that you had a problem with the project?

Lisa: I didn't realise there was so much work. So, can I have a assistant?

Ravi: I'm sorry, it's not just possible. Why don't you give some of the work to sales?

Lisa: OK, I'll think around it.

Ravi: I think you should spoke to the Sales Manager. I can call him for you.

Lisa: OK, thanks. That's a idea good.

B Work in pairs. Student A is the Project Manager and Student B is the Project Director. The Project Manager explains to the Project Director why they need new equipment.

Project Director: *I understand you want some new equipment.*

Project Manager: *Yes, the machine we have is too old.*

Project Manager

You want the Project Director to buy two new machines to complete the project.

- The existing machines are too old.
- They are very slow, and the project won't finish on schedule.
- You didn't discuss the problem in the project meeting because you wanted to check the machines.
- New machines could finish the project sooner.
- The new machines could cut costs on future projects.

Project Director

You don't want to spend money on new equipment. If necessary, there is enough money in the budget to buy one new machine. Try to persuade the manager to use the old machines to finish the project.

- It would cost a lot of money to buy new machines.
- The Project Manager didn't mention the problem in the project meeting last week. Why?
- Suggest that the project team works longer hours to finish the project sooner.
- Decide whether to buy a new machine or ask the Project Manager to work with the old machines.

RESOURCE BANK – Speaking

Advertising

PARTICIPATING IN DISCUSSIONS

A   Match two sentences (1–8) to each heading (a–d).

a   Agreeing

b   Disagreeing

c   Giving an opinion

d   Making a suggestion

1   I think we need to sell this in supermarkets.

2   You're right.

3   I'm afraid I don't agree.

4   What about using a green bottle?

5   I'm not sure I agree with you.

6   That's a good idea.

7   How about selling it for €6.50?

8   In my opinion, we should target young professionals.

B   Work in small groups. You work on the marketing team for a company that makes hair products. The company wants to launch a new shampoo. Role-play a meeting to discuss these points.

- What does the new shampoo smell like? What colour is it?
- What is the best target market?
- What is the selling price?
- Agree on a name for the product.
- Design the bottle and think of a good slogan.
- What is the best outlet to sell the product?
- Suggest ways to advertise the shampoo.

C   Present your ideas to another group. At the end of the other group's presentation, do one of the following:

- give an opinion: *I really like the slogan.*
- think of a question: *Why did you choose that name?*
- make a suggestion: *What about selling it on the Internet?*

Companies

STARTING A PRESENTATION

A Complete the introduction below to a talk about customer services using the words in the box.

> By the end of my talk   finally   good to see you all   Secondly
> subject of my presentation   three sections

Hi, I'm Nadim and I'm a customer services trainer. It's ....[1] here today. The ....[2] is how to deal with complaints. My talk is in ....[3]. Firstly, I'll explain why customers complain. ....[4], we'll look at how customer services should respond. And ....[5], we'll discuss what we can learn from complaints. ....[6], you will understand how to help customers effectively and calmly.

B Work in pairs. Use the information below to prepare a short introduction to a presentation to a customer services department. Then present the introduction to each other. Listen to your partner's presentation and complete the checklist.

Student A		
You are:	Customer Services Manager	
Topic:	talking to customers on the phone	
Plan:	1	How to listen to what customers want
	2	Useful phrases to use on the phone
	3	How to deal with problem calls
Aim:	1	To speak confidently on the phone
	2	To improve customer-service calls for customers

Student B		
You are:	Customer Services Consultant	
Topic:	the department's move to Singapore	
Plan:	1	Look at the planned dates of the move
	2	Housing allowance and bonuses for staff who are moving
	3	How to communicate the move to customers
Aim:	1	You will know more about the details of the move.
	2	You will know how to deal with any questions from customers.

Checklist

Tick the things that your partner does.

1 Introduces himself/herself. ☐
2 Says his/her job title. ☐
3 Greets the audience. ☐
4 Gives a plan of his/her talk. ☐
5 Says what the aim of the talk is. ☐
6 Speaks slowly and clearly. ☐
7 Makes eye contact with the audience. ☐

RESOURCE BANK – Speaking

Communication

MAKING ARRANGEMENTS

A Put these sentences in the correct order to form a phone conversation to arrange a meeting.

a) How about 2.30?

b) Yes, I can make Wednesday. What time suits you?

c) Sure, what day is good for you?

d) I'm sorry, I can't do Tuesday afternoon. Is Wednesday OK for you?

e) Hi, it's Jan Mathews. Can we meet next week to discuss the project?   *1*

f) Yes, Wednesday at 2.30 is fine for me. See you then.

g) How about Tuesday afternoon?

B Work in pairs. Use the diaries below to role-play this situation. Student A telephones Student B to arrange a meeting for next week. The meeting will last an hour and a half and will be at Student B's office.

A: *Hello. It's … here. Can we meet next week to discuss the project? What day is good for you?*

C Student B needs to change the day or time of the meeting. Telephone Student A. Apologise and rearrange the appointment.

B: *Hello. It's … here. Sorry, but I need to change the time of our meeting …*

Student A's diary		Student B's diary	
Monday 10th	10–11.15 a.m. Marketing meeting	Monday 10th	12–2.30 p.m. Lunch meeting 3– 5 p.m. Presentation
Tuesday 11th	9.30 a.m.–12 p.m. Visit new advertising agency 2–4.30 p.m. See accountant	Tuesday 11th	2.30–5 p.m. Meet new client
Wednesday 12th	10–11.00 a.m. Dentist	Wednesday 12th	7.30 a.m. Fly to Bulgaria Return 10 p.m.
Thursday 13th	11 a.m.–2.30 p.m. Meet visitors from head office	Thursday 13th	10.30 a.m.–1.30 p.m. Product demonstration
Friday 14th	11.30 a.m.–12.30 p.m. Team meeting 5.30 p.m. Fly to Dubai	Friday 14th	11.00 a.m.–2.15 p.m. Choose new office furniture

Cultures

IDENTIFYING PROBLEMS AND AGREEING ACTION

A Write the sentences below (1–8) under the correct heading of the table.

OPENING	STATING THE TOPIC	SUGGESTING ACTION	RESPONDING TO SUGGESTIONS

1 The best thing to do is to talk to your manager.
2 Yes, I think that would be very helpful.
3 Could I have a word with you?
4 There's a problem with my hours.
5 Well, I'm not sure about that.
6 One thing we could do is find another supplier.
7 There's something I'd like to talk to you about.
8 The problem is, the office is too small.

B Work in groups of four. Read Sam Rowland's e-mail. Discuss his main problems and suggest solutions. Choose two things that you think Sam should do.

> Dear Jo,
>
> Could I ask your advice? I recently moved office and I now share a room with six people. I find it very difficult to work because it's very noisy. I'm new to the department, and it's difficult to talk to anyone about this problem. My colleagues are friendly and they often come and talk to me at my desk. I don't want to be unfriendly, but it takes me longer to finish my work. In my last office, I was on my own. It was very quiet, and I worked very quickly and efficiently. Now I sometimes miss deadlines, and my boss is unhappy with me. What do you think I should do?
>
> Sam

C Work in pairs. Role-play a conversation between Sam and Jo.

Student A: You are Sam. Explain the problem and respond to your friend's suggestions.
Student B: You are Jo. Listen to the problem and suggest some solutions.

INTERVIEW SKILLS

A Match the interview questions (1–6) to the answers (a–f).

1 Why did you leave your last job?
2 What are you good at?
3 Can you work under pressure?
4 What are your main interests?
5 Where do you want to be in 10 years' time?
6 Do you have any questions?

a) My main skills are in research and analysis.
b) Yes. When does the job start?
c) I hope to be head of the department.
d) Yes, I always work calmly and effectively.
e) I wanted a challenge and to use my skills.
f) I really enjoy learning languages.

B Work in pairs. Student A is the Human Resources Director. Student B is a candidate. Role-play the interview. The Human Resources Director is interviewing the candidate for the job of Department Manager.

Human Resources Director

Introduce yourself and use these ideas to make questions to ask the candidate.

1 How long / been in / present job?
2 Why / leave / last job?
3 What skills / have?
4 Where / want to be in five years' time?
5 What / do in / free time?

Choose one of the answers in italics to respond to the candidate's questions.

1 Job starts in a *week* /*month*.
2 annual holiday: *14* /*31* days
3 company car after *three* /*six* months
4 salary: *€42,000* /*€75,000* a year plus bonus

Candidate

Introduce yourself and choose one of the answers in italics and respond to the interviewer's questions.

1 Been Assistant Manager for *two* /*five* years.
2 Left last job because wanted *a challenge / to use my skills*.
3 Main skills: *languages and IT* /*planning and organisation*.
4 Plan to be *a good director* /*a CEO*.
5 Enjoy *playing tennis* / *travelling*.

Use these ideas to make questions to ask the interviewer.

1 When / job start?
2 How long / annual holiday?
3 Will / company car?
4 What / salary?

RESOURCE BANK – Speaking

Introductions

JEREMY KEELEY, CONSULTANT AND SPECIALIST IN CHANGE LEADERSHIP

A ◀)) CD 1.8 **Listen to the first part of the interview and match the two halves of these sentences.**

1	Can you	**a)**	to make decisions.
2	My name is	**b)**	Jeremy Keeley.
3	I live in	**c)**	to feel welcome.
4	I help leaders	**d)**	a small city.
5	Do you always	**e)**	shake hands?
6	I like people	**f)**	introduce yourself?

B ◀)) CD 1.8 **Listen to the first part again. Read the audio script and correct the seven mistakes.**

My name is Jeremy Keeley. I live in a small city in Scotland near London called St Albans. I have four teenage children, and I run my own large business, which works for organisations across the USA and in Africa, where I help employees to make decisions together and to improve the quality of my leadership.

C ◀)) CD 1.9 **Listen to the second part of the interview. Choose the best word (a–c) to complete the questions that Jeremy asks.**

1 .... are you?

   a) Who **b)** How **c)** What

2 Where do you come ....?

   a) to   **b)** by   **c)** from

3 What do you ....?

   a) do   **b)** work **c)** be

D **Match each of the questions in Exercise C (1–3) to one of these responses (a–c).**

  a) I'm from Lublin in Poland, but I live in Fortaleza in Brazil.

  b) I'm a engineer at a large electronics company.

  c) Fine thanks, and you?

E ◀)) CD 1.9 **Listen to the second part again. Tick the points that are mentioned.**

When he meets a new business contact, Jeremy Keeley:

1 asks questions to start the conversation.

2 always offers tea or coffee.

3 finds out what is important to the person.

4 waits until they ask him a question before he talks about himself.

5 invites them to visit his house.

6 waits until the person offers him their business card.

Work and leisure

ROS POMEROY, CONSULTANT AND EXECUTIVE COACH

A ◀)) CD 1.22 **Listen to the first part of the interview and decide whether these statements are true (T) or false (F).**

1 At work, Ros Pomeroy does the same thing every day.

2 She works for different clients on different projects.

3 She never has meetings.

4 Sometimes she runs a workshop.

5 She's often in her office.

6 She never takes phone calls at work.

B ◀)) CD 1.23 **Listen to the second part. Choose the correct word in italics to complete these extracts.**

1 I do work very *short /long* hours.

2 I also have *teenage /young* children.

3 It's *difficult /easy* to find enough time for leisure.

4 To *ask /answer* your question ...

C ◀)) CD 1.24 **Listen to the third part. Choose the best answer (a–c) for each question.**

1 What does Ros often do on Saturday and Sunday?

  a) writes for a newspaper

  b) reads the newspaper

  c) listens to the news

2 What other activity does she do?

  a) running

  b) swimming

  c) walking

3 She says this activity doesn't sound ...

  a) interesting.

  b) relaxing.

  c) fun.

4 What does Ros think it is important to do?

  a) stay inside and sleep

  b) go out and visit friends

  c) get outside and see the countryside

D ◀)) CD 1.24 **Complete the extract below using the words from the box. Then listen to the third part again to check.**

go into run not that that's time very week weekends

At the ....^{1}, I spend a lot of my ....^{2} reading the newspaper. I catch up on the news from the previous ....^{3}. And also I try to ....^{4} out running. Now, running may ....^{5} sound like something ....^{6} is very relaxing, but I think that it's ....^{7} important to get outside ....^{8} the fresh air and see the countryside. So ....^{9} why I ....^{10}.

Problems

JEREMY KEELEY, CONSULTANT AND SPECIALIST IN CHANGE LEADERSHIP

A ◀)) CD 1.34 **Listen to the first part of the interview and match the two parts of the expressions.**

1	work	a)	job
2	own	b)	business
3	enough	c)	time
4	good	d)	problems
5	urgent	e)	busy
6	very	f)	requests

B **Complete these sentences using the expressions in Exercise A.**

1 I don't have my ...., I work for a multinational company.

2 Is there .... to finish the report before the meeting?

3 Mr Cole is .... today, but you can see him tomorrow.

4 If you have any ...., you can ask the HR department to help resolve them.

5 We use these builders a lot because they always do a ....

6 Our client has some ...., so we need to do the work quickly.

C ◀)) CD 1.35 **Listen to the second part. Tick the words that Jeremy Keeley mentions.**

companies	❏	meetings	❏
managers	❏	equipment	❏
change	❏	property	❏
resources	❏	computers	❏
offices	❏	money	❏
staff	❏	prices	❏

D ◀)) CD 1.35 **Listen to the second part again. Choose the correct word in italics to make true statements.**

1 Jeremy Keeley usually works with *big /small* companies.

2 The companies go through change *slowly /fast*.

3 The companies find it *difficult /easy* to plan for their needs.

4 They need to *satisfy /change* their customers.

5 Their customers expect them to *reduce /increase* prices.

E ◀)) CD 1.36 **Listen to the third part. Complete the missing words in these sentences.**

1 My customers u _ _ _ _ _ _ ask me to help them solve complicated problems.

2 Recently, there was a c _ _ _ _ _ _ _ system that had to be introduced ...

3 ... that affected millions of c _ _ _ _ _ _ _ _ and their bills.

4 I brought the technical team, the business team, the p _ _ _ _ _ _ team and the suppliers together in one room.

5 We came up with the s _ _ _ _ _ _ _ that solved the problem altogether.

RESOURCE BANK – Listening

LIZ CREDÉ, CONSULTANT IN ORGANISATION DEVELOPMENT

A 🔊 CD 1.59 **Listen to the first part of the interview, then match the verbs and verb phrases in the left column (1–5) to the phrases in the right column (a–e).**

1	work	a)	by phone and video conferencing
2	travel	b)	in the old town
3	visit	c)	to Amsterdam
4	contact	d)	with my clients
5	it's based	e)	colleagues in Singapore

B 🔊 CD 1.59 **Listen to the first part again and decide whether these statements are true (T) or false (F). Correct the false ones.**

1 Liz goes on business trips all over the world to visit clients.
2 Currently, she travels to Amsterdam every week.
3 She travels to Singapore and China twice a year.
4 She contacts colleagues by phone and video conferencing.
5 Her favourite location is the office in Singapore.
6 The office is based in the business district.

C 🔊 CD 1.60 **Listen to the second part. Number the information in the order that Liz Credé mentions it.**

a) She has a meal before she flies. ☐
b) They remember what her favourite drink is. ☐
c) They know her name. ☐
d) Her favourite way of travelling is to fly business class. ☐
e) She travels a lot. ☐
f) She has a seat that turns into a bed. ☐

D 🔊 CD 1.60 **Listen to the second part again and answer these questions.**

1 Where can she go before she flies?
2 Why does she like her seat that turns into a bed?
3 Does she prefer to stay in different hotels?
4 Where is one of her favourite hotels?

JEREMY KEELEY, CONSULTANT AND SPECIALIST IN CHANGE LEADERSHIP

A ◀)) CD 1.66 **Listen to the first part of the interview. Which meals and drinks does Jeremy Keeley mention?**

B ◀)) CD 1.66 **Listen again and tick the words that he mentions.**

furniture	❑	information	❑
contacts	❑	water	❑
milk	❑	office	❑
client	❑	a glass of milk	❑
staff	❑	park	❑

C ◀)) CD 1.67 **Listen to the second part and answer these questions.**

1 Why is a meal a good way to entertain business contacts?

2 What is Jeremy careful about during the meal?

D ◀)) CD 1.67 **Listen to the second part again and complete these notes.**

- Don't take out a c _ _ _ _ _¹ you don't like.
- Don't waste the t _ _ _².
- Don't take a client to a restaurant where they c _ _ _³ eat the food.
- Don't spend too m _ _ _⁴ money.

E ◀)) CD 1.68 **Listen to the third part and choose the correct words in italics to complete this extract.**

I get to know what they *can /can't*¹ eat and what they *can /can't*² eat, and what they *like / don't like*³, from them personally. I *ask /tell* ⁴ them, I *do /don't*⁵ assume. I then plan it *quickly / carefully*⁶, but I also relax, so that they *can /can't*⁷ relax and *eat /enjoy*⁸ it.

RESOURCE BANK – Listening

Buying and selling

ROS POMEROY, CONSULTANT AND EXECUTIVE COACH

A CD 1.76 **Listen to the first part and choose the best answer (a–c) to complete these sentences.**

1 Ros thinks it is a good idea to .... time to build business relationships.

a) take   b) see   c) enjoy

2 It's important to .... the product or service you're selling.

a) understand   b) remember   c) arrive

3 It's not a good idea to sell customers something that they don't .... or want.

a) know   b) need   c) work

4 Customers like to be .... to.

a) explained   b) asked   c) listened

5 Customers don't like to be .... at.

a) talked   b) looked   c) explained

B CD 1.77 **Listen to the second part and match the two halves of these expressions.**

1 successful   a) price
2 maximum   b) quotation
3 written   c) volume
4 additional   d) buyer
5 higher   e) away
6 walk   f) extras

C Now match the expressions in Exercise B (1–6) to these explanations.

a) more of something
b) decide not to buy something
c) a person who buys a product for their company at a good price
d) more things included in a deal
e) the most money you will pay
f) a document that gives a price for products or services

D CD 1.78 **Listen to the third part and answer these questions.**

1 What was the best thing that Ros ever bought?
2 How many years ago did she buy it?
3 Was her first offer accepted?
4 How long did the negotiation take?
5 Which of these describes what she paid?

a) a higher price than the owner asked
b) the price that the owner asked
c) a lower price than the owner asked

ROS POMEROY, CONSULTANT AND EXECUTIVE COACH

A 🔊 CD 2.1 **Listen to the first part of the interview. Match the expressions on the left (1–6) to the ones on the right (a–f) to make true sentences about Ros Pomeroy.**

1	She likes working with	a)	who are reliable.
2	In particular, she likes	b)	who give up easily.
3	Most of all, she likes people	c)	all kinds of people.
4	Reliable people	d)	creative people.
5	She also likes working with	e)	do what they say they are going to do.
6	She doesn't like people	f)	working with hard-working people.

B 🔊 CD 2.1 **Listen to the first part again and correct the seven mistakes in this audio script.**

I like working with all kinds of products. In particular, I like working with people who aren't hard-working and, most of all, people who are relaxed; that is, those that do what they say they are going to do and at time. But I never like working with creative people, people who are willing to find old ways to solve problems. And I really like people who give up too easily.

C 🔊 CD 2.2 **Listen to the second part. Choose the correct alternative to replace the expression in italics so that the sentence has a similar meaning.**

1 One manager often *criticised members of her team* in front of others.
   a) said positive things about a people
   b) said negative things about people

2 This meant her team members *hid information from her*.
   a) didn't show her information
   b) gave her information

3 It also meant they *were not prepared to take any risks*.
   a) only made dangerous decisions
   b) only made safe decisions

4 If something went wrong, she would not *support* them.
   a) help
   b) talk to

D 🔊 CD 2.3 **Listen to the third part and decide if these statements are true (T) or false (F) according to Ros Pomeroy.**

A good manager ...
1 will delegate and allow a team member to complete a task.
2 is always involved with how the task is done.
3 sets clear objectives.
4 doesn't need to say what results they expect.
5 only gives feedback when things go wrong.

RESOURCE BANK – Listening

LIZ CREDÉ, CONSULTANT IN ORGANISATION DEVELOPMENT

A ◄)) CD 2.12 **Listen to the first part of the interview. Choose the best answer (a–c) for each question.**

1 What does Liz think of the advert?

   a) She doesn't like it.   **b)** She likes it.   **c)** It's her favourite.

2 When would you eat the product in the advert?

   a) at breakfast   **b)** between meals   **c)** for dessert

3 The advert shows a man choosing whether he loves the product more than his …

   a) car.   **b)** phone.   **c)** partner.

4 How does Liz describe the advert?

   a) not realistic and too long   **b)** short and not funny   **c)** badly acted

B ◄)) CD 2.13 **Listen to the second part. Which of these words does Liz mention? Which of the words are adjectives and which are nouns?**

effective   funny   memorable   message

easy   interesting   cars   advert

bad   flowers   engine   intelligent

C ◄)) CD 2.13 **Listen to the second part again. Decide whether these statements are true (T) or false (F) according to Liz.**

1 Memorable adverts aren't effective.

2 You remember the main message or product in an effective advert.

3 Liz particularly likes an advert for a travel company.

4 The advertisement uses pictures of towers and buildings.

5 The advert gives a modern message about the product.

D ◄)) CD 2.14 **Listen to the final part and identify the six mistakes in this audio script.**

Yes, I think that products shouldn't use claims or pictures that don't seem to be delivered at work. I'm thinking particularly about washing products, which claim to clean stains, but they don't do it when I make them at home.

RESOURCE BANK – Listening

Companies

A ◀)) CD 2.17 **Listen to the first part of the interview and decide whether these statements are true (T) or false (F).**

1 Jeremy Keeley's favourite company sells private banking services.

2 He likes the leaders of the company.

3 The company looks after its staff.

4 The company doesn't care about its customers' needs.

5 The environment is important to the company.

6 The employees believe that they are helping people.

B ◀)) CD 2.18 **Listen to the second part. Choose the best answer (a–c).**

1 Jeremy Keeley would like to work for a company that has a …
   a) large profit.
   b) big purpose.
   c) bigger office.

2 What does Jeremy think the best companies have in common?
   a) strong leadership
   b) good products
   c) low prices

3 How do these companies treat their employees?
   a) They look for young graduates.
   b) They look into ways to cut salaries.
   c) They look after their staff.

4 What do these companies think about customers?
   a) They don't care how many customers they have.
   b) They care about their customers' needs.
   c) They care how much the customers pay.

5 What other things do these companies care about?
   a) taxes and bonuses
   b) media and technology
   c) the environment and the world

C ◀)) CD 2.19 **Listen to the third part and complete these notes.**

● He doesn't k _ _ _ [1] which company is going to do well in the future.
● Rolls Royce is famous for the quality of its l _ _ _ _ _ _ _ _ [2].
● Apple is famous for its innovation and c _ _ _ _ _ _ _ _ [3].
● Google invests time in i _ _ _ _ _ _ _ _ [4] new products.
● Fairtrade is famous for looking after p _ _ _ _ _ [5] in the world.
● Body Shop is environmentally f _ _ _ _ _ _ _ [6].

UNIT **10** Communication

ROS POMEROY, CONSULTANT AND EXECUTIVE COACH

A 🔊 CD 2.27 **Listen to the first part of the interview. Choose the best word in italics to complete these sentences.**

1 Ros Pomeroy uses a *professor* / *professional* networking site.
2 She's connected *to* / *by* over a hundred people.
3 Some people she knows have more than five *thousand* / *hundred* contacts in this way.
4 She also uses a *couple* / *double* of specialist networking sites.
5 She uses these for sharing knowledge and *experts* / *expertise* about topics.

B 🔊 CD 2.28 **Listen to the second part. Match the two halves of these expressions.**

1	advantages	**a)**	in touch
2	keep	**b)**	and disadvantages
3	professional	**c)**	in
4	made	**d)**	me something
5	interested	**e)**	field
6	sell	**f)**	contact

C **Complete these sentences with expressions from Exercise B.**

1 I don't like it when I go into a store and the assistant immediately tries to ....
2 He's very .... science and technology.
3 The Internet makes it easy to .... with friends and family in different countries.
4 What are the .... of moving our factory to Taiwan?
5 The conference was useful because we .... with some interesting suppliers.
6 Greg's an accountant and Lois is a lawyer, so they don't work in the same ....

D 🔊 CD 2.29 **Listen to the third part. Which of these things does Ros mention about her ex-boss?**

He ...
a) had a passion for his subject.
b) made contact by e-mail and phone.
c) was enthusiastic.
d) knew his subject well.
e) spoke slowly and calmly.
f) made the audience feel important.
g) asked the audience questions.

E 🔊 CD 2.30 **Listen to the final part. Match each form of communication (1–3) to Ros's opinion of it (a–c).**

1 face-to-face
2 e-mail
3 corporate newsletter/magazine

a) gets the company message across, but often isn't very interesting
b) best for getting information across and getting things done in business
c) good for making people aware of what is going on

LIZ CREDÉ, CONSULTANT IN ORGANISATION DEVELOPMENT
JEREMY KEELEY, CONSULTANT AND SPECIALIST IN CHANGE LEADERSHIP
ROS POMEROY, CONSULTANT AND EXECUTIVE COACH

A ◀)) CD 2.40 **Listen to Liz Credé and decide whether these statements are true (T) or false (F).**

1 Liz thinks that differences in communication style can result in mistakes.

2 She gives an example about working with a colleague from Holland.

3 Liz's colleague sent her a letter.

4 He wrote to say that he liked the design.

5 They had a conversation to discuss what he wanted to happen.

6 Liz didn't make the changes that her colleague wanted.

B ◀)) CD 2.40 **Listen again and find words that mean the following.**

1 something that isn't correct: m _ _ _ _ _ _

2 making no effort to be friendly: a _ _ _ _ _

3 not polite: r _ _ _

4 something that is easy to understand: c _ _ _ _

C ◀)) CD 2.41 **Listen to Jeremy Keeley and choose the correct word (a–c) to make true sentences.**

1 He was working with people in East ....

   a) Asia   **b)** Africa   **c)** Europe

2 They had .... problems to solve.

   a) many   **b)** urgent   **c)** unusual

3 Jeremy's mistake was that he got .... onto business.

   a) slowly   **b)** back   **c)** straight

4 The people he was working with wanted to talk about what was going on in their ....

   a) lives   **b)** homes   **c)** jobs

5 Jeremy found it .... to get on with work until he gave them their space to talk.

   a) easy   **b)** slow   **c)** hard

D ◀)) CD 2.42 **Listen to Ros Pomeroy and number these topics in the order that she mentions them.**

a) People in other countries find it confusing.

b) She leaves the important parts of the message until the end.

c) The humour confuses them, and what she says is often ignored.

d) They don't understand why she isn't being direct.

e) She usually writes long e-mails.

f) She normally includes a funny comment.

RESOURCE BANK – Listening

A ◀)) CD 2.47 **Listen to the first part of the interview. Match the two halves of the expressions.**

1	current	a)	laugh
2	long	b)	them
3	a good	c)	hours
4	treated	d)	of (years)
5	involve	e)	people very well
6	a couple	f)	job

B **Replace the words in italics in each of these sentences with an expression from Exercise A.**

1 Charles plans to travel in Asia for *two* months.

2 I enjoy working with my colleagues because we have *a lot of fun*.

3 She often works *from 7 a.m till 7.30 p.m.*

4 To motivate staff, we need to *listen to their opinions* when we make decisions.

5 What do you enjoy about your *occupation at the moment*?

6 Graduates wanted to work for the company, because it *was always good to its employees*.

C ◀)) CD 2.48 **Listen to the second part and complete these two extracts with what Liz says.**

I think my s _ _ _ _ _ _ _ _1 come from my work as a c _ _ _ _ _ _ _ _ _2 over the last t _ _ _ _ _3 years. I understand how companies work through looking at their l _ _ _ _ _ _ _ _4, their culture and their b _ _ _ _ _ _5 strategy …

I think my main w _ _ _ _ _ _6 is that I can see a s _ _ _ _ _ _ _7 from many different s _ _ _ _8, and sometimes that makes it h _ _ _9 to make d _ _ _ _ _ _ _10.

D ◀)) CD 2.49 **Listen to the final part. Number these statements in the order that Liz mentions the topics. Which advice is about starting work, and which is for job interviews?**

a) Build relationships across the organisation.

b) Show that you have done some research into the organisation.

c) Ask a question to demonstrate your interest in a company.

d) Take the opportunities you are given and learn from them.

e) Ask a question about the company culture.

f) Listen and pay attention to what people say.

RESOURCE BANK LISTENING KEY

Unit 1

A

1 f   2 b   3 d   4 a   5 e   6 c

B

My name is Jeremy Keeley. I live in a small city in **England** near London called St Albans. I have **three** teenage children, and I run my own **small** business, which works for organisations across the **UK** and in **Europe**, where I help **leaders** to make decisions together and to improve the quality of **their** leadership.

C

1 b   2 c   3 a

D

1 c   2 a   3 b

E

He mentions 1, 3, 4, and 6.

Unit 2

A

1 F   2 T   3 F   4 T   5 T   6 F

B

1 long   2 teenage   3 difficult   4 answer

C

1 b   2 a   3 b   4 c

D

1 weekends   2 time   3 week   4 go   5 not   6 that
7 very   8 into   9 that's   10 run

Unit 3

A

1 d   2 b   3 c   4 a   5 f   6 e

B

1 own business   2 enough time   3 very busy
4 work problems   5 good job   6 urgent requests

C

Jeremy Keeley mentions: companies, change, resources, staff, equipment, property, money, prices.

D

1 big   2 fast   3 difficult   4 satisfy   5 reduce

E

1 usually   2 computer   3 customers   4 project
5 solution

Unit 4

A

1 d   2 c   3 e   4 a   5 b

B

1 T   2 F (week month)   3 F (China Chicago)   4 T   5 T
6 F (business district old town)

C

a) 2   b) 6   c) 5   d) 1   e) 4   f) 3

D

1   She can go into the business lounge.
2   She can sleep.
3   No, she prefers to stay in the same hotel.
4   Amsterdam

Unit 5

A

He mentions: lunch and dinner (meals) and tea and coffee (drinks).

B

He mentions: contacts, client, office, park.

C

1   It gives you the chance to talk to them and find out about them.
2   He is careful about the noise level and how private it is.

D

1 client   2 time   3 can't   4 much

E

1 can   2 can't   3 like   4 ask   5 don't   6 carefully
7 can   8 enjoy

Unit 6

A

1 a   2 a   3 b   4 c   5 a

B

1 d   2 a   3 b   4 f   5 c   6 e

C

1 higher volume   2 walk away   3 successful buyer
4 additional extras   5 maximum price
6 written quotation

D

1 a house   2 eight years ago   3 no   4 18 months   5 c

Unit 7

A

1 c 2 f 3 a 4 e 5 d 6 b

B

I like working with all kinds of **people**. In particular, I like working with people who **are** hard-working and, most of all, people who are **reliable**; that is, those that do what they say they are going to do and **on** time. But I **also** like working with creative people, people who are willing to find **new** ways to solve problems. And I **don't** like people who give up too easily.

C

1 b 2 a 3 b 4 a

D

1 T 2 F 3 T 4 F 5 F

Unit 8

A

1 a 2 b 3 c 4 a

B

Liz mentions: effective, memorable, message, cars, advert, flowers, engine.

Adjectives: effective, funny, memorable, easy, interesting, bad, intelligent

Nouns: message, cars, advert, flowers, engine

C

1 F 2 T 3 F 4 F 5 T

D

Yes, I think that **adverts** shouldn't use claims or **promises** that don't seem to be delivered at **home**. I'm thinking particularly about **cleaning** products, which claim to **remove** stains, but they don't do it when I **try** them at home.

Unit 9

A

1 F 2 T 3 T 4 F 5 T 6 T

B

1 b 2 a 3 c 4 b 5 c

C

1 know 2 leadership 3 creativity 4 inventing
5 people 6 friendly

Unit 10

A

1 professional 2 to 3 hundred 4 couple 5 expertise

B

1 b 2 a 3 e 4 f 5 c 6 d

C

1   sell me something
2   interested in
3   keep in touch
4   advantages and disadvantages
5   made contact
6   professional field

D

a, c, d, f

E

1 b 2 c 3 a

Unit 11

A

1 T 2 T 3 F 4 F 5 T 6 F

B

1 mistake 2 abrupt 3 rude 4 clear

C

1 b 2 b 3 c 4 a 5 c

D

a 4 b 2 c 6 d 5 e 1 f 3

Unit 12

A

1 f 2 c 3 a 4 e 5 b 6 d

B

1 a couple of 2 a good laugh 3 long hours
4 involve them 5 current job
6 treated people very well

C

1 strengths 2 consultant 3 twenty 4 leadership
5 business 6 weakness 7 situation 8 sides 9 hard
10 decisions

D

a 3 b 5 c 4 d 1 e 6 f 2

Advice about starting work: d, f, a

Advice for job interviews: c, b, e

Introductions

CASE STUDY WRITING TASK: MODEL ANSWER

To:	Bob Evans
From:	Sue Price
Subject:	Assistant to the Sales Manager

Hi Bob,

I met an interesting person at a conference in Singapore. Here is some information about him:

David Chong is a university graduate. He is 24 years old and he has work experience as a web designer. He speaks fluent Chinese and English.

I think he is a good candidate to be your assistant.

Let me know if you need any more information.

Best wishes

Sue Price

(See the Writing file, Course Book page 126, for information about e-mails.)

A **Write an e-mail from Bob Evans to Sue Price. Include the following information:**

- Thank Sue for her e-mail.
- Say that David Chong seems like a good candidate.
- Use these prompts to write questions:

Where /David from?

What /he like?

What /his interests?

What /his e-mail address?

B **Work in pairs. Swap the e-mails that you wrote in Exercise A and write Sue's reply to Bob.**

RESOURCE BANK – Writing

Work and leisure

CASE STUDY WRITING TASK: MODEL ANSWER

To:	HR Team
From:	Tim Rogers
Subject:	Information about my job

There's a lot of variety in my job. I travel and meet clients, and my colleagues are friendly. The office is in a great location in the city.

But there are some problems. Sometimes I don't leave work until 10 p.m. My boss wants me to be in the office every day at 8 a.m., and I get tired.

I think the company should let staff work flexible hours. This is a good idea for my team because we often work late on projects.

I hope these ideas are useful.

Regards

Tim

(See the Writing file, Course Book page 126, for information about e-mails.)

A You are a member of the HR team. Write an e-mail to the management team about one of the people on page 135 of the Course Book – the receptionist, the website developer, the writer or the graphic designer.

- Briefly summarise the problems they have with the company.
- Suggest ways that the company can help them.

B The company agrees to make the changes you suggest. Write an e-mail from the employee to the HR team.

- Thank the HR team for their help.
- Say what you like about your job now.

Problems

CASE STUDY WRITING TASK: MODEL ANSWER

To:	Jason Parker, Head Office
From:	Diana Nolan
Subject:	Complaints from guests

Hello Jason,

There are a lot of complaints from our guests at the moment. Here are some of the problems they have:

- The bedrooms are too small and dark.
- The bathrooms aren't well equipped, and the showers don't work well.
- The sitting rooms don't have enough furniture, and the terraces have no furniture.
- Some guests say that the gym has no equipment and the pool is too small.
- They say that the apartments are noisy.
- The Internet is too expensive.
- Guests want TVs with satellite programmes.
- Some guests complain about the view. The advertisement shows apartments near the beach. One guests complained that the beach is 20 kilometres away.

Can we arrange a meeting with the Director of Marketing to discuss these problems? I also want to discuss High-Style Business Rentals' future advertising policy.

Thank you for your help with this.

Regards

Diana Nolan

(See the Writing file, Course Book page 126, for information about e-mails.)

A You are Jason Parker. Write an e-mail to Diana Nolan.

- Thank her for bringing the problems to your attention.
- Suggest a date and time when you can have a meeting.
- Ask her to write a letter to guests to apologise for the problems.
- Ask her to keep you informed about any other comments from guests.

B You are Diana Nolan. Write an e-mail to the guest at the High-Style Business Rentals on page 29 of the Course Book.

- Thank the guest for their telephone call.
- Apologise for the problems in their apartment.
- Say that the company plans to make improvements to the apartments.
- Offer the guest a free night in the apartment with their next booking.

CASE STUDY WRITING TASK: MODEL ANSWER

To:	Victoria Wallis, Elegant Ways Beauty Products
From:	The Gustav Conference Centre
Subject:	Conference booking

Dear Ms Wallis,

Thank you for your telephone enquiry today concerning conference bookings. Here are the details of your stay.

Date of arrival: Friday, 7th July

Date of leaving: Sunday, 9th July

As requested, you have one meeting room and two seminar rooms each day.

We can offer you the Rossini Room. This is our largest room and has excellent facilities. It has a very large screen (5m x 4m) for video conferencing, and we can offer technical support at all times. I'm afraid that it does not have direct access to the garden, but it has an excellent view.

We hope you enjoy your visit to the Gustav Conference Centre. Please do not hesitate to contact me if you have any questions.

Regards,

Chiara Carpini

(See the Writing file, Course Book page 126, for information about e-mails.)

A You are Sam Clark, the conference organiser at Minnesota Chemicals. You want to make some changes to your booking. Write an e-mail to Chiara Carpini at the Gustav Conference Centre.

- Say you want to change your conference dates.
- Ask to book a conference room and a meeting room from 14th to 16th July.
- Say which conference room you would like and what facilities you need.
- Thank her for her help.

B You are the conference organiser for the TVL Group. You want to organise a conference. Write an e-mail to the Gustav Conference Centre to get some information.

- You want to organise a conference for 40 people.
- Dates: 20th–22nd September
- You need a conference room and two meeting rooms.
- Include the facilities you need (video conferencing, laptops, technical support).
- Ask if rooms are available.
- Request a response as soon as possible.

Food and entertaining

CASE STUDY WRITING TASK: MODEL ANSWER

To:	Hanna West
From:	Zoe Lewis, Organic 3000
Subject:	Dinner invitation

Dear Hanna,

I would like to invite you for a meal on Wednesday at 7.30 p.m.

The restaurant is really good. It's called the Kerala Sands and it serves a variety of South Indian dishes. They have vegetable curries and some delicious desserts.

It's about five miles from the city centre. We can go by taxi.

I hope you can come.

Best wishes,

Zoe

(See the Writing file, Course Book page 126, for information about e-mails.)

A **Write a reply to Zoe. Look at your diary to see if it is possible.**

Wednesday	Thursday	Friday
7 p.m. Office party	6–7 p.m. Finish report	5–6 p.m. Meet Jake for coffee

- Thank her for the invitation.
- Comment on the restaurant. (*It sounds …*)
- Say if it is possible or not. (If not, give a reason.)
- If Wednesday isn't possible, suggest another day and time.

B **Write an e-mail to one of the three restaurants on pages 50–51 of the Course Book. You want to book a table for an office celebration.**

- You need a table for 15 people.
- Include the date and time.
- Ask if they have any tables available.
- Ask the restaurant to send you a menu.

CASE STUDY WRITING TASK: MODEL ANSWER

To:	Sales department
From:	PeterWoods@NPI
Subject:	Product query

Dear Sir/Madam,

I work for a company called NPI, which sells gifts for the home, office and travel.

I am interested in buying your RC1 spaceship to sell in our store. Could you send me a catalogue and a price list? Can I also have a sample of the RC1, please?

What is the delivery date if we place an order?

Thank you for your help.

Yours faithfully,

Peter Woods

(See the Writing file, Course Book page 126, for information about e-mails.)

A Choose the best word in italics to complete the reply to Peter Woods' e-mail.

Dear Mr Woods,

Thank you *for / to* your e-mail. Please find *attached / attaching* our latest catalogue and price list. A sample of the RC1 is *on / in* the post.

If you place an order, we *are / can* deliver in five days.

Please let me know if you need any more information *about / around* our products.

Wishes / Best wishes

Jay Parks

Jay Parks
Sales Manager

B Choose another product on page 59 of the Course Book. Write to the manufacturer to ask for the following information.

- cost
- colours
- weight
- features

Office Life Message Board

Business Today

I can understand why you are upset with your colleague, Thomas. However, if you complain to your boss, you will look bad. Firstly, why don't you speak to your colleague and say that you want to share the clients? If that doesn't work, I think you should arrange a meeting with your manager. Explain that you do a lot of the work with clients and would like more opportunities to take them to see the properties. You could also ask to go on a training course to improve your sales skills. This will help you to be more confident. I'm sure your boss will be pleased to have two good salespeople on the team.

(See the Writing file, Course Book page 126, for information about e-mails. The message board would use a similar informal style.)

A Use the information below to write a message for the message board at Office Life. Describe the problem.

- You share an office with a colleague. He is friendly and likes to chat to you.
- You are preparing for an important project.
- It is difficult to work because he talks so much.
- You don't want to upset your colleague or change offices.

B Write a reply to the problem in Exercise A. Give your reason for the action you suggest.

RESOURCE BANK – Writing

Advertising

CASE STUDY WRITING TASK: MODEL ANSWER

Product launch plans

Dreamland chocolate bar

Slogan
- The slogan for the product will be 'Join us in Dreamland'.

Advertising
- We will have 30-second TV ads in prime-time slots, starting on September 18th.
- The advertisement will show a woman sitting at her desk eating a Dreamland bar. Suddenly she is on an exotic beach with a Hollywood star sitting next to her. He smiles and hands her another Dreamland chocolate bar.

Endorsement
- We will offer the actor Doug Miles the opportunity to endorse the product and appear in the advertisement. We are arranging a meeting with his agent.

Special events
- We will give out free Dreamland chocolate bars at major film festivals in Dubai, Asia and Europe.
- There will be competitions with free tickets to each of the film festivals and a chance to meet the film directors and stars.

(See the Writing file, Course Book page 127, for information about product launch plans.)

A Read the information below about a product launch. Write a launch plan. Organise the information into headings and bullet points. Leave out any unnecessary words or phrases.

Bubble Fun is a new shampoo for the children's market. Our slogan is 'No more bathtime tears.' We will advertise the product on family websites and on TV during children's programmes. We will offer Hi-Jump, a teenage dance act, sponsorship on their tour in return for product endorsement. The event will be launched with a party at the London Aquarium. There will also be a Bubble Fun dance competition, and the winner will have the opportunity to appear in the company's ads.

B Write an e-mail to the writer of the product launch plan in Exercise A. Say which idea(s) you like and which idea(s) you disagree with. Give reasons for your comments.

Companies

Company profile

Our mission

Omnia Supermarkets is a leading group of supermarket and convenience stores based in France. We sell food, household products and furniture. Our company employs around 1,500 people. We want to be the number-one supermarket chain in Europe.

Turnover and profit

We have a turnover of approximately €220 million. Last year, our profits were €18.4 million.

Future plans

We want to continue offering our customers excellent service. To do this, we want to build more convenience stores. We also want to increase our range of own-label products to offer our customers even better value.

(See the Writing file, Course Book page 129, for information about short company profiles.)

A Write a brief profile of your company or a company you know well. Look at the company brochure or website and summarise key information.

- Describe what the company does.
- How many employees does it have?
- Include information about turnover or profits.

B You are a business journalist. You are writing an article about one of the organisations – Omnia Supermarkets, Miriam Palmer Heathcare or The Forest Life Trust. Look at the information on pages 133, 142 or 143 of the Course Book. Write a letter to the PR Officer for the organisation.

- Explain that you plan to write an article about the company.
- Ask three questions about the company.
- Ask for an interview (suggest a date and time).
- Thank the PR Officer for their help.

CASE STUDY WRITING TASK: MODEL ANSWER

To:	All staff
From:	Managing Director

As you know, the company is currently considering changes that we will need to make in the future.

You are invited to a meeting to discuss the present situation of the company. The meeting will be on Friday 14th October in Conference Room 6.

All the directors will attend, and we will answer any questions you have. We will talk about the company's plans for improving profits.

I look forward to seeing you all on Friday.

Regards

Geoff Harper

Managing Director

(See the Writing file, Course Book page 126, for information about e-mails.)

A You are the Managing Director of Blakelock Engineering. Write an e-mail to the shareholders to tell them how you plan to do these things:

- Choose who will leave the company.
- Help employees who will be leaving Blakelock Engineering.

B You are going on a business trip next week. Write a list of things you need to do before you leave. (See Writing File, Lists, Course Book page 127.) Then write an e-mail to a friend to tell them where you are going and what you need to do.

CASE STUDY WRITING TASK: MODEL ANSWER

Far Eastern Traders

Subject: New ideas from Head Office   Date: May 10th

Participants: Dev Anish, Gemma Agnew, Sasha Kalvis, Lukas Moretti

	Agenda item	Decision	Reason	Action	Name
1	Staff to use first names	agreed	A more relaxed style will help the company's image.	Department managers to talk to staff.	DA
2	Staff to dress casually on Fridays only	agreed	Idea is popular with staff.	Try a 'casual Friday' next month and get staff feedback.	SK
3	Introduce a system of flexible working hours	not agreed	Difficult to organise at present (discuss further in next meeting).	Send a questionnaire to staff to see what they think about this idea.	LM
4	Keep all meetings to 30 minutes only	not agreed	Longer meetings good for decision-making.	None	
5	Introduce 'hot-desking' to open-plan offices	agreed	Reduces office costs.	Marketing department to try the new system and report back.	GA
6	'Open-door' policy – staff can see manager at any time	not agreed	Some staff will feel uncomfortable with this policy.	None	

(See the Writing file, Course Book page 128, for information about action minutes.)

A You are a director of Far Eastern Traders. Write an e-mail to Stuart Adams at Head Office. Summarise the main changes and give reasons.

B You are a department head at Far Eastern Traders. Write an e-mail to your staff. Choose two of the ideas on the agenda and ask staff if they think they are good ideas. Ask them to reply to you as soon as possible.

CASE STUDY WRITING TASK: MODEL ANSWER

Jason Thomas
247 Coleford Avenue
Philadelphia
PA 89087

17 June

Dear Mr. Thomas,

Re: Job application

We are pleased to inform you that you have been successful in your application for the position of Marketing Manager at Nelson & Harper Inc.

As agreed in the interview, we would like you to start on July 20th in our Philadelphia office. Your starting salary will be $50,000 per annum. You can take two weeks' annual leave. We can also offer the use of a company car and health insurance.

Please find enclosed a copy of your contract. Please could you sign it and return it to me as soon as possible.

We look forward to hearing from you soon.

Yours sincerely

Melissa Webb

Melissa Webb

Vice-President, Human Resources

Enc: Contract

(See the Writing file, Course Book page 128, for information about letters.)

A **You have been offered a job at Nelson & Harper (decide what job you have been offered). Write a letter to Melissa Webb in Human Resources.**

- Thank her for her letter.
- Decide whether you want to accept or decline the job offer and give reasons.
- Say you have enclosed the contract (if you accept the job).
- End the letter politely.

B **Write a letter to a company that you are interested in working for.**

- Say why you like the company.
- Briefly outline your skills or work experience.
- Ask whether any suitable positions are available at the moment.
- Thank the person for taking the time to consider your application.